Collaborating
for Success With the
Common Core

A Toolkit for
**PROFESSIONAL LEARNING
COMMUNITIES
AT WORK™**

Kim Bailey
Chris Jakicic
Jeanne Spiller

Solution Tree | Press

a division of
Solution Tree

555 North Morton Street
Bloomington, IN 47404
800.733.6786 (toll free) / 812.336.7700
FAX: 812.336.7790

email: info@solution-tree.com
solution-tree.com

Visit **go.solution-tree.com/commoncore** to download the reproducibles in this book.

Printed in the United States of America

17 16 15 14 13   1 2 3 4 5

Library of Congress Cataloging-in-Publication Data

Bailey, Kim.
  Collaborating for success with the common core : a toolkit for professional learning communities at work / Kim Bailey, Chris Jakicic, Jeanne Spiller.
      pages cm
  Includes bibliographical references and index.
  ISBN 978-1-936764-72-3 (perfect bound) 1. Education--Standards--United States. 2. Professional learning communities. 3. Teaching teams. I. Title.
  LB3060.83.B35 2014
  379.1'580973--dc23
                                      2013020125

Solution Tree
Jeffrey C. Jones, CEO
Edmund M. Ackerman, President

Solution Tree Press
President: Douglas M. Rife
Publisher: Robert D. Clouse
Editorial Director: Lesley Bolton
Managing Production Editor: Caroline Weiss
Senior Production Editor: Joan Irwin
Copy Editor: Sarah Payne-Mills
Proofreader: Elisabeth Abrams
Text and Cover Designer: Jenn Taylor

Acknowledgments

I'm constantly reminded how blessed I am to be in this profession. Working alongside gifted and caring educators, including the teachers of my own children and my colleagues in Capistrano Unified School District, provides inspiration on a daily basis. Adding to that inspiration are my writing partners, Chris and Jeanne, who have mastered the art of stretching my thinking while making me laugh. I am grateful for the incredible support I receive from my family and friends, which bolsters me continuously. Finally, I can never fully express my gratitude to my husband, Randy, also a gifted educator, whose never-ending patience, flexibility, and endurance for my "what about…?" questions are a true statement of unconditional love.

Kim Bailey

Because there were no real "experts" about the Common Core State Standards for schools and districts jumping early into the implementation of these standards, we all faced a potentially overwhelming challenge. These were new standards for everyone; standards that required new ways of thinking about teaching and new ways of assessing student understanding. I am especially grateful to all of the teachers who willingly embraced this new challenge and allowed me to be a part of the process with them. Thanks especially to the teachers in Kildeer District 96 who shared their insights and experiences with me. Your willingness to take risks and learn from the work you're doing exemplifies the idea of continuous improvement and far surpasses anything I've seen in other districts. The same can be said of my favorite co-writers, Kim and Jeanne. Working with you has been both professionally rewarding and just out and out fun! I also thank my husband, John, for willingly sharing this journey with me.

Chris Jakicic

I have the great fortune to work with the incredibly talented, dedicated teachers and administrators in Kildeer District 96 who live and breathe the ideas in this book every day. I am so grateful to work in a place that exemplifies what it means to be a professional learning community, a place where high levels of collaboration and a laser-like focus on results and student learning are the norm. There are so many of you that have shared your knowledge, thoughts, concerns, and celebrations with me. I have learned so much from all of you, and I am extremely thankful for that. To my writing buddies Kim and Chris, this journey has been much like our ride up Mulholland Drive with exhilarating twists and turns on the way up, and the most rewarding, magnificent view at the top. Thank you for all of your support and guidance on the way up. Above all, I want to thank my husband Dave and my kids Brandon and Breton, who supported and encouraged me in spite of all the time it took me away from them.

Jeanne Spiller

Solution Tree Press would like to thank the following reviewers:

Alysson Keelen
Principal
The Adelphia School
Freehold, New Jersey

Cindy Koss
Chief Academic Officer
Deer Creek Public Schools
Edmond, Oklahoma

Katherine Perez
Director of Professional Development and Outreach
School of Education
Saint Mary's College of California
Moraga, California

Peg Portscheller
President
Portscheller and Associates: Pathways to Results
Aurora, Colorado

Jonathan G. VanderEls
Principal
Memorial Elementary School
Newton, New Hampshire

Visit **go.solution-tree.com/commoncore**
to download the reproducibles in this book.

Table of Contents

Reproducible pages are in italics.

About the Authors

Kim Bailey is director of instructional support and professional learning for the Capistrano Unified School District in southern California. Her leadership has been instrumental in uniting and guiding educators throughout the district's fifty-six schools in their journey to becoming professional learning communities (PLCs). In addition to her role at Capistrano, Kim works with schools and districts across the United States, providing guidance and support to move forward with their own development as PLCs. Kim is passionate about empowering teams to do the important work inherent in effective learning communities, including the development of common formative assessments and the alignment of standards, assessment, interventions, and instruction.

Kim's education background spans over thirty years, and her work at Capistrano has won national praise in the United States. The National School Boards Association (NSBA) recognized Kim's leadership in coordinating and implementing the district's Professional Development Academies. The academies received the distinguished American School Board Journal Magna Award and the California School Boards Association Golden Bell Award. She has also taught courses in educational leadership as an adjunct faculty member at Chapman University in Orange, California, and she is coauthor of *Starting Strong: Surviving and Thriving as a New Teacher* and *Common Formative Assessment: A Toolkit for Professional Learning Communities at Work™*.

To learn more about Kim's work, visit http://kbailey4learning.wordpress.com, or follow her on Twitter @bailey4learning.

Chris Jakicic, EdD, served as principal of Woodlawn Middle School in Long Grove, Illinois, from its opening day in 1999 through the spring of 2007. Under her leadership, the staff shifted toward a collaborative culture focused on learning and implemented formative assessment practices to shape their instructional strategies. Student motivation and performance also increased. Chris began her career teaching middle school science before serving as principal of Willow Grove Elementary in Buffalo Grove, Illinois, for nine years. Her experience as a practitioner guides her work with schools; she wants teachers to feel confident that they have the skills and the ability to make a difference for their students. Through her work with teachers and administrators across the United States, Chris emphasizes that effective teaming is the heart of PLCs. She also shares practical knowledge about how to use data conversations to interpret classroom information for effective instruction.

Chris has written articles for the *Journal of Staff Development* and *Illinois School Research and Development Journal*, detailing her experiences with common assessments and PLCs. She has worked as an adjunct instructor at National Louis University, as well as Loyola University Chicago, where she earned a doctor of education. She is also coauthor of *Common Formative Assessment: A Toolkit for Professional Learning Communities at Work.*

To learn more about Chris, visit www.chrisjakicic.com, or follow her on Twitter @cjakicic.

Jeanne Spiller is the Assistant Superintendent for Teaching and Learning in Kildeer Countryside School District 96, located in Buffalo Grove, Illinois. Her recent work has been largely focused on implementation of the Common Core State Standards. Jeanne has led the process of unpacking, powering, scaling, and pacing the English Language Arts Common Core standards with numerous schools, districts, and teacher teams.

Jeanne's work with teachers and administrators in District 96 as well as with several school districts throughout the country is focused on clarity regarding what students should know and be able to do as well as the development of aligned assessments and assessment practices that help teachers determine how to approach instruction so that all students succeed.

Jeanne has served as a middle school classroom teacher, building staff developer, team leader, and middle school assistant principal. She is the current President of the Illinois affiliate of Learning Forward (formerly the National Staff Development Council), and is passionate about the importance of high quality professional learning for every educator so that all students succeed.

Jeanne earned a Master of Arts degree in Educational Teaching and Leadership from St. Xavier University in Chicago, a second Master of Arts degree in Educational Administration from Loyola University Chicago, and is currently pursuing a doctorate degree in administrative leadership from Northern Illinois University in DeKalb, Illinois. You can follow Jeanne on Twitter @jeeneemarie.

To book Kim Bailey, Chris Jakicic, or Jeanne Spiller for professional development, contact pd@solution -tree.com.

Introduction

We have had the privilege to work with collaborative teams across the United States as they implement the practices of professional learning communities (PLCs). During this process, we've worked with people assigned leadership roles, such as Curriculum Directors, Staff Developers, and Team Leaders, in school districts as well as with informal teacher leaders—teachers who are recognized as leaders by their colleagues and collaborative teams. We recognize the hard work it takes to make change happen and to commit to a belief that *all* students can learn at high levels. We've also been able to watch and support the work as these teams embrace and begin teaching the Common Core State Standards (CCSS; NGA & CCSSO, 2010g). In our work with these high-performing teams, we've learned a great deal about the collaborative process it takes to make this significant transition. This book is a product of our own learning: learning about the process and the CCSS themselves.

We've noticed that there are some processes that remain the same in this change. Good teams function well when they have a common mission to ensure learning for all and a common vision of what learning will look like when it happens for their students in their grade level or course. Team members make commitments to each other and to their students—commitments that they are accountable for. They set stretch goals for success—goals that challenge them to reach higher than they thought might be possible.

High-performing teams also know that they must do some things differently as they make this change. The culture of continuous improvement in a PLC will help your team meet these new levels of rigor for learning and will allow you to embrace new instructional strategies needed to support this rigor. Your team must be willing to look at your current common assessments and intervention processes to see how they must change to achieve deeper learning around more complex text, embedded mathematical practices, and literacy expectations in all subjects. Knowing that you are a part of a team makes the change less threatening.

This book is intended to help stimulate your team's work by providing ideas about how team members can support and facilitate change, examples of how other teams have successfully implemented the CCSS, and tools and templates for your team to use and modify to make CCSS implementation work in your own setting. We've written the book to support teams who are already answering the four critical questions of a PLC using their own state standards and who want to make the shift to the Common Core State Standards as smooth as possible. Richard DuFour, Rebecca DuFour, Robert Eaker, and Thomas Many (2010) identify the four critical questions of a PLC that provide a foundation for the work of collaborative planning teams.

1. What do we want our students to learn?
2. How will we know if our students are learning?
3. How will we respond when some students don't learn?
4. How will we extend and enrich the learning for students who are already proficient?

At the end of each chapter, we have included specific information for teams who are new to the PLC process and who want to capitalize on the benefits of making this significant change in a collaborative way. These suggestions appear in the feature "Tips for Teams New to the PLC Process." We've included suggestions about how to get started and discussed other issues you might want to consider as you begin. Finally, we also know that principals and other leaders will look at this change through a different lens than classroom teachers. For these readers, we've included a feature: "Tips for Principals and Leaders."

The book is divided into four parts: (1) Setting the Stage, (2) Getting on the Same Page, (3) Planning for Learning, and (4) Working on the Work. Each section represents a major *chunk* of information your team will want to consider as you begin this work. Figure I.1 lays out the organization of these parts and provides a visual of the information included in each section. These parts follow the typical order you might consider as you move through this transition—that is, the first part addresses topics and concerns that usually rise at the beginning of the transition process, and the last part explores those matters that are likely to happen much later in the process.

Setting the Stage

- Establish the mindset and expectation for collaboration around the CCSS.
- Refresh teams' understanding and focus on the purpose and guiding questions that drive PLCs.
- Support developing teams as they refine their processes for collaboration, including norms for working together and the cycle of improvement.
- Build initial awareness of the CCSS.
- Design district or site CCSS transition efforts with consideration of the change process.

Getting on the Same Page

- Build common clarity about the structure and content of the CCSS across teams, with emphasis on those standards that are deemed essential.
- Facilitate and support the unwrapping of standards to build collective clarity about their intent and specific focus, and break them down into specific learning targets.
- Examine the notion of scaling learning targets in support of accurate assessment and differentiated instruction.

Planning for Learning

- Identify and communicate pacing of standards to inform instruction, assessment, and interventions.
- Develop integrated units of instruction containing aligned assessments and embedding best practices.
- Develop and refine scoring guides and rubrics.

Working on the Work

- Examine collective results of instruction, making adjustments to ensure learning of all students.
- Provide targeted and efficient interventions based on the outcomes of formative and summative assessments.
- Analyze patterns of student learning and apply new knowledge across teams.
- Support team growth and professional learning.

Awareness	Implementation	Integration	Refinement

Figure I.1: The collaborative journey to success with the CCSS.

In the first part, Setting the Stage, we look at what this transition really entails: the shifts in thinking and planning that will be vital to your success. We also examine the value of using a collaborative process in approaching this transition to the Common Core State Standards. Chapter 1 helps your team see the link between the work you are already doing as a part of a PLC and the transition that will be required as you move to this set of rigorous standards. The four critical questions that guide the work of collaborative teams (DuFour et al., 2010) will be instrumental in supporting this transition. Teams who have relied on these four questions for their work in the past, however, will find that the CCSS require several shifts in thinking and behavior. In the past, teams learned together but often relied on the wisdom of experienced teachers to understand the state standards and their meaning. With the Common Core, everyone is *inexperienced* in his or her understanding of what these standards mean and in the implications of implementation. Chapter 2 extends this discussion by looking at the issue of change. Despite the fact that many teachers recognize the value of the CCSS and look forward to having a more coherent and aligned set of standards to work with, this transition is a significant change for everyone at the school and district levels. However, this change is manageable when accommodations are made for your team to have time to work and learn together and when they have appropriate support. In this chapter, we provide descriptions of what those accommodations might be.

We've designed the second part, Getting on the Same Page, to help you familiarize yourself with the CCSS. How can your team most effectively learn what implications the standards will have for your work? We help you explore the ways that your team will answer the first critical question collaborative teams ask themselves: What do we want our students to learn? Chapter 3 begins with the process of understanding how the CCSS are designed and the information that your team needs to develop common understanding—collective clarity—of their meaning and the implications for instruction and assessment. We explain the process that your team can use to identify your *essential* or *power standards* and include some specific suggestions for making this process practical. Teams using the four critical questions of a PLC know that the answer to question one is more complex than just saying we want our students to know the standards. These teams identify essential or power standards which reflect the most important content that *all* students must know. For example, in the Common Core ELA, we know that standard one in every grade level in reading is essential for all students. They must be able to read closely, answer text-dependent questions, and cite the place in the text where they got their answer. In chapter 4, we help teams learn even more specifically about what the CCSS will mean for instruction and assessments through the process of *unwrapping* the standards into learning targets. We explain this process and make suggestions about how this might be different from what you have done with state standards. Chapter 5 looks at the process of *scaling* the learning targets. The scaling process will help your team identify what proficiency will look like for each learning target, ensuring that all teachers on the team have the same expectations for their students. Scaling also helps you lay out both the simpler and the more complex content for each target so that you can discuss how to help students who are experiencing difficulty or those who can benefit from additional challenge.

The third part, Planning for Learning, provides strategies your team can use to cement the shift from teaching to learning, the concept that PLCs are built on. We'll explore how your team can most effectively answer the second critical question collaborative teams ask: How will we know if our students are learning? This part begins with chapter 6, which explores ways your team can approach curriculum pacing and mapping with the CCSS to effectively put learning targets together to create coherent units of instruction. Chapter 7 tackles the issue of how assessment practices must change when teams work with the Common Core. The CCSS are rigorous; they require more complex texts, more analysis, and more problem solving than many previous state standards. The assessments to support them will require more than just multiple-choice questions. In this chapter, we provide information and resources about other types of assessment items that can provide the information teams need to make good decisions about what to do next for their students. With the use of performance tasks and constructed-response questions, your team will want to design quality rubrics so that teachers are scoring their students' responses in the same way. Chapter 8 looks at how teams can construct rubrics for both teacher use and student use, so they know what quality work looks like. When fully implemented, these strategies help ensure that your team will know what your students have and have not learned and how to best respond.

In the fourth part, Working on the Work, we take a deeper look into the work of collaborative teams as teachers plan their instruction—particularly as they ensure that students are able to meet the more rigorous expectations of the CCSS. We make suggestions for teams who want to learn more about how to use the results of their assessments to plan quality responses to their common formative assessments (CFAs). While the Professional Learning Communities at Work™ model doesn't include the question about instruction, we introduce an additional question we call question 2.5 which asks, What effective practices will lead to student learning of essential skills and concepts, including 21st century skills? We believe that the teams who will be most successful in making this transition are those who ask themselves what instructional strategies they must use to support this effort and how they can learn to use these new strategies in a collaborative way. To encourage this, in chapter 9, we provide some initial thinking about this necessary shift. This part also examines teams' responses to critical questions three and four: How will we respond when some students don't learn? How will we extend and enrich the learning for students who are already proficient? Chapter 10 explores how your team can move from gathering assessment data to planning corrective instruction for students who didn't learn specific targets the first time. We know that if assessments are designed properly, you will have the right data to make these decisions. To make that process seamless, this chapter looks at some specific steps a team can take to move from data to action. At the same time, collaborative teams want to provide challenging activities for the students who have already mastered the learning targets being taught in a unit. Chapter 11 discusses how teams can manage this. Using preassessment strategies and scales you've developed around learning targets, your teams will be able to plan quality opportunities for each unit of instruction. No longer is enrichment an *add-on*; rather, it is an integral part of the teaching-learning process.

Whether you are a member of a collaborative teaching team, a principal, or a central office leader, we encourage your team to read the chapters in order or to start wherever makes most sense to you. For example, teacher teams might want to read chapter 3 as they begin the process of identifying their essential or power standards and then subsequent chapters as they move forward with their work; a curriculum director might want to read the entire book in order to understand the big picture before he or she begins planning for professional development. Collaborative Connections, a feature at the beginning of each chapter, outlines key ideas that you may find helpful in determining how you will read the book. As noted, we conclude each chapter with two features—"Tips for Teams New to the PLC Process" and "Tips for Principals and Leaders." These features offer advice about some of the thorny issues collaborative teams and leaders encounter as they work through the challenges that come with implementation of the Common Core. Lastly, the reproducible tools and protocols in the appendix serve as samples for you to use as written or to adjust and make better—that's the power of working as a team and continually improving processes.

We hope we've provided the catalyst to help you and your colleagues move forward to higher achievement and learning. Remember, this work is ongoing and takes time to accomplish. Even the most experienced, most high-performing teams will not be able to do it all in their first year. It's a journey for us all. Happy learning!

Part One

Setting the Stage

1

Understanding the Common Core State Standards

Collaborative Connections

- The CCSS will require a shift not only in what students learn but also in how they learn.
- The guiding questions of a professional learning community are a powerful framework for guiding curriculum, instruction, and assessment in the CCSS.
- Teachers working as a collaborative team within a professional learning community can work smarter, not harder, as they strive to understand and incorporate strategies that lead to high levels of learning.

We begin our book with a quick survey. Nobody but you will see this. Nobody will evaluate you based on your answer. In other words, you can be brutally honest! Here's the question: When you first heard that your state adopted the Common Core State Standards, which of these statements came to mind?

1. I love change, and I can't wait to tackle an entire new set of standards!

2. I think the CCSS make a lot of sense, but I'm pretty worried that I won't be up to the challenge.

3. This too shall pass. I'll just stay under the radar until the next new initiative comes around.

4. How can I possibly figure out all of this on my own?

5. How long before I can retire?

If you picked any answer other than number one, please know that you're probably in good company. We get it. A major change initiative such as the Common Core can bring about any number of emotions.

In unprecedented fashion, an overwhelming majority of states have accepted the challenge to align their educational curriculum to the CCSS—standards that are designed with a focus on rigor and relevance and ones that specifically target the skills and concepts needed to prepare our students not only for college and career but also for the 21st century. The stakes are high not simply from an accountability standpoint but from the standpoint of students' preparedness for college and the world of work and on an even larger scale: the United States' economic well-being. While these states have agreed on the common ground of the standards they embrace for their students, individual states, districts, and schools are taking different journeys as they work to make sense of the CCSS and begin to integrate them in classrooms. Some systems have created elaborate checklists, and others have compiled complicated documents to help teachers know what to teach and when. It's safe to say that there are no silver bullets. While schools across the United States have begun their Common Core journey, it's clear that the supports and guidelines for teachers are inconsistent.

Feeling overwhelmed and uncertain about how to move forward is understandable. In fact, it would be surprising if you *weren't* overwhelmed, particularly in light of the incredible amount of information coming at educators during this transition to the Common Core. Educators have been hit with a fire hose of articles, advertisements, and invitations to workshops. Their inboxes are full of emails touting the "next best thing" to help them teach the CCSS and help their students achieve the skills needed in the 21st century. Textbook publishers have numerous products advertised as "Common Core aligned" and are encouraging schools and teachers to purchase these. Depending on one's state, district, or school, there may be a *perception* of support for these shifts or a feeling of desertion, which has further led teachers to feel that they're on their own to sink or swim.

Regardless of your personal level of enthusiasm for the Common Core, any significant change in a school requires a significant proportion of its teachers to adopt the new initiatives. In other words, to orchestrate the shifts required to effectively impact student learning around the CCSS, a systematic approach designed to empower and support all teachers is necessary.

We know that these shifts aren't going to take place overnight, nor will they all be met with open arms. Without a doubt, educators will be grappling with some of the shifts alluded to in the CCSS—shifts required in instructional practice, in the assessment of student learning, in the level of rigor reflected in what is taught, and in the picture of student success. One thing is certain: To successfully implement these critical shifts and achieve the "end in mind" of the CCSS, all educators need guidance as they dig into the content of the standards, and ongoing embedded support to continuously adjust their professional practice.

Achieving these shifts will take time. We know effective professional development can't be accomplished by having teachers attend a one-day workshop that encompasses everything needed to effectively teach in a way consistent with the desired outcome—in this case, meeting the expectations of the CCSS. In fact, Joellen Killion (2011), senior advisor for Learning Forward, an international organization that advocates for quality professional development, states, "To make substantive changes in teaching and learning, professional learning must be a continuous process sustained over a period of time that engages educators in learning from experts and with and from one another." Shifting to the CCSS will require exactly that: a continuous process embedded in our daily work in which all educators in a school system learn from experts and each other.

So, what if there is another choice in the survey you just took? What if one of the response options is, "I'm really glad to be working as part of a collaborative team so that we can figure this out together." If you could answer with this choice, we assert that facing the many unknowns and shifts that the adoption of the Common Core State Standards triggers would seem significantly less overwhelming. Of course, what we're describing here is the work of collaborative teams within a professional learning community. These teams work with absolute commitment to high levels of learning and with the understanding that by working together their students can achieve high levels of learning, especially when they capture the best of what their collective practice has to offer.

In their book *Leaders of Learning*, Richard DuFour and Robert Marzano (2011) remind us that the only way a school's curriculum can truly be guaranteed is when teachers work collaboratively to do the following.

- Study the intended curriculum.
- Agree on priorities within the curriculum.

- Clarify how the curriculum translates into student knowledge and skills.

- Establish general pacing guidelines for delivering the curriculum.

- Commit to one another that they will, in fact, teach the agreed-on curriculum.

Collaborative teams establish a clear, agreed-on curriculum by using the following four guiding questions, which shape the team's inquiry and instructional practice (DuFour et al., 2010).

1. What do we want our students to learn?

2. How will we know if our students are learning?

3. How will we respond when some students don't learn?

4. How will we extend and enrich the learning for students who are already proficient?

These questions are familiar friends of collaborative teams. They have served as a beacon for work focused on improvements in student learning and will continue to do so during the transition to the CCSS. Without question, the journey of implementing the CCSS will require rethinking what students need to know and do as well as the context in which they demonstrate that knowledge and skill. It will require reexamining how we monitor student learning. It will require retooling how we deliver instruction and support learning for all students, including those who struggle and those who are ready for increased opportunities for challenge. In other words, to succeed in this process, teams must continue to use the guiding questions that are inherent in PLCs. They are the proverbial glue that will guide teams to deeper understanding of the content, context, and dispositions we are seeking through the implementation of the CCSS. In light of the instructional shifts that the CCSS require, however, we have taken the liberty to make one addition to these compelling questions. We strongly urge teams to consider the instructional practices that will engage learners in successful learning by asking what we call question 2.5: What effective practices will lead to student learning of essential skills and concepts, including 21st century skills? By adding this question to the conversation, collaborative teams will proactively engage in conversations that assist with the design of their instruction so that students are more likely to attain the skills and concepts that are targeted.

Figure 1.1 (page 10) illustrates the process that collaborative teams might take as they work to answer the guiding questions. Starting at the top of the diagram with question one, What do we really want students to know and be able to do?, teams can progress in a clockwise fashion to address each question. This ongoing process keeps the guiding questions in the forefront. The process implies a backward learning design, embedding an additional question that asks teams to proactively and collaboratively plan for best *first* instruction.

Throughout this book, we will walk through the processes aligned to each of these guiding questions. You'll answer the first question—What do we want our students to learn?—by prioritizing the standards, unwrapping them to reveal specific learning targets, and developing scales that will define levels of proficiency. Second, we must envision the end in mind and, based on that picture of success, design assessments that will be used to accurately measure whether students have attained the target (How will we know if our students are learning?). These assessments are designed to not only measure learning at the end of the instructional unit in a summative fashion but also along the way, using formative measures. Next, we use what we know about quality first instruction to design a learning pathway that is likely to yield success for students. (What effective practices will lead to student learning of essential skills and concepts, including 21st century skills?). We feel strongly that some of the shifts inherent in the CCSS

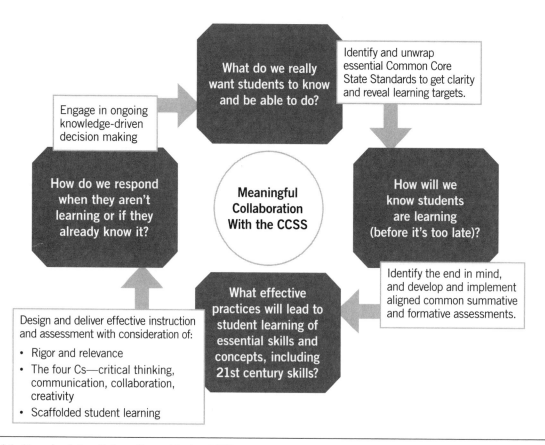

Figure 1.1: Meaningful collaboration with the CCSS.

will require a thoughtful, intentional examination of *how* student learning is facilitated. We also assert that it's impossible to get deep understanding of the CCSS without actually *applying them*, reflecting on the instructional processes used and the results in student learning. By looking at the results of our practice and assessment of student learning, we also gain information on students' needs for differentiated support. (How do we respond when they aren't learning or if they already know it?)

As practitioners, we have seen firsthand the impact that collaborative teams working in a professional learning community can make on the level of clarity and confidence that teachers attain when addressing the content of the CCSS and the assessments that measure their achievement. We are confident that this is the structure and the mindset for moving forward with the CCSS. When educators are truly collaborating, they find that there's not just safety in numbers—there's *clarity* in numbers! We hope that as you move through this book and examine the power of collaborative teams within a PLC, you'll see that it really is the only model that can work in the context of these ongoing and multiple shifts needed for an effective transition to the Common Core. If you're new to the concepts and work of professional learning communities, we recommend referencing the documents mentioned in this chapter's "Tips for Teams New to the PLC Process" (page 16). These resources provide guidance about the *why* and *how* of professional learning communities.

Shifts in Transitioning to the CCSS

The National Governors Association Center for Best Practices (NGA) and the Council of Chief State School Officers (CCSSO), authors of the Common Core, take painstaking measures to ensure that the standards align to those skills and dispositions that are deemed essential for success in college and careers. The anchor standards for each strand—Reading, Writing, Speaking and Listening, and Language—in the Common Core English language arts/literacy define those skills and dispositions (NGA & CCSSO, 2010a). They are the end in mind for all students, and the standards provide a *staircase* framework of skills and concepts that will lead the students there.

The *staircase* organization of the standards in the Reading strand focuses on increasing text complexity throughout the grades. Students are expected to develop skill in analyzing a wide range of cognitively demanding literary and informational texts as they progress from beginning reading to the college and career readiness level.

Similarly in the CCSS for mathematics, the Standards for Mathematical Practice (NGA & CCSSO, 2010e) define habits of mind that are essential for success in school and life. Figure 1.2 provides a summary of the overarching goals in both literacy and mathematics. When you examine them closely, you will see there are many parallels between the ELA/literacy and mathematics standards. In the center of the figure are the *big ideas* in both sets of the standards. These big ideas are consistent—they are the center of a Venn diagram, so to speak. Regardless of the content or topic, a significant focus is evident on critical thinking and problem solving, on relevance and application, on the integration of multiple skills, and on high-level literacy.

English Language Arts/Literacy

To be ready for college and careers, we want students to be able to:

- Read a diverse and increasingly complex array of literature as well as challenging informational texts in a range of subjects

- Write logical arguments based on substantive claims, sound reasoning, and relevant evidence, particularly in the text

- Conduct relevant research, analyzing and evaluating the credibility of sources and presenting the findings using a variety of media and tools

Common Big Ideas About What We Want for Students

- We want students to persist when problems are challenging.

- We want students to know the why behind what they are learning and the strategies they use to solve problems.

- We want students to engage in real-life problems and work with others to identify innovative solutions.

- We want students to be good consumers of information of all types and good communicators about the information they are sharing.

- We want students to engage in activities that require application of high-level thinking.

Mathematics

To be ready for college and careers, we want students to be able to:

- Make sense of problems and persevere in solving them.

- Reason abstractly and quantitatively.

- Construct viable arguments and critique the reasoning of others.

- Model with mathematics.

- Use appropriate tools strategically.

- Attend to precision.

- Look for and make use of structure.

- Look for and express regularity in repeated reasoning.

Source: Adapted from NGA & CCSSO, 2010a, pp. 10 and 18; NGA & CCSSO, 2010e, pp. 6–8.

Figure 1.2: CCSS expectations for English language arts/literacy and mathematics.

What will it take for us to get our students to these levels? It's clear that there will be shifts not only in what we teach but also in how we teach and how we assess. Table 1.1 provides our attempt to summarize these shifts, knowing that they won't necessarily fit into neat little boxes.

Table 1.1: A Summary of Shifts in the CCSS

Shift	Implications for Designing and Delivering Instruction	Implications for Designing and Delivering Assessment
We want students to persist when problems get challenging.	Instruction should focus on empowering students with strategies for breaking down difficult text, mathematics problems, or other information so that they can clearly understand the content.	Assessments should require high-level thinking and problem solving. Novel problems should be provided.
We want students to demonstrate deep understanding of a variety of increasingly complex texts to gain information from a number of resources, including those that are digital. We want them to persist when text becomes challenging.	Discussions should be driven by a variety of texts that engage students at a high level. Instruction should provide a balance of text types with increasing complexity and a shift to the use of informational text as students advance in the grades. This focus on text complexity needs to be embedded in all content areas at all grade levels.	Assessments should utilize multiple pieces and types of text with increasing complexity. Students should be required to reference and analyze text in critical reading. This requires a shift from student *text-to-self* questions to more *text-dependent* assessment questions in which students have to dig into the reading to answer questions and make appropriate inferences. Assessment tasks should require students to conduct close reading of complex texts.
We want students to know the *why* behind what they are learning and to have the experience of using what they learn to solve real-life issues whenever possible.	Instruction should allow students more time for in-depth experiences to develop deeper conceptual understanding.	Assessments should focus less on formulas and algorithms and more on having students explain their thinking or showing it within the context of real-life issues.
We want students to integrate a number of skills and apply them in realistic contexts beyond the classroom.	Instruction should expose students to complex scenarios, problems, and projects that require them to integrate a number of skills in a more realistic context.	Rather than only assessing skills in isolation, the assessment process should incorporate integrated tasks that require students to demonstrate application of multiple standards and resolve an authentic or realistic problem. Students should be expected to conduct research and write reports based on their findings.
We want students to think at high levels, create, innovate, and communicate. We want them to research, investigate, and communicate their findings.	Instruction should place less focus on the *right* answer and more emphasis on engaging students in the development of creative and innovative solutions to problems.	Assessments should place more emphasis on performance tasks that provide opportunities for students to demonstrate creativity and innovation.

*Visit **go.solution-tree.com/commoncore** for a reproducible version of this table.*

At first glance, these major shifts may seem overwhelming. Our experience is, however, that when collaborative teams begin doing this work, they are energized with the idea that their work is important and valuable. Teachers are no longer teaching students to fill in bubbles and to eliminate the answer choices they know are wrong and guess between those remaining. These teachers are involved in practices that led them to the teaching profession in the first place. In addition, relying on the four guiding questions (page 9), they organize their work in manageable chunks and use the process in the planning of instructional units throughout the year.

Becoming Familiar With the CCSS

So, how does a team get started on this important work? We recommend building awareness of the structure and general content of the CCSS (www.corestandards.org/the-standards) as an important first step, and one that will lead the team to answering the first critical question, What do we want our students to learn? In the two sections that follow, we define the structure of the ELA/literacy and mathematics standards.

Learn the Structure of the CCSS ELA/Literacy

The Common Core State Standards for English language arts/literacy (NGA & CCSSO, 2010a) comprise three main sections: (1) grades K–5 English language arts standards, (2) grades 6–12 English language arts standards, and (3) grades 6–12 standards for literacy in history / social studies, science, and technical subjects. Three appendices accompany the main document: (1) "Appendix A: Research Supporting Key Elements of the Standards and Glossary of Key Terms," (2) "Appendix B: Text Exemplars and Sample Performance Tasks," and (3) "Appendix C: Samples of Student Writing" (NGA & CCSSO, 2010b, 2010c, 2010d).

The work of your teams will be effective if members are conversant with the organization of these standards. They should know the meanings of key terms—*strands, anchor standards, domains, grade-specific standards,* and *grade bands.*

- **Strands** are the main divisions for grades K–5 and 6–12: Reading, Writing, Speaking and Listening, and Language. At these levels, the Reading strand has two parts: Reading Standards for Literature (RL) and Reading Standards for Informational Text (RI). Foundational Skills (RF) are a third set of standards in the Reading strand for K–5 (see NGA & CCSSO, 2010a, pp. 15–17). The Literacy standards for history and social studies, science, and technical subjects have two strands—Reading (RH and RST) and Writing (WH and WST; see NGA & CCSSO, 2010a, pp. 60–66).

- **Anchor standards** define expectations for college and career readiness (CCRA). They define general, cross-disciplinary expectations for each strand—Reading, Writing, Speaking and Listening, and Language—as well as the two strands in the Literacy standards. The anchor standards are numbered consecutively for each strand. For example, CCSS ELA-Literacy.CCRA.R.1 signifies college and career readiness anchor standard (CCRA), Reading strand (R), and anchor standard one (1). In this book, we use a simplified version of the standard designation; in this case, that designation is CCRA.R.1. The Reading and Writing strands for literacy in history and social studies, science, and technical subjects have anchor standards. For example, WHST.9–10.4 signifies Writing strand (W), history (H), science (S), technical subjects (T), grade band (9–10), anchor standard four (4).

- **Domains** define categories of anchor standards for each of the ELA/literacy strands. The domains are consistent across the grades and ensure continuity as the standards increase in rigor and complexity. The four domains in the Writing strand are (1) Text Types and Purposes, (2) Production and Distribution of Writing, (3) Research to Build and Present Knowledge, and (4) Range of Writing (see NGA & CCSSO, 2010a, p. 18).

- **Grade-specific standards** define what students should understand and be able to do at the end of the year. These standards correspond to anchor standards with the same number designation. For example, RL.6.1 signifies Reading Standards for Literature (RL), grade six (6), and standard one (1) in the domain Key Ideas and Details. Similarly, SL.6.1 signifies Speaking and Listening (SL), grade six (6), and standard one (1) in the domain Comprehension and Collaboration.

- **Grade bands** are groupings of standards by grade levels: K–2, 3–5, 6–8, 9–10, and 11–12.

Learn the Structure of the CCSS for Mathematics

The Common Core State Standards for mathematics consist of two parts: (1) Standards for Mathematical Practice and (2) Standards for Mathematical Content. The content standards have three sections: (1) standards for grades K–8 and high school, (2) a glossary, and (3) a sample of works consulted. "Appendix A: Designing High School Mathematics Courses Based on the Common Core State Standards" is another component (see NGA & CCSSO, 2010f).

Having a common vocabulary facilitates the work of your collaborative teams. Members should be conversant with these key terms in the Common Core mathematics: *Mathematical Practices*, *standards*, *clusters*, *domains*, *critical areas*, and *conceptual categories*.

- **Mathematical Practices** are the habits of mind or areas of expertise that students need to develop to understand and use mathematics effectively. These practices are integral to the development of mathematics content at all grade levels. The eight Mathematical Practices are (1) Make sense of problems and persevere in solving them, (2) Reason abstractly and quantitatively, (3) Construct viable arguments and critique the reasoning of others, (4) Model with mathematics, (5) Use appropriate tools strategically, (6) Attend to precision, (7) Look for and make use of structure, and (8) Look for and express regularity in repeated reasoning (see NGA & CCSSO, 2010e, pp. 6–8).

- **Standards** define what students should understand and be able to do.

- **Clusters** are groups of related standards. Because mathematics is a connected subject, standards from different clusters may sometimes be closely related.

- **Domains** are larger groups of related standards. Standards from different domains may sometimes be closely related. For example, the domains for grade 4 are Operations and Algebraic Thinking (4.OA), Number and Operations in Base Ten (4.NBT), Number and Operations—Fractions (4.NF), Measurement and Data (4.MD), and Geometry (4.G). The domains each carry a designation that signifies the grade level and the symbol for the domain.

- **Critical areas** define topics for particular focus for mathematics instruction in K–8. For example, the critical areas for kindergarten are: "(1) representing, relating, and operating on whole numbers, initially with sets of objects; (2) describing shapes and space. More learning time in Kindergarten should be devoted to number than to other topics" (NGA & CCSSO, 2010e, p. 9).

- **Conceptual categories** are the listings for the high school mathematics content standards. These categories present "a coherent view of high school mathematics; a student's work with functions, for example, crosses a number of traditional course boundaries, potentially up through and including calculus" (NGA & CCSSO, 2010e, p. 57). The six conceptual categories are:

  a. Number and Quantity (N)

  b. Algebra (A)

  c. Functions (F)

  d. Modeling

  e. Geometry (G)

  f. Statistics and Probability (S)

Each conceptual category, with the exception of Modeling, consists of domains containing two or more clusters. For example, the conceptual category Algebra (A) has four domains: (1) Seeing Structure in Expressions (A-SSE), (2) Arithmetic With Polynomials and Rational Expressions (A-APR), (3) Creating Equations (A-CED), and (4) Reasoning With Equations and Inequalities (A-REI). The domain Seeing Structure in Expressions (A-SSE) has two content standard clusters: (1) *Interpret the structure of expressions*, which has two standards, and (2) *Write expressions in equivalent forms to solve problems*, which also has two standards. The standards are numbered consecutively in the domains. For example, A-SSE.1 designates the conceptual category Algebra (A), the domain Seeing Structure in Expressions (SSE), and the first standard (1) in the cluster *Interpret the structure of expressions* (see NGA & CCSSO, 2010e, p. 64).

Explore the CCSS ELA/Literacy and Mathematics

While there are a number of ways to accomplish the task of becoming familiar with the CCSS, there are four easily implemented approaches that provide opportunities for team members to interact with each other as they examine the Common Core resources: (1) vertical standards walks, (2) end-in-mind skills exploration, (3) assessment exploration, and (4) scavenger hunts.

Vertical Standards Walks

As a team whose members represent different grade levels, conduct a vertical exploration of the Common Core ELA/literacy and mathematics standards. For a *strand walk* in language arts, take one of the strands—Reading, Writing, Speaking and Listening, or Language—and post the standards for the grade band the team represents. This activity for the mathematics standards will be a *domain walk*. Similarly, team members take one of the domains (for example, Operations and Algebraic Thinking) and post standards for the grade band represented. Teams can then *walk the room* and using sticky notes post observations about the shifts they observe in *what students should know and do*, how they will demonstrate or apply this knowledge, and implications for assessment. Additionally, the teams may note some of the differences in the academic language and terms used in the CCSS. It's useful to take careful note of the verbs the standards use, as they indicate the rigor of thinking you will expect from your students. Using this vertical activity serves to spark conversations about teaching and learning across grade levels or content areas within the entire school and helps to increase awareness of the staircase design of the standards.

End-in-Mind Skills Exploration

As a school or team, examine the Common Core ELA/literacy anchor standards or the Mathematical Practices in the mathematics standards. These components are the bases for the grade-level standards in each discipline and represent the *end-in-mind* skills and dispositions desired for all students. As you examine standards, discuss your grade level's role toward their accomplishment and the standards that aligned to this anchor standard or mathematical practice at your grade level. Discuss the importance of the selected anchor standard or mathematical practice, particularly as it supports the preparedness of students for the demands of college and career.

Assessment Exploration

Two consortia—the Partnership for Assessment of Readiness for College and Careers (PARCC) and the Smarter Balanced Assessment Consortium (SBAC)—are working with state representatives to develop K–12 assessments of English and mathematics aligned with the CCSS by the 2014–15 school year. (Visit www.parcconline.org and www.smarterbalanced.org for information about the work of the consortia and their released questions.)

As a grade-level or course team or on a schoolwide basis, examine the released questions and blueprints available through your state's assessment consortium (either PARCC or SBAC). Doing so will serve as an eye-opener. After seeing the task demands, context, and level of skill application contained within these samples, any teachers who might have been working under the illusion that the CCSS won't require a change in practice will definitely get the idea that this isn't business as usual. Following are some guiding questions for your team to consider as you examine the released items.

- As you look at the items compared to the traditional standardized assessments, what differences do you notice in terms of what students need to know and do?

- What challenges do you think students will face as they encounter these assessments?

- Given the differences and potential challenges, what implications might there be for your instruction and assessment practice within your course, discipline, or grade level?

Scavenger Hunts

Conduct CCSS scavenger hunts to engage staff in the process of digging into the standards for both English language arts and mathematics. Figure 1.3 presents questions for a scavenger hunt of the CCSS ELA/literacy; figure 1.4 (page 18) presents questions for a scavenger hunt of the CCSS for mathematics. Use the questions to jumpstart further dialogue.

Tips for Teams New to the PLC Process

We understand that teams may bring varied experiences to the table when first reading this book. First of all, if you and your team are just beginning, we applaud you for picking up this book. We truly believe that the best way to move forward with the CCSS is by working with others to focus on student learning.

The Common Core State Standards for ELA/literacy comprise three main sections: (1) grades K–5 English language arts standards, (2) grades 6–12 English language arts standards, and (3) grades 6–12 standards for literacy in history/social studies, science, and technical subjects. Three appendices accompany the main document: (1) "Appendix A: Research Supporting Key Elements of the Standards and Glossary of Key Terms," (2) "Appendix B: Text Exemplars and Sample Performance Tasks," and (3) "Appendix C: Samples of Student Writing." (See www.corestandards.org/ELA-Literacy for the standards.)

Strands

- What is a strand?
- What are the strands in the Common Core ELA/literacy?
- How does the Reading strand differ from the other strands?
- What do you observe about ways in which the strands overlap with one another? What is an example at your grade level?
- What are the strands in the standards for literacy in history and social studies, science, and technical subjects for grades 6–12?

Anchor Standards

- What are anchor standards?
- What is the standard for your grade level that connects to anchor standard eight in the Reading strand?
- What is a domain?
- How are domains related to anchor standards?
- What are the domains in the Language strand?

Standards

- What is a standard?
- How many standards can you find for your grade level that include the word *analyze*?
- What are the types of writing you will teach in your grade level?
- Compare your grade level Reading standard three to the grade below yours and the grade above yours.

Terminology

- What is text complexity? How is it determined?
- What are text exemplars?
- What are domain-specific words and phrases?
- What is a grade band?
- What are Lexile ranges? What is the Lexile range for your grade level?

Figure 1.3: CCSS English language arts/literacy scavenger hunt.

Visit go.solution-tree.com/commoncore for a reproducible version of this figure.

You've made a great choice! Here are some pointers to get started. If your team is just developing, or if you are unclear about what a PLC is all about, we suggest starting with a couple of resources.

Our first recommendation is that teams obtain a copy of *Learning by Doing: A Handbook for Professional Learning Communities at Work*™ (DuFour et al., 2010), a resource that walks teams through the PLC concepts and practices, clarifying the purpose of collaborative teams and providing guidelines and processes for *doing the work*. Among its many resources, the book contains processes for establishing time to meet, creating collective commitments, organizing team meeting time, and building consensus among its members.

Another resource is the first chapter in *Common Formative Assessment: A Toolkit for Professional Learning Communities at Work*™ (Bailey & Jakicic, 2012), which is devoted to synthesizing the background and guiding principles of professional learning communities and includes indicators of effective teams.

We strongly recommend Parry Graham and Bill Ferriter's (2010) book *Building a Professional Learning Community at Work*™: *A Guide to the First Year*. This practical book takes teams on the journey of implementing professional learning communities, giving useful insights and guidance from the perspective of practitioners.

The Common Core State Standards for mathematics consist of two parts: (1) Standards for Mathematical Practice and (2) Standards for Mathematical Content. The content standards have three sections: (1) standards for grades K–8 and high school (organized by conceptual categories), (2) glossary, and (3) sample of works consulted (see www.corestandards.org/Math for the standards). "Appendix A: Designing High School Mathematics Courses Based on the Common Core State Standards" is another component.

Domains

- What is a domain?

- What are the domains for your grade level?

- Which domains in the grade level before yours are the same? Different?

- Which domains in the grade level after yours are the same? Different?

- Examine one domain that is in your grade level and in the grade level before. What will students already know in that domain when they come to your grade level?

Clusters

- What is a cluster?

- Which domain in your grade level has the most clusters? The fewest?

Standards

- What is a standard?

- How many standards are there in your grade level?

- Which one standard is new at your grade level?

- Which one standard is no longer taught at your grade level?

- How many standards begin with the word *understand*?

Terminology

- What are the Standards for Mathematical Practice? How are they connected to the Standards for Mathematical Content?

- What are the critical areas? What are the critical areas for your grade level?

- What is a grade band?

- What is a conceptual category?

Figure 1.4: CCSS for mathematics scavenger hunt.

*Visit **go.solution-tree.com/commoncore** for a reproducible version of this figure.*

Finally, we encourage you to visit the website AllThingsPLC (www.allthingsplc.info), where you will find tools and resources, articles and research, and stories of educators participating in the PLC journey.

At a minimum, to be effective a team should have the following:

- Regular, dedicated time to work together

- Commitments or norms for how members will interact, communicate, and prioritize their efforts and decisions

- A clear understanding of the team's core purpose—to help students learn

Teams may benefit from having support during their initial meetings. We suggest that schools beginning the process consider bringing all teams together in a common room, so that they can connect and share their products and processes. In addition, this configuration allows for someone to assist teams as a lead facilitator.

Tips for Principals and Leaders

As you begin this work, be sure to make *explicit* connections between the work of collaborative planning teams and the need to transition to the CCSS. While the connection may seem obvious, there is a risk that some teams may see the transition to new standards as something disconnected to the work of collaborative teams within the PLC. Additionally, some or all team members may be new to the process.

Consequently, without intentionally reviewing the *why* behind the work, you can't ensure that everyone is on the same page and understands the purpose, process, and point of the team and the PLC process.

As part of this review, we strongly suggest *refreshing* teams early on to ensure common clarity about why they are collaborating, effective practices of teams, and your expectations for team outcomes or products. You may ask teams to review their norms and provide you a copy of their initial statement or revision.

To support teams' understanding of the nature and purpose of their work, continue to frame all discussions, professional development activities, and support products along the guiding questions of a PLC (see page 9).

2

Supporting Change to Facilitate Shifts to the CCSS

Collaborative Connections

- Making the transition to the CCSS involves a change that would be more difficult if collaborative teams didn't have each other for support.

- Building strong collaborative practices will help teachers embrace this change.

- Teams will need time to work together to make this change happen; therefore, embedded time to work together will provide the best professional development.

Education changes constantly. We often talk about the pendulum swings that occur in our profession as though they belong on the list of Newton's laws of motion—something that we can't control and that we expect to always happen. We have become so accustomed to change that many teachers believe that, if they wait long enough, the change will go away and be replaced with something new, or something that was once declared passé will be rejuvenated. Unfortunately, this culture in our profession has allowed us to see every change with the same perspective and to embrace only those changes that resonate with our own personal beliefs. If we want to help teachers embrace the changes that are a part of the new expectations we have for learning, there are some ways we can plan and support teachers as they get started.

We feel strongly that districts, schools, and teams must first understand *why* they are making this change. In his book *Start With Why*, Simon Sinek (2009) discusses how organizations can inspire people to action by making sure they focus first on *why* a change is necessary. He makes the case that change in practice occurs more easily when people understand the reasons why this change is necessary or beneficial. For example, consider the idea of college and career readiness, which is paramount in the CCSS. Teachers may not realize the importance of this emphasis, especially if they are not working at the high school level. The findings of a study from the Georgetown University Center on Education and the Workforce (Carnevale, Smith, & Strohl, 2010) address this issue. The research shows that by 2018, 63 percent of all jobs will require more than a high school diploma (Carnevale et al., 2010). No longer can we set graduation from high school as the end goal for students.

This need is also borne out when you consider the issue of 21st century skills. How often have you heard the term *21st century skills* in reference to the future of education? The reality is that we have already lived more than 10 percent of the 21st century, yet many teachers don't feel like they've had time or training to change how they teach to prepare students for the future. In fact, as educators, we know that we are preparing our students for a world that is likely to be very different from the one in which we're currently living. However, it's challenging to provide the necessary preparation when we don't really know what that world will be. We've all heard the numbers about how quickly the amount of information available is accruing. In fact, Ken Kay (2010), president of the Partnership for 21st Century Skills, observes that while technical information was doubling every twenty-four months in 2010, he expects that by 2020, it will double every seventy-two days. He further explains, "Only people who have the knowledge and skills to negotiate constant change and reinvent themselves for new situations will succeed" (Kay, 2010).

Effective Transition to the CCSS

What changes must we make to ensure that the transition to the CCSS is effective? Let's examine the shifts inherent in the CCSS ELA/literacy and mathematics. From our examination of the ELA/literacy and mathematics standards, we see that significant changes are required in school curricula. Both sets of standards imply a different instructional approach in order to meet the level of rigor built into the standards. Here's a quick way to highlight the shift in rigor. Take one strand in the English language arts standards or one domain in the mathematics standards for a selected grade level and simply circle all the verbs. Then compare those verbs to those you use in your current state standards. We're guessing that the change in rigor is readily apparent. Additionally, not only do the standards have heightened rigor but also an expectation for significant changes in how and when standards are taught and the pacing of instruction. Let's look at the most significant shifts found within the CCSS for English language arts/literacy and mathematics.

Changes in Expectations for the CCSS ELA/Literacy

We describe seven features of the ELA/literacy standards that have significant implications for what teachers will teach and how students will learn: text complexity, informational text, interdisciplinary literacy, close reading, text analysis, argumentative writing, and academic vocabulary and language.

1. **Text complexity:** The first change most teachers notice is the expectation for increased text complexity in the reading matter provided for students at all grade levels. In the Reading strand at all grade levels, anchor standard ten addresses this issue.

    > Read and comprehend complex literary and informational texts independently and proficiently. (R.CCRA.10) (NGA & CCSSO, 2010a, p. 10)

    The Common Core for English language arts contains two resources that support teachers in working with this standard: (1) appendix A of the Common Core (NGA & CCSSO, 2010b) explains why text complexity matters and how it is determined, and (2) appendix B of the Common Core (NGA & CCSSO, 2010c) provides examples of various types of text organized by grade bands K–1, 2–3, 4–5, 6–8, 9–10, and 11–12, as well as sample performance tasks for each type of text. In order for teachers to be able to make this change, they will need time to work collaboratively to learn about text complexity, to find new pieces of text to meet the high expectations for students, and to learn together about how to incorporate these in their language arts programs (Davis, 2012).

2. **Informational text:** These standards are consistent with the distribution of literary and informational text in the framework of the National Assessment of Educational Progress (NAEP). Table 2.1 shows this distribution for grades 4, 8, and 12.

Table 2.1: Grade Distribution of Literary and Informational Passages in the 2009 NAEP Framework

Grade	Literary	Informational
4	50 percent	50 percent
8	45 percent	55 percent
12	30 percent	70 percent

Source: Adapted from NGA & CCSSO, 2010a, p. 5.

In the elementary grades, the balance between these forms of text is about 50 percent for each type. However, this distribution changes at the high school level, in which approximately 70 percent of the curriculum is expected to be based on informational text. While many elementary and middle schools have been making this transition, this may be the first time that high schools have to think about how such courses as American literature and British literature will change. Although there is an expectation that more literary nonfiction will be included in the English programs, the emphasis on informational text in the higher grades applies across the curriculum. Teams in middle and secondary schools will have to have time to work with their colleagues in science, technical subjects, and social studies to compare and share new resources (EngageNY, 2012).

3. **Interdisciplinary literacy:** There is an expectation that the ELA standards will be embedded into other classes including science, technical subjects, history, and social studies. NGA and CCSSO (2010a) specify, "The Standards insist that instruction in reading, writing, speaking, listening, and language be a shared responsibility within the school" (p. 4). Prior to grade 6, the ELA standards for informational text are written to include materials and activities that might be typically taught in a science or social studies lesson. For example, consider this third-grade standard in the Reading Standards for Informational Text.

> Describe the relationship between a series of historical events, scientific ideas or concepts, or steps in technical procedures in a text, using language that pertains to time, sequence, and cause/effect. (RI.3.3) (NGA & CCSSO, 2010a, p. 14)

The standards for grades 6–12 have two sections, one for English language arts and another for literacy in history and social studies, science, and technical subjects (see NGA & CCSSO, 2010a, pp. 60–66). Teachers in those content areas will now have to address the literacy standards for reading and writing as well as their own content standards. For example, consider this standard for grades 6–8 in the Reading Standards for Literacy in History/Social Studies.

> Identify key steps in a text's description of a process related to history/social studies (for example, how a bill becomes law, how interest rates are raised or lowered). (RH.6–8.3) (NGA & CCSSO, 2010a, p. 61)

Consequently, it will be important for content-area teachers and ELA teachers to work together to learn about specific strategies being taught in ELA classes that can be used in other content-area classes. For example, content teachers will want to know how to help students understand point of view, bias, and support in order to make sense of the texts used in their courses. For this to happen, teams will have to be organized horizontally—across disciplines—and will need time to meet together to share information.

4. **Close reading:** The first anchor standard in the Reading strand sends a clear message about close reading of text.

    > Read closely to determine what the text says explicitly and to make logical inferences
    > from it; cite specific textual evidence when writing or speaking to support conclusions
    > drawn from the text. (R.CCRA.1) (NGA & CCSSO, 2010a, p. 10)

    This standard signals that teachers will need to provide explicit instruction to enable students to achieve this standard. For many years, teachers have taught reading by helping students access their prior knowledge before beginning to read a piece of text. Furthermore, that approach encourages students to relate the text to their own experiences rather than requiring them to scrutinize the text for evidence. Often, through these discussions, students learn most of the content of the text before they even begin to read it. The CCSS ELA make clear that students should be able to read a text independently and understand what the author is saying as well as what the author may be implying with word choice, sentence construction, figurative language, and so on. Consequently, many teachers may need additional training about how to prepare students for close reading. To develop this skill, teams may want to use peer teaching relationships, such as those in the lesson study approach (see www.tc.columbia.edu/lesson study/lessonstudy.html).

5. **Text analysis:** Reading anchor standard one (R.CCRA.1) also demonstrates the importance of students being able to cite specific examples from the text to support their facts, inferences, or conclusions. In other words, textual evidence will be an important part of any answer a student provides about the text he or she has read. While many teachers likely have asked students to provide text-based information in their answers, it will become vitally important that *all* teachers share this expectation and adjust their instruction accordingly. The ability to analyze text effectively is linked to the ability to do close reading, which leads to deep comprehension.

6. **Argumentative writing:** The Common Core ELA Writing strand focuses on three types of writing: (1) argumentative, (2) informational or explanatory, and (3) narrative. Of these three types, the standards place "particular emphasis on students' ability to write sound arguments on substantive topics and issues, as this ability is critical to college and career readiness" (NGA & CCSSO, 2010b, p. 24). This emphasis involves moving away from personal opinion and replacing it with facts and ideas that information and evidence support. For some teachers, this may be a more significant change than for others, depending on what they have focused on in the past. Some teachers, for example, taught specific strategies—such as *bandwagon,* an emotional appeal to go along with popular opinion—to help their students understand how to create an emotional appeal in their writing (Davis, 2012). These teachers will have to revise

their units of instruction to shift from a personal or emotional focus to a logical or reasoned focus. Teachers will need to have the time to work with their colleagues as they make this shift. They will want to find writing samples that will demonstrate good writing as well as to create activities and prompts that will help students become better writers of this genre. A useful resource for teachers seeking writing samples is appendix C of the Common Core ELA (NGA & CCSSO, 2010d). Here you will find samples of student writing representative of the three types defined in the Writing strand. The samples stipulate the criteria required to meet the standards for each type of writing in grades K–12.

7. **Academic vocabulary and language:** The Language strand in the Common Core ELA highlights the importance of explicit vocabulary development. Anchor standard six specifies the types of words—*academic* and *domain specific*—that are essential to students' success in school and beyond.

> Acquire and use accurately a range of general academic and domain-specific words and phrases sufficient for reading, writing, speaking, and listening at the college and career readiness level; demonstrate independence in gathering vocabulary knowledge when encountering an unknown term important to comprehension or expression. (L.CCRA.6) (NGA & CCSSO, 2010a, p. 25)

Based on the work of Isabel Beck, Margaret G. McKeown, and Linda Kucan (2002, 2008), the ELA standards define three tiers of words. Students often acquire tier one words in speaking and listening in the early grades K–2. Tier two words are academic words students learn through reading both literature and informational texts. They are often generalizable across several different content areas. Tier three words are domain-specific words that students often learn through reading informational texts (NGA & CCSSO, 2010b). The standards for acquiring vocabulary are intended to support students as they read complex texts and move toward achieving *lexical dexterity* (NGA & CCSSO, 2010b).

When teacher teams spend time really digging into the implications of the new ELA/literacy standards, they recognize that this set of standards includes more than just new content; there will be many implications for both the use of different instructional strategies as well as the need for acquiring new text resources. Additionally, teachers will likely need to rethink their use of instructional time to add more opportunities for students to write. Whether we are teachers, principals, curriculum designers, or staff developers, these standards will have an impact on our work.

Changes in Expectations in the CCSS for Mathematics

The mathematics standards have comparable changes in expectations to those we identified in the Common Core ELA. We describe four features, which have significant implications for the content teachers will teach and the skills students will learn: (1) fewer but more focused standards, (2) habits of mind, (3) progression of skills and concepts, and (4) procedural fluency.

1. **Fewer but more focused standards:** The Common Core mathematics standards are purposely more focused with the result that fewer standards are presented for the elementary and middle school grades and high school courses. NGA and CCSSO (2010e) explain that these standards are intended to create a focused and coherent set of expectations that allow students the time to develop deep understanding of each standard. The adage *less is more* characterizes

the Common Core mathematics. For teachers who are accustomed to using a curriculum or textbook that addresses all of the typical mathematical domains during a school year, this new focus means understanding more deeply each of the domains that they will be teaching. For example, students have often been taught how to use an algorithm to solve a problem. They may have been able to fill in the numbers and complete the sequence of steps to get to the right answer. However, they often were unable to explain what they were doing and why; they lacked clear understanding of the process and concept. The CCSS require students to focus on justifying why they used each step in solving the problem—that is, they must deeply understand the solution process. For this change to happen, it is essential that mathematics teachers have the time and the professional development they need to be able to provide opportunities to build these reasoning skills for their students. The professional development support for mathematics teachers will need to enable them to enhance their knowledge of mathematical concepts and processes so that they can adapt their instruction to fulfill the expectations of the CCSS. Many schools and districts are moving to incorporating coaches and coaching time into their professional development practices in order to help teachers with these new understandings.

2. **Habits of mind:** The challenge implicit in these standards is teaching students to think like mathematicians. The Standards for Mathematical Practice (NGA & CCSSO, 2010e) define six behaviors that students need to develop in order to apply problem-solving skills in real-world situations. The habits of mind—persevering, reasoning, forming arguments, modeling, communicating precisely, and using structure—formed through the Mathematical Practices enable students to become "practitioners of the discipline of mathematics" (NGA & CCSSO, 2010e, p. 8). Teachers will be seeking out more real-life applications and specific problems to ensure their students are able to meet these new expectations. Again, adding coaching support as teachers develop and learn these new skills will be important.

3. **Progression of skills and concepts:** The Common Core mathematics standards are built on the concept of *coherence* from one grade to the next. This means that students must acquire certain skills and knowledge as the foundation for what will be coming in the next grade level. For teachers, it will be important to study certain progressions in the Standards for Mathematical Content. For example, consider how the standards demonstrate progression in the development of the concept of fractions over three grade levels: fractions are formally introduced in grade 3; equivalent fractions are presented in grade 4; addition and subtraction of fractions are presented in grade 5. Understanding the concept of *progressions* will be important as teachers work with the Common Core mathematics standards. Teachers will be served well by reading the progressions that apply to the grade levels they teach (see http://math.arizona.edu/~ime/progressions for *Progressions Documents for the Common Core Math Standards*; Common Core Standards Writing Team, 2012).

4. **Procedural fluency:** Students are expected to be able to carry out certain calculations with speed and accuracy. This expectation will require teachers to provide enough repetition for students to practice and achieve this fluency. This expectation for fluency begins in kindergarten with students being able to add and subtract fluently up to five and with greater expectations each year. Students are expected to be able to fluently multiply multidigit numbers in grade 5 and to compute fluently in grade 6. By grade 7, they are expected to solve equations fluently. Procedural fluency is a hallmark of the Standards for Mathematical Practice (EngageNY, 2012).

As with the ELA standards, the implications of these new mathematics standards go beyond just a change in the content of what teachers will teach. Allowing students the time to think about—and especially to talk about—how they are solving a problem requires a real shift away from teacher-directed lessons. Finding quality mathematics tasks will likely be a high priority as teams work together to infuse the Standards for Mathematical Practice into their instruction. Assessments will need to move from having students demonstrate that they can apply the correct algorithm, to having students make a conjecture solving a realistic problem and then justify their reasoning.

Getting Aboard the Change Train

The good news is that teachers with whom we've worked in their transition to the CCSS feel strongly that the standards make a great deal of sense and incorporate many of the things that will be important for students in the future. The problem is, however, that these same teachers are being bombarded with changes from all directions and feel overwhelmed with everything they have to do, especially considering the limited amount of time they have for collaborative planning. Linda Darling-Hammond (2010) provides a comparison to teachers in other countries that supports this lack of planning time: U.S. teachers spend about 80 percent of their working time in the classroom with students, leaving only 20 percent for professional development, planning, and working collaboratively. This is in contrast to how teachers in other countries spend their time; they spend about 60 percent of their time working with students, leaving 40 percent for professional development, planning, and working collaboratively. Those teachers have much more time for their own learning. The scope of change evident with the CCSS demands that schools and districts are intentional about how this change will happen. The ramifications are significant: *what* teachers will be teaching, *how* they will be teaching, and *how* students will be learning.

Transitioning to teaching and assessing the CCSS and ensuring that students have learned them could be perceived as overwhelming changes for teachers, schools, and districts. Teachers will likely rewrite or revise their curriculum and units of instruction, change their pacing, use new instructional strategies, and create new plans for supporting students with more time and differentiated tasks. Any of these would be a significant change by itself, and together they certainly represent what is often called *second-order change*, that is, a change that is not incremental but one that requires new thinking and a new direction for the school organization (Marzano, Waters, & McNulty, 2003). Second-order change is significantly different than first-order change (usually incremental in scope) in that it requires a change in the culture in order to make it happen.

As we think about how to make this change manageable and effective, let's first consider what we know about how change successfully happens for schools and other organizations. John Kotter's (1996) study of how successful organizations make changes happen suggests a multistep process to be successful. (Visit www.mindtools.com for more information about Kotter's change model [MindTools, n.d.].)

Step One: Create a Sense of Urgency

Kotter (1996) explains how complacency often derails the change process and recommends that the first step involves creating a sense of urgency for the people involved in the change. Overcoming complacency requires teachers to understand the reason for the change and believe that it will make a difference for their students. If we apply this first step to the work we do in schools, it may appear fairly easy to create a sense of urgency given that many schools are failing to meet their adequate yearly progress (AYP) requirements and are facing sanctions as a result. Many schools and districts have used this threat of sanctions to create urgency for change. However, as we've found, this threat makes teachers comply with the rules but hasn't always led to greater achievement or willingness to work collaboratively to accomplish the necessary changes.

Other schools and districts, knowing their students will be taking the new PARCC or SBAC assessments on the Common Core in 2014–2015, have rushed to start using the new standards with little planning for the deep implementation that is needed. This may leave teachers feeling that they are ill-prepared for this work and worry that their students will be unprepared for these new "high stakes" tests.

Both of these scenarios create the sense of urgency and help teachers overcome complacency. Unfortunately, however, they also both replace that complacency with fear—fear that can inhibit people from taking action. We believe there is a better way. First, we'll explore the research about the concerns that teachers have when facing any change. We'll follow that by suggesting ways to create a sense of urgency that doesn't rely on emphasizing fear.

As we've worked with teachers, schools, and districts implementing change including the transition to the Common Core, we've often referred to the Concerns-Based Adoption Model (CBAM) research (Hall & Hord, 2006) to consider how to help teachers move through change more easily. The model suggests three stages of concern individuals experience as they go through any change. These concerns relate to self, tasks, and impact.

Understand and Manage Self-Concerns

At the beginning of any change when individuals become aware of what the change will be, Gene Hall and Shirley Hord (2006) suggest that they become focused on *self*-concerns and how the change will impact their own practices. They may be uncomfortable not knowing if they will like, or be good at, the new innovation. We often see this reaction in our work with teachers who are just learning about the Common Core standards. Because they have heard about the increased rigor of these standards, they are often worried that they may not be able to help students learn at this higher level. Often they've already struggled with helping all students reach proficiency and wonder if it's possible with these new, more rigorous standards.

One recommendation to help teachers at this stage is to assure them that these concerns are normal when facing such a significant change. We've found that many teachers, particularly those who have a great deal of experience, are uncomfortable admitting that they don't have all the answers. When they learn that it is natural to feel insecure early in implementation, they are more likely to embrace the uncertainty.

So what would help teachers move through their self-concerns as they embrace the Common Core and work on new curriculum and instructional strategies? First, it is important to focus on the support the collaborative team structure provides. No teacher is trying to do (or is expected to do) this work independently. By design, developing understanding of the standards, choosing the essential standards, writing common formative assessments, and designing corrective instruction are all done collaboratively. If teachers know that they are going to be able to rely on each other and to have the time they need, they will more easily overcome their self-concerns.

To alleviate self-concerns at this stage, leaders need to provide collaborative teams with some basic information: the nature and structure of the CCSS, a draft timeline for how the transition will occur, and reassurance that they will have the information and training needed to make this transition. We've seen many schools and districts shift the roles of instructional specialists into coaching roles as they prepared professional development plans to support this transition. For schools using this model, teachers need to know how these coaches will be helpful for the adult learning that needs to happen. Self-concerns will likely spill over into the next stage: *task concerns*.

Understand and Manage Task Concerns

During this stage of transitioning to the Common Core State Standards, teams are concerned about the amount of work they see ahead of them: new curriculum, new instructional strategies, new common formative assessments, new intervention and extension strategies, and so on. They will need assurance from their administrators that the plan for this transition is manageable. Having a process in place that lays out an attainable timeline will help teams stay focused on the work they need to do without feeling overwhelmed with the entire process. Presenting the big picture will enable teams to see that each step of the change process has a purpose and that it is important to keep moving forward in order to complete the implementation. During this step, it is important that the leadership team for the school and district meet regularly to discuss and share successes and roadblocks. Teacher teams must feel that they have some say in the process and some control over the timeline. This is where the issues of *loose and tight* relationships become critical. The Professional Learning Communities at Work model explains the relationship in this way: "A leadership concept in which leaders encourage autonomy and creativity (loose) within well-defined parameters and priorities that must be honored (tight)" (DuFour, DuFour, & Eaker, 2008, p. 470). There will always be some tension between the leadership and teachers about what a realistic timeline will look like. The leadership team must keep the focus on student learning and must ensure that the transition occurs smoothly. We provide additional observations about loose-tight relationships in step four on page 32. See also the reproducible "Loose Versus Tight Decisions" on page 186.

Sometimes teams will need more time to accomplish a particular step. For example, in a district working to identify essential standards, the work of one high school English department team came to a screeching halt when talking about the ELA standards in the Language strand for grades 9–12. The team members realized that there was no common belief about how grammar should be taught or how much grammar was important for students to learn. For this group, accomplishing the task of identifying essential standards had to include some time to work through a philosophy about teaching grammar. Although all of the K–8 grade levels in the district had completed their list of essential standards, and the issue of vertical alignment across the district had to be postponed until high school, English teachers were able to build consensus about grammar.

In addition to having an overall timeline, teachers need to understand the priorities and believe that their administrators have the same priorities. It would be unrealistic and unproductive to add all of this new work to the list of things teams should be focusing on without taking away something. Being overt about what tasks and expectations will be *taken off* the to-do list could make a difference in how teams respond to the plans for change.

Understand and Manage Impact Concerns

As teams get more involved in the new innovation, they will experience additional concerns about the *impact* of the change and about how they can make sure to sustain the innovation. At this point, the support that teachers need includes some coaching, some opportunities for leadership, and increased opportunities for collaboration.

Strategies to Create a Sense of Urgency

Although the research on stages of concern (Hall & Hord, 2006) is helpful in understanding factors that affect a sense of urgency, we suggest that schools and districts create a sense of urgency in a different way as they begin this transition. We recommend that they start by examining the need for change from the students' perspective. For example, many schools we've worked with use their data in a more personal way. The teachers translate the numbers into students' names and faces. Rather than seeing that 17 percent of their students didn't meet expectations, they see the names of students who didn't meet expectations. When teachers personally know the students who haven't mastered the standards, they are more likely to understand why this change is so important. This emphasis redirects attention away from the personal concerns of self, task, and impact.

In this context, we recommend that leadership and teacher teams examine their current school culture. Most schools and districts that have embraced the professional learning community model have worked to develop a culture that supports the belief that all students can learn at high levels. In some cases, schools get so caught up in the work they are doing in answering the four guiding questions they neglect to attend to their culture—to making sure that everyone understands and behaves in a way to support this work. Do teachers in your school see their responsibility to help maintain this culture? For example, in a meeting we attended, a group of elementary teacher leaders was discussing the issue of *resisters*—colleagues who didn't always believe that all students can learn at high levels. One colleague asked, "How do you respond, when these teachers question what we're doing?" One teacher leader responded by saying that she actually appreciated those colleagues who questioned her because it forced her to think deeply about why she believed what she was doing was the right thing.

Creating a sense of urgency in positive and constructive ways is vital to ensuring the success collaborative teams will experience as they embark on the process of change. School leaders can do much to support teams and individual teachers in addressing self, task, and impact concerns. Essentially, the leaders need to use strategies that allow teams to embrace change rather than fear it.

Step Two: Build a Guiding Coalition

Kotter (1996) observes that change happens most easily when a *guiding coalition* directs it.

A guiding coalition, often called the *school leadership team*, is the group of people who will lead the change process and includes both the formal leaders (for example, administrators, department chairpersons, and team leaders) and the informal leaders (teachers highly regarded by their colleagues) within the system.

In a professional learning community, this group typically comprises a representative group of teachers and administrators in a school who oversee and help to strategize and energize the ongoing implementation of the school's efforts to meet its mission, vision, values, and goals. We see this body as crucial to the organization of a school's transition to the CCSS, with one caveat. That caveat refers to decisions about who will be on the leadership team.

We recommend that leadership teams consider whether they have the right people in place to lead this new initiative or whether they need to add new members. We know that the leadership team should include people who have levels of expertise like content knowledge or communication skills that will foster collaborative efforts. Do we need to seek out other individuals for team membership? Can we help create people with expertise through additional training? In elementary schools, the leadership team should include members who have a high level of expertise in reading, writing, and mathematics, as these are the standards that will be their focus. For schools that are using coaches to support the work, the team should have a member who can provide information about the coaching process. By bringing in representatives of all stakeholder groups—content-area experts, grade-level teachers, veteran and new teachers, special education teachers, and guidance counselors—your guiding coalition will benefit from a broadened circle of ideas and expertise.

Of course, when this expanded leadership team comes together to do its work, members need to make sure that they are using the appropriate processes that ensure high-functioning teams: clarifying the team's purpose, establishing team norms, setting team goals, defining team member roles (for example, facilitator, notetaker, and time keeper), and focusing on the work ahead. (Visit **go.solution-tree.com /commoncore** for the reproducible "Critical Issues for Team Consideration" for more ideas about features of high-functioning teams.)

Step Three: Create and Communicate a Vision

The next step is to develop and communicate the vision. Hopefully, your school has created a culture where everyone believes that all students can learn at high levels. This culture will indeed support the transition to the Common Core State Standards. However, your school or district vision will likely need to be updated to include new ideas related to implementation of the CCSS. At this point, it's healthy to let people dream about a different future for your school and students and discuss what this ideal future will be. This discussion should include opportunities for teachers to describe how they envision the school if all students are to be successful with the rigorous expectations of the CCSS. Revisiting and communicating the vision starts with the leadership team clarifying how this change will happen in each team, school, or district. Teachers need to understand why the school is making this change, how the change process will occur, and what the expectations for each teacher or team will be. We recommend that all teachers be part of the conversation and refinement of the school's vision for learning.

To accomplish this, it will be important for participants in the conversation to learn more about the level of expectations and shifts contained in the Common Core. Building this shared knowledge will lead to deeper conversations that include considering potential challenges for how the CCSS will affect current practice in order to fulfill the vision. Conversations about what the standards will actually *look like* for students must occur. For example, English teachers will likely begin to examine the amount of informational text reading and writing in their grades or courses. Middle and high school teams in the subject areas—history, social studies, science, and technical subjects—might begin to discuss how they can build the expertise, resources, and time to include the literacy standards they are now expected to *own*. Mathematics teachers will begin to wrestle with the question of how the Mathematical Practices impact current mathematics instruction.

Prior to working with the professional learning community model, individual teachers may have made decisions for their own classrooms in order to meet these new expectations. Now, your collaborative teams will be the focus for this change. Having a clear vision that everyone subscribes to will help make this change a reality.

Step Four: Empower Everyone

The fourth step in building a successful change process is to empower *all* the stakeholders in the process. When teachers feel that something is being *done to them*, it is much harder for them to support change. On the other hand, when teachers are participants in collaborative teams, they feel empowered because they are contributing to plans for change. This starts with the process of identifying *essential or power standards* (see chapter 3, page 39) and continues as teams write and use common formative assessments. Based on assessment results, teachers pace instruction in order to provide additional time and support for students who haven't learned concepts or to provide additional challenge for students who can benefit from it.

Professional learning community principles include establishing a *loose-tight* relationship between leadership decisions and the resulting team products. DuFour and Marzano (2011) discuss the importance of building shared leadership responsibilities so that a collaborative team makes some, but not all, decisions.

Teams are empowered to complete their work in whatever way works best for them around *loose* expectations but they must follow the expectations of the leadership when completing *tight* tasks. Of course the leadership team must be clear about what will be tight as their schools move through this process. They must decide how and when they will determine the essential or power standards. Will a representative group of teachers do the work, or will all teachers be involved in the process? What subject will be completed first, next, and so on? What are the expectations about changing or revising the common formative assessments? If your district is using benchmark assessments written around your current state standards, who will revise these? When will they be revised? Will the current systematic response system in place need to be revised?

We provide an activity that your leadership team could complete to initiate the conversation around loose-tight issues. The reproducible "Loose Versus Tight Decisions" (page 186) invites you to consider various tasks, processes, and activities that require decisions about who will be responsible for completing or deciding this issue—the leadership or the teachers. For example, some districts will be leading the change around the transition to the CCSS, and some schools will take responsibility. Either way, the collaborative teams of teachers must know what they will be expected to decide and what their school or district leadership team will hold tight.

This step also requires that your collaborative teams begin the work. While this sounds simplistic, we sometimes work in schools where teams of teachers get stuck before they even get started. These teams want to plan everything out so that they know they won't make any mistakes. They are afraid that mistakes might derail them. We know that getting started can be scary. We also know that you will learn from whatever mistakes you make. Remember that the process isn't linear. You will want to decide on your power/essential standards during year one and use them in draft form. For the second year, you'll want to revise these standards. So, get started! Learn together!

Step Five: Celebrate Short-Term Wins

Creating short-term targets helps to sustain teams' interest and motivation. Kotter (1996) recommends celebrating short-term wins. Successful schools and districts will make sure they stop frequently to recognize and celebrate their accomplishments. Your collaborative team will need to do the same. Teachers tend to be much better at celebrating student success, but this is a time to celebrate how the work of the team is helping you move forward. Team meetings, faculty meetings, and regular communication with parents and the public must all feature information about tasks accomplished, people who have demonstrated leadership, and new learning the teachers have embraced.

Implications for Professional Development

The specifics of changes required in making the transition to the Common Core State Standards have several implications for professional development. The first is very obvious to everyone—collaborative teams and individual teachers will need time to make these changes. Schools and districts will need to be explicit about how the changes will happen. For example, some schools and districts have built-in professional development days when all teachers are available for this work and students have the day off. It will be important to set aside this time for work that must occur between collaborative teams—the vertical and horizontal alignment activities for identifying the priority standards as well as the discussions about how the literacy standards will be taught in science, technical subjects, history, and social studies.

Collaborative teams must have time to do the work of learning about new instructional strategies, finding new resources for instruction, working together to unwrap and understand the standards with more clarity, and studying support documents including the CCSS ELA/literacy appendices, the progressions in mathematics, and items from the assessment consortia (Common Core Standards Writing Team, 2012; NGA & CCSSO, 2010b, 2010c, 2010d; PARCC, 2012b; SBAC, 2012c). We strongly support the notion of embedded professional development by teams as they *do the work*; however, we also recognize the need for *jumpstart* training in strategies or practices that are unfamiliar to teachers. A number of vehicles exist to provide this training, including in-person workshops, book studies, online professional learning, and targeted coaching.

Building support with other teachers will also be important. Coaching relationships will help teachers acquire and refine new instructional strategies. Connecting with other teachers who are also learning about the CCSS will be very important. Many teachers are making these connections not only with other teachers in their same districts but also with others in the same content area. These teachers are reaching out through professional organizations and social media. Since we are using the same standards in many states, teachers are finding that they are no longer limited to making connections with teachers in their own school, district, or state.

Leading the Charge of Continuous Improvement

In this chapter, we've discussed the shifts reflected in the CCSS and their implications for change. We also discussed the change process and the fact that how schools roll out and support these initiatives can make or break whether or not those changes actually take place. What gives us hope is the notion that schools and districts operating as professional learning communities already embrace the power of continuous improvement. They are constantly seeking ways to improve their own work and their own learning. Transitioning to the Common Core requires a culture that seeks continuous improvement and supports the concept of team learning. So what might these teams need from their leaders to support that continuous improvement and collective learning? Let's go back to the fundamentals.

- Teams need time to work together, time to try out strategies with their students, and time for professional learning and reflection on the impact of those practices across their course or grade level.

- Teams need clear expectations about what they will be doing and the reasons (the *why*) behind those expectations.

- Teams need support. They need leaders to guide them in these shifts with reasonable support that takes their learning needs into account.

Remember, we're asking teacher teams to rebuild the plane as they're flying it! We know that when resources are scarce, these needs might seem challenging. Yet the potential consequences of not making these needed changes are sobering. School leaders in concert with their guiding coalition—the leadership team—must examine how they might organize their efforts to not overwhelm their teams with everything at once. We like the motto "Think big. Start small!" Providing the various kinds of support for teams and individual teachers as they deal with the shifts in the CCSS has implications for teams that are new to the PLC process as well as for principals and school leaders.

Tips for Teams New to the PLC Process

This chapter is about change, and you're undergoing a significant change just transitioning to the CCSS. You might be wondering whether you should consider making both changes at the same time—transitioning to the Common Core State Standards and organizing collaborative teams to engage in this transition. We believe that this is the right time to make both changes and that the collaborative process will make the transition to the Common Core easier. However, be aware that you will likely have some teachers question this decision. Remember that people in every change begin with self-concerns. They will need lots of support during this time and will need to know that you understand their fear of this major transition. Your teachers will need to know that you are going to *stay the course* throughout the process.

Whenever we work with teams who are just beginning the PLC process, we remind them that getting started is the most important goal. If they wait until they have everything planned and prepared for, they will likely never get started. With that in mind, it's important that you consider who will be on each collaborative team and who will be on the leadership team for the school. Collaborative teams should include teachers who teach the same content area: often grade-level teams in elementary school and teams organized around subject areas in middle and high school. For your leadership team, or guiding coalition, you'll want to carefully consider the recommendations from step two (pages 30–31). Who are the teacher leaders that peers respect? Who has the expertise that will be helpful in leading this change? Create a guiding coalition that will be able to communicate the vision and help facilitate the work of the teams.

Creating and communicating the vision (step three, pages 31–32) is a great place to start. What kind of school or district do you want to become? As you lay out this vision, consider the shifts that the CCSS will require—attention to college and career readiness, more rigorous curriculum, more text complexity, and so on. How will the vision you have now make this a reality? Be honest that this won't be accomplished overnight. In fact, this change will likely evolve over several years and will require a change in school culture. Don't be discouraged if things aren't perfect; they wouldn't be perfect without teams!

Pay attention to step five—celebrate short-term wins (page 33). It is really important to acknowledge successes as they happen so that teachers don't get discouraged when things don't happen quickly or easily.

Tips for Principals and Leaders

As you consider this process, you will likely realize that this change, no matter how it is done, will be one of the more significant changes you'll undertake in your career. There are no effective shortcuts! So having a strong leadership team to work with and to help you manage the process is vital to your success. Make sure that you've identified the right people to be a part of your leadership team—your guiding coalition. Do you have people with the right leadership skills? Do you have people with the expertise that will be needed to lead this change in the areas of English language arts, literacy in the subject areas, and mathematics? If not, what will you need to do—help individuals develop the appropriate skills or identify other individuals who have the desired skills and knowledge?

Consider how you will use your leadership team in a shared leadership capacity. As you work through the process of what you'll be *loose* about and what you'll hold *tight*, work with your leadership team to make sure that the members understand and will support these decisions.

Pay careful attention to your school culture during this transition. Remember that the focus should be on learning—learning for students as well as learning for the adults in the building.

Importantly, be overt and upfront about timelines and expectations. Most importantly, be realistic about timelines and expectations. This is not a change that *can* or *should* take place overnight. It will likely take years of work to ultimately put all of the pieces in place successfully. Choose your priorities and make your timelines visible and flexible.

Part Two
Getting on the Same Page

3

Powering the CCSS

Collaborative Connections

- When teams go through the process of identifying their essential or power standards, they are setting the stage to deliver a guaranteed and viable curriculum.

- Building consensus on the essential or power standards requires teams to clarify what each standard means.

- Collaboratively choosing essential or power standards helps teams commit to being responsible for all students.

- When teams vertically align their essential or power standards, they are making commitments to each other and to their students about what's most important.

As your collaborative team begins the work of transitioning to the Common Core, we suggest you start by asking and answering the first critical question for PLC teams: "What do we want our students to learn?" If your team has never done this work before, you may feel that you have sufficient answers: "We'll use our state standards, of course!" or "The Common Core State Standards must be the focus of this work." However, if your team simply accepts either of those premises, each teacher will be inclined to interpret and apply the standards in a different way. Instead, we advise that teams spend time working with their standards on the process we describe in this chapter. This chapter will guide you through conversations to help clarify and understand the meaning of the CCSS. In fact, we believe that teams' work around this first question will have significant impact on their success in making this transition.

This first question requires your team to review all standards, Common Core and any others for which you have responsibility to teach, to determine which ones will be considered *power* or *essential* standards. Power or essential standards are the standards your team believes all students must possess for either deep understanding or the ability to perform. They are the ones that will receive the most emphasis in your instruction, the ones around which your collaborative team will develop common formative assessments, and those for which you will provide additional time and support when students struggle to learn them. Whether your team has already done this work or not with your current state standards, it will be an important learning experience to do this collaboratively with the CCSS.

The terms *power standard* and *essential standard* are used interchangeably in this book because their purpose in a PLC is the same. These standards are those that have been identified as the ones the team guarantees all students will know. They are the standards that common formative assessments are written around.

Too Much to Teach

We often begin powering standards by asking teachers to consider all the information they have about what they are expected to teach. As they list items such as pacing guides, curriculum maps, state standards, teacher guides for their textbooks, high-stakes testing information, and standards-based report cards, they begin to realize how difficult it is to juggle all these documents as they try to fit everything into their curriculum. Sometimes *fitting everything in* seems a bit like a fraternity prank designed to see how many people can be stuffed into a small car! Consider the fact that many states have had extensive lists of standards for their teachers; some as many as fifty or sixty standards in a single subject. For example, in the 2008 Math Standards, Arizona teachers had fifty-six performance objectives to teach. In their current Science Standards, Minnesota eighth-grade teachers have sixty-three performance standards to teach. Recognizing that the school year is typically 180 days, this translates into a very unlikely possibility that teachers could cover each standard in depth. This results in what Mike Schmoker and Robert Marzano (1999) call *curriculum chaos*—every teacher making these decisions in isolation based on what he or she feels is most important. Curriculum delivered to students in this chaotic fashion means one thing: what students learn often depends on which teacher they're assigned to.

We further contend that when individual teachers make decisions in isolation, students in a grade level or course are prepared *differently* for the next level. For example, think about the role of mathematics facts at the elementary level. If one third-grade teacher spends considerable time making sure his or her students have had lots of practice knowing the multiplication tables, and another believes that it is more important to work on problem solving with multiplication, these students are not equally prepared for the next grade level. Their receiving fourth-grade teacher must review and scaffold for both groups of students as they teach new material. In contrast to this decision making in isolation, teams working collaboratively to make decisions about priorities agree to make sure all students are *equally* prepared for the next level.

As we look at the importance of choosing power standards, we also should consider the research that supports it. In his book *What Works in Schools*, Marzano (2003) discusses the research on what makes some schools more effective than others. He reports that the number-one factor in high-performing schools is that they have a guaranteed and viable curriculum. Most teachers understand what it means to have a guaranteed curriculum—the curriculum is the same no matter which teacher a student is assigned. However, we often fail to consider if our curriculum is viable—if we have enough time to teach it. When states have extensive lists of standards for each grade level or each subject, the curriculum is not very likely to be viable.

As we look at the CCSS, we must consider whether the number of standards is appropriate to develop a viable curriculum. For example, the ELA standards for grade 6 total sixty-nine: the Reading strand has nineteen standards, the Writing strand has twenty-four standards, the Speaking and Listening strand has nine standards, and the Language strand has seventeen standards. These numbers include components defined for some standards; for example, standard one for sixth grade in the Writing strand has five components.

1. Write arguments to support claims with clear reasons and relevant evidence.

   a. Introduce claim(s) and organize the reasons and evidence clearly.

   b. Support claim(s) with clear reasons and relevant evidence, using credible sources and demonstrating an understanding of the topic or text.

   c. Use words, phrases, and clauses to clarify the relationships among claim(s) and reasons.

   d. Establish and maintain a formal style.

   e. Provide a concluding statement or section that follows from the argument presented. (W.6.1) (NGA & CCSSO, 2010a, p. 42)

If the team wants to teach a standard in depth, assess whether the students have learned it, and provide time and support for students who need more instruction, there obviously isn't enough time to do it all for every standard on the list. Even if we consider the fact that the NGA and CCSSO (2010a) make clear that "each standard need not be a separate focus for instruction and assessment. Often, several standards can be addressed with a single rich task" (p. 5), there is still too much to teach to ensure every student has learned every standard. With previous state standards, teachers would have compensated for this reality either by *covering* the curriculum by rushing through everything (and leaving out some of the important things because they run out of time) or by picking and choosing those standards they believed to be the most important or ones they were most comfortable with. Neither of these scenarios results in students receiving a guaranteed and viable curriculum.

We believe that a better option is for teams to work collaboratively to make decisions about which standards should be prioritized. While still teaching all of the standards, teams choosing this option will identify which of the standards they will teach in depth and assess using a common formative assessment. They will then use the data from that assessment to diagnose what their students need next. They recognize that they can't do this for everything they teach, so they create their list of essential standards together so that their students are commonly prepared for the next grade or course.

As we began this discussion, we used the example of the number of ELA/literacy standards for sixth grade. We would be remiss if we didn't recognize that the number of mathematics standards in the Common Core for each grade level is significantly less than for ELA. In fact, mathematics standards range from as few as twenty-three at grade 1 to forty-two at grade 6. However, as teams review the mathematics standards, they will see that there are significant expectations for the amount of depth teachers devote to concepts. We know that each of those standards will require more instructional time and more opportunities for practice and application than likely happened with previous state standards. When students must build conceptual understanding, the time required to ensure they are learning is far more than when students had only to apply an algorithm to a problem.

It is also interesting to consider how the process of choosing the power standards for the CCSS is different for teachers than if they did this work on their own state standards. When going through the process of prioritizing their current state standards, teachers likely had already become familiar with their content, how the standards fit together, and even how much time it took to teach them. With the transition to the CCSS, all teachers are beginning the work with much less familiarity than before. Because they haven't fully experienced the CCSS, they may not know which standards fit together or how much time they will need to teach them. Therefore, it is important that this process not only help teams in answering the first critical question for their collaborative work but also begin the process of getting clarity and understanding about what the CCSS mean for their grade levels or subjects.

What Powering Isn't

At times, we've heard schools and districts express concerns about whether they are allowed to *power* their standards. Sometimes these concerns have come about because their state education department or another organization advised them *not* to identify power or essential standards. We recognize that there are different schools of thought, but we believe that some of the conflicting opinions might have occurred because of a misperception about the definition of *powering*—what the process *is* and what it *is not*. It is critical to understand that powering is not about identifying which standards teachers will teach and which standards they will not! Let us be clear: each standard in both the Common Core ELA and mathematics is important, and our students need to know each of them in order to learn at high levels and be prepared for college or careers after high school. In no way are we suggesting that schools eliminate any standards—by design, we can't eliminate any of them. The Common Core standards are designed to build on each other. If we don't teach them all, our students will have gaps in their learning and a weak foundation as they leave a particular grade level or course.

So what is the point of powering the standards? The powering process provides the opportunity for teams to collaboratively look at the big picture of the standards, discuss their importance, and reach agreement about which of them will be taught in greater depth. Building this clarity about which standards are the highest priority ensures that everyone on the team is teaching to achieve the same outcome. What happens when teams don't have these collaborative conversations and haven't made collective decisions about what's important? Here's the reality: We know that individual teachers simply possessing the list of standards without a collaborative conversation will result in individual decisions about what is important, and as a result, will be preparing their students differently when compared to other teachers at their same grade level or course (Schmoker & Marzano, 1999). Consider this example of teachers individually interpreting the standards and determining their own priorities. Two first-grade teachers are both teaching the first standard in the mathematics domain Operations and Algebraic Thinking (1.OA):

> Use addition and subtraction within 20 to solve word problems involving situations of
> adding to, taking from, putting together, taking apart, and comparing with unknowns
> in all positions; for example, by using objects, drawing, and equations with a symbol
> for the unknown number to represent the problem. (NGA & CCSSO, 2010e, p. 15)

One teacher sets up centers in her classroom with flash cards to help students practice their addition and subtraction facts. Another teacher helps students build conceptual understanding around addition and subtraction in real-life situations, by having students practice counting on and counting back. Both teachers believe they are teaching the standard, yet they are teaching very different concepts. When those students move to second grade, the receiving teacher will not have students who are commonly prepared with their understanding of addition and subtraction or perhaps even fluent with mathematical facts. We assert that there is no way to ensure a guaranteed and viable curriculum without teams making these decisions, not individual teachers working in isolation.

What Powering Is

Remember, your team will teach all of the standards. This process helps ensure that what teachers teach and what students learn are the same no matter which teacher on the team the students are assigned to. Individual teachers won't interpret the standards differently, nor will they have different definitions for proficiency. These are the standards on which your team will write its common formative assessments. These are the standards that will enable your collaborative team to determine how you will differentiate instruction by providing extra time and support for students who haven't learned them and creating new challenges for students who have mastered them.

Implications of Powering the CCSS

Leaders engaging teams in decisions about powering the CCSS should be aware of several important considerations. Who will be responsible for powering the standards—a district-based team or a school-based team? What is the appropriate configuration of the team who will be responsible for determining which standards are essential? What must team members know about the CCSS ELA and mathematics so that they make good decisions? What is the best way to get started? Answers to these questions provide the foundation for using the four-step powering process we describe later in this chapter (see pages 47–52).

Responsibility for Powering the CCSS

The first decision school or district leadership teams need to make is whether each school or whether the district will systematically identify power standards. There are benefits to both processes. If each school chooses its own set of power standards, every teacher will be involved in the process. Every teacher will have an opportunity to discuss the CCSS and what they mean. The work can be done, for the most part, during the collaborative teams' common planning time. The downside to this choice is that when each school chooses its own set of power standards, the district loses the common emphasis from school to school. Some districts use benchmark assessments to make sure that the schools are all getting to the same place at the same time with the curriculum. This is not a possibility if each school is working with a different set of power standards.

If your district selects representative teachers to come together to choose power standards, the curriculum will be more consistent districtwide. However, individual teachers who are not part of that process will not have the same awareness of the standards as their colleagues who are part of the district team. When making this choice, districts must ensure the representative teachers bring the draft list of power standards back to the school teams for input and consideration. Larry Ainsworth (2003) calls this the *accordion model*. This process will require district representatives to have a common release time or professional day to complete the work. For example, we have completed the process of identifying the power standards for either ELA or mathematics with a group of teachers in one full day.

We also suggest that your team makes an agreement at the beginning of this work to review the power standards again at the end of the first year. Over time, as your team and your students become familiar with the Common Core, power standards may change. For example, one district we worked with chose the grade level standard connected to anchor standard one in the Reading strand to be a power standard for each grade level.

Read closely to determine what the text says explicitly and to make logical references from it; cite specific textual evidence when writing or speaking to support conclusions drawn from the text. (R.CCRA.1) (NGA & CCSSO, 2010a, p. 10)

The teachers carefully taught and assessed the standard throughout each grade level in their elementary school. By the third trimester, most students were very capable of providing evidence from the text for their inferences and conclusions. Consequently, the teachers decided that this standard no longer had to be powered at every grade level.

The configuration of teams assigned to powering the standards is an important consideration for the principal/school leadership team or the district leadership team. You will want to make sure to configure your teams in the right way to produce the best possible products. This means that teams should be made up of teachers who teach the same content; for example, first-grade reading teachers, sixth-grade mathematics teachers, or ninth-grade geography teachers; each comprise a team that will work together on their standards. We suggest that elementary grade-level teams start with one subject—English language arts/literacy or mathematics—rather than trying to do both content areas at once. You'll find that your team will learn the powering process with the first subject and will be able to work more efficiently through the second set of standards when you're ready to do so. In choosing which subject to pursue first, you may want to consider which area needs the most immediate attention by thinking through the strengths and limitations of the existing programs and student performance within those programs.

We suggest that subject-area teachers in grades 6–12 be responsible for powering the ELA and literacy standards in the subjects they teach. We recommend that each grade level (for example, sixth-grade social studies) go through the process using the standards for its grade band (for example, grades 6–8) and identify those standards teachers believe are most important for their grade level. By looking at the standards across the grade band, teams will gain understanding of the learning progressions for the strands. Later during the powering process, the teams can have vertical discussions about which standards are most appropriate at each grade in that grade band. Teachers who teach more than one course might be members of more than one team.

We recognize that it's important that someone have a "big picture" view—perhaps a district leader or leadership team—to ensure that collaborative teams keep the coherence of the standards from grade level to grade level in mind. This person or group must have an understanding about the coherence of the standards—both ELA and mathematics—as well as how they are designed. Most importantly, they will want to understand the implications for professional development, access to new resources, planning for communication across schools, and so on. This person or team is likely already familiar with the standards and supporting documents we discuss in this section including the standards themselves, the appendices, and the frameworks from either SBAC or PARCC.

Responsibility for Knowing the CCSS ELA/Literacy

A second implication of the powering process relates to each collaborative team's familiarity with the CCSS for its grade level. In working through this process with several schools, we've found that building teachers' general understanding of the way the CCSS are designed is a vital step.

Once the decision—districtwide or schoolwide—about responsibility for developing the power standards is in place, the first step is to examine the CCSS and the materials your collaborative team will be using. You and your teams will need copies of all the components of the CCSS ELA. This includes the standards documents as well as the appropriate appendices for the subject the team is working on. Chapter 1 contains descriptions of the structure of the Common Core ELA/literacy along with explanations of relevant terms (see pages 13–14). To jumpstart your process, you might find it helpful to review this information with the team. We offer additional suggestions for ways to ensure that team members are conversant with the organization of the CCSS and companion resources.

You'll find that the ELA/literacy standards are written with a clear picture of the end in mind for students. The anchor standards in each strand describe the skills students are expected to develop to be college and career ready. The section "Key Design Considerations" (see NGA & CCSSO, 2010a, p. 4) describes the importance of the anchor standards, the grade-level structure, and the emphasis on results rather than teaching strategies, which allows teachers to determine how they will deliver instruction. Furthermore, this section provides insight into the integration of standards across the Reading, Writing, Speaking and Listening, and Language strands, as well as the importance of shared responsibility for students' literacy development across the curriculum. Each team should have the overall understanding about the design of the standards but will need to become much more familiar with their own grade-level standards.

The three appendices accompanying the Common Core ELA/literacy will become increasingly important as collaborative teams learn more about the standards. Appendix A (NGA & CCSSO, 2010b) includes resources for each strand—Reading, Writing, Speaking and Listening, and Language; here you'll find evidence to support your decisions about essential standards. The Reading strand resources include in-depth descriptions of text complexity and the Reading Foundational Skills. Descriptions of the three writing types—argumentative, informative and explanatory, and narrative—and the special place of argument are resources in the Writing strand. The importance of oral language development in K–5 and the effective use of read-alouds are the focus of resources for the Speaking and Listening strand. The grade-by-grade language progression skills define those skills in the Language strand that require repetition over time. This material along with information about vocabulary acquisition and development will be invaluable as your teams work to select the power standards. This resource provides the background teams need prior to beginning to select their power standards.

While we suggest your team becomes familiar with appendix B (NGA & CCSSO, 2010c) and appendix C (NGA & CCSSO, 2010d) of the CCSS, we think these documents will likely prove more relevant as you begin to design assessments and choose your instructional strategies. Appendix B includes text exemplars and sample performance tasks for each grade band. This document establishes a picture of the end in mind for the literacy skills students will be expected to perform and the text types they will encounter. Also, the sample performance tasks provide representative examples of what students might find on Common Core tests and can serve as formative assessments for teams. Appendix C includes sample student writing. While we wish appendix C included examples of both proficient and weak writing, there are explanations for what makes the writing proficient that are helpful. This information will help your team as you develop writing rubrics. You will find that you do not need to read these appendices prior to selecting the power standards but instead should be aware of the materials they contain.

Responsibility for Knowing the CCSS for Mathematics

The structure of the Common Core for mathematics is less complex than the ELA/literacy. The introduction to the mathematics standards includes an explanation of how to read the grade-level standards and defines three key terms—*standard*, *cluster*, and *domain*. We introduced these and other terms in chapter 1 (see pages 13–14), so you may want to review as you prepare to study the standards in more depth. A description of the Standards for Mathematical Practice follows the introduction. As your teams become more familiar with these overarching standards of practice, the descriptions of the Mathematical Practices and how they relate to the content standards will become critical; however, a general understanding will suffice as you begin your work on determining which standards are essential.

Appendix A of the CCSS for mathematics (NGA & CCSSO, 2010f) is specific to high school. It lays out how the standards can be used with either a traditional high school mathematics pathway, such as, algebra 1, geometry, algebra 2, and fourth course; or an integrated pathway, such as, mathematics 1, mathematics 2, mathematics 3, and fourth course. This fourth course might include Pre-calculus, Calculus, Advanced Statistics, Discrete Mathematics, Advanced Quantitative Reasoning or another course needed for technical classes. Whichever pathway your school chooses, this appendix provides a delineation of which standards you will include in each course.

Responsibility for Knowing the CCSS Assessments

The PARCC and SBAC, the consortia developing the CCSS assessments, provide support materials that will be valuable as you go through the powering process. Visit the consortia's websites for information about your state (see www.parcconline.org and www.smarterbalanced.org). Note that some states belong to both consortia.

Each consortium has released sample assessment items for review. While this first step of choosing your power standards isn't about writing assessments, having sample questions may help your team better understand the meaning behind each standard. We recommend your teams download the appropriate support documents for your consortium: the PARCC Model Content Frameworks and the SBAC Content Specifications for the Summative Assessment of the Common Core State Standards (visit **go.solution -tree.com/commoncore** to access these resources).

We aren't trying to overwhelm you by sharing information on these materials. Our goal is empowerment—equipping you with the resources to do your work. This is about being familiar with CCSS structures, content, and resources so that you can draw on them to support your work. By knowing what resources are available and having copies on hand, teams can look up information as needed during work sessions.

Resources to Support Powering the CCSS

Visit **go.solution-tree.com/commoncore** to access the following resources.

English Language Arts/Literacy

Common Core State Standards for English Language Arts & Literacy in History/Social Studies, Science, and Technical Subjects (NGA & CCSSO, 2010a)

Common Core State Standards for English Language Arts & Literacy in History/Social Studies, Science, and Technical Subjects: Appendix A—Research Supporting Key Elements of the Standards and Glossary of Key Terms (NGA & CCSSO, 2010b)

Common Core State Standards for English Language Arts & Literacy in History/Social Studies, Science, and Technical Subjects: Appendix B—Text Exemplars and Sample Performance Tasks (NGA & CCSSO, 2010c)

Common Core State Standards for English Language Arts & Literacy in History/Social Studies, Science, and Technical Subjects: Appendix C—Samples of Student Writing (NGA & CCSSO, 2010d)

Application of Common Core State Standards for English Language Learners (NGA & CCSSO, n.d.a)

Application to Students with Disabilities (NGA & CCSSO, n.d.b)

Framework for English Language Proficiency Development Standards Corresponding to the Common Core State Standards and the Next Generation Science Standards (CCSSO, 2012)

Common Core State Standards Official Identifiers and XML Representation (NGA & CCSSO, 2012)

Mathematics

Common Core State Standards for Mathematics (NGA & CCSSO, 2010e)

Common Core State Standards for Mathematics: Appendix A—Designing High School Mathematics Courses Based on the Common Core State Standards (NGA & CCSSO, 2010f)

Progressions Documents for the Common Core Math Standards (Common Core Standards Writing Team, 2012)

Assessment

Partnership for Assessment of Readiness for College and Careers (www.parcconline.org)

PARCC Model Content Frameworks (PARCC, 2012c)

PARCC Model Content Frameworks: English Language Arts/Literacy—Grades 3–11 (PARCC, 2012d)

PARCC Model Content Frameworks: Mathematics—Grades 3–11 (PARCC, 2012e)

Smarter Balanced Assessment Consortium (www.smarterbalanced.org)

Content Specifications for the Summative Assessment of the Common Core State Standards for English Language Arts and Literacy in History/Social Studies, Science, and Technical Subjects (SBAC, 2012a)

Content Specifications for the Summative Assessment of the Common Core State Standards for Mathematics (SBAC, 2012b)

The Four-Step Powering Process

Before embarking on the powering process, teams need to decide where to begin. In working with the elementary (K–5) ELA standards, we suggest teams first start with the Reading strand. This strand includes both the Literature and Informational Text standards as well as standards for Foundational Skills. After finishing the first two steps in the powering process with this strand, teams can then follow the same process consecutively with the Writing strand, the Speaking and Listening strand, and the Language strand. Similarly, we recommend the same sequence for working with the ELA standards in grades 6–12. We recommend this sequence because the Speaking and Listening standards and Language standards often have connections to the Reading and Writing standards. As you work through each strand and become aware of connections, your team will likely go back and make changes to the power standards you've identified.

The literacy standards for history, social studies, science, and technical subjects may present a new sphere of activity for grades 6–12 teachers in those subject areas. You will still be responsible for the subject matter standards you've had in the past, but will also be responsible for Reading and Writing standards connected to your curriculum. For you, the Reading strand has two parts: (1) Reading Standards for Literacy in History/Social Studies and (2) Reading Standards for Literacy in Science and Technical Subjects for each grade band (6–8, 9–10, and 11–12). The Writing strand contains one set of standards that encompasses all the subject areas across the grade bands. We recommend that each team (for example, sixth-grade science) look at all of the Reading and Writing standards they should be teaching to choose what they believe are their essential standards. Then, they can vertically align their selected standards with their science colleagues in grades 7–8.

As you examine and become familiar with these new standards, you'll likely notice that they reflect important ways that students acquire and communicate information. For example, being able to read and understand a technical manual is a skill important to your students and one you may have addressed previously. However, now it's explicitly included in your curriculum. In social studies, understanding the difference between primary and secondary source documents is likely a concept you've worked on with students as well. You, just like any other team, determine which are the most important for all students to know.

We highly recommend that teachers have the opportunity to talk and share ways to teach these standards with cross-curricular connections. For example, interdisciplinary teams at the middle school level might share a research project designed by both the ELA and science teachers. High school history and English teachers might want to work together on connected projects around the important seminal U.S. documents.

The structure of the Writing strand invites conversations among teachers from both the science and social studies departments. If writing in these two content areas has not been previously emphasized in your school, teachers need to understand the types of writing their students will be expected to do in your classes: argumentative, informative, and explanatory. In addition, students will be expected to do research and write about it. If this is the case for your team, we recommend that a good start for year one is at least powering standards one, two, and seven for your grade levels, which include writing arguments, informative/explanatory texts, and conducting short research projects. This will allow you to become more familiar with ways to incorporate writing into your regular lessons.

You will choose the appropriate grade-level standard for each of the following anchor standards:

> Write arguments to support claims in an analysis of substantive topics or texts using valid reasoning and relevant and sufficient evidence. (CCRA.W.HST.1)
>
> Write informative/explanatory texts to examine and convey complex ideas and information clearly and accurately through the effective selection, organization, and analysis of content. (CCRA.W.HST.2)
>
> Conduct short as well as sustained research projects based on focused questions, demonstrating understanding of the subject under investigation. (CCRA.W.HST.7) (NGA & CCSSO, 2010a, p. 63)

The mathematics standards have four or five domains for each grade K–8 and six conceptual categories for high school. Your teams will likely be able to work through all of the domains and conceptual categories during each step of the powering process unlike the ELA standards where teams work with one strand at a time. For example, in mathematics, a third-grade team will begin with step one—choosing the essential or power standards using the filtering criteria. Each member will work through all of the standards together including the domains: Operations and Algebraic Thinking, Number and Operations in Base Ten, Number and Operations—Fractions, Measurement and Data, and Geometry.

The Standards for Mathematical Practice have connections throughout each grade level's content standards. It would be impossible to choose essential standards from this group as they will all be important at every grade level. Thus, each grade level will ensure that they are using and assessing all eight Standards for Mathematical Practice.

We suggest schools and districts use the four-step powering process. Our experience provides suggestions for *chunking* the tasks so that teams are more effective in choosing their power standards. The reproducible "Protocol for Powering the Common Core" (page 187) describes the materials needed for the process and summarizes the steps (see the appendix, page 187, and online at **go.solution-tree.com /commoncore**). You may find it helpful to provide copies of the protocol to teams as they begin and follow through the powering process.

Step One: Identify Potential Power Standards Based on Filtering Criteria

Step one asks individual teachers on the team to first identify for themselves which standards they believe are the power or essential standards. We recommend using Doug Reeves's (2002) three criteria to determine what is necessary for a power standard: endurance, leverage, and readiness for the next level of learning. The standard must meet one of these criteria:

1. **Endurance** means that the standard reflects learning that will be important now and for a long time to come. For example, in mathematics, a deep understanding of place value is important for students over their entire lifetime. It isn't something that they will need to know only for a grade level or for a summative assessment.

2. **Leverage** refers to learning that has cross-curricular implications; something that is taught in one subject but used in another subject. For example, we teach students about unit rate in mathematics but use that concept to solve problems in physical science classes.

3. **Readiness for the next level of learning** identifies prerequisite skills. For example, students are taught letter and sound recognition in early literacy, which is an important skill when learning to read. Students who don't learn letter and sound recognition have a difficult time with future reading skills. The readiness criterion applies to the progressions of skills in both language arts and mathematics.

During this step, each teacher on your team will have a copy of the standards for which he or she is responsible. Each team member *independently* goes through the standards, marking those that he or she believes meet one or more of these criteria. We suggest that this first step must have a time limit, typically twenty minutes. Our experience shows that given too much time, teachers will find a way to mark each of the standards as important. Remind teachers to keep Reeves's (2002) three criteria in mind, using them as a filter for their initial decision making.

Step Two: Develop a First Draft Based on Team Members' Recommendations

To facilitate step two, we recommend that you use a chart or document camera to display the entire set of standards you are examining. This allows all team members to see the standards and reference them during the discussion. Team members can place marks by the standards they individually identify as being essential, or one member can compile all of the individual tallies onto the chart. Having access to the entire list invites suggestions for changes and tends to foster meaningful discussion.

Now comes the interesting part: the conversation about what's on the list and what's not. The desired outcome of step two is a draft list of power standards. Consensus during this part of the process about what is essential isn't necessarily linear. For example, as you first look at the individual responses compiled on a single chart, you may find that there are some standards around which you have 100 percent agreement: either everyone marked it as essential or no one marked it as essential. Yet not all standards will be viewed in such a black-and-white fashion. When things get gray, the more difficult work begins. Your team will need to work through each standard one at a time and ask each team member why it was marked or not marked as a power standard. During this discussion, team members will clarify for each other their understanding of the meaning of the standard and how they feel it applies at the grade level. For example, it is common for teachers to discuss the connection between literature and informational text in the ELA standards. They might decide to power a standard in literature but not its companion standard in informational text because they will assess it in one area and teach its application in the other. For example, consider the third-grade level standard six which addresses point of view in reading literature and reading informational text.

> Distinguish their own point of view from that of the narrator or those of the characters. (RL.3.6) (NGA & CCSSO, 2010a, p. 12)

> Distinguish their own point of view from that of the author of the text. (RI.3.6) (NGA & CCSSO, 2010a, p. 14)

The team may assess this standard in one area only (perhaps literature). However, you must make sure the team members connect the knowledge and skill in the other area (perhaps informational text).

It's important to note that this second step of this process involves building consensus and agreement on the power standards draft among all team members. In a PLC, the term *consensus* has a specific definition. DuFour et al. (2008) define *consensus* in this way: "Consensus is achieved when (1) all points of view have been heard and (2) the will of the group is evident even to those who most oppose it" (p. 465). Using this framework for decision making implies a specific process and guidelines or norms for how the team conducts itself during these conversations. While teams can build consensus in a number of different ways, it is important that all of the teachers have a voice in the final list. Discussion and respectful debate will lead to a better product. If you are the leader, it's important that you pay careful attention to make sure that all teachers engage in this process, including those who are new to your team. For the collaborative team, you will find that your norms for working together will foster how well your team works to build consensus. What we don't want is for some teachers to exclude themselves from the process of conversing about the standards merely because they are afraid to speak up if they disagree.

When teachers are having a hard time resolving disagreement, we recommend they go back to step one and review the criteria for endurance, leverage, and readiness to help them make a decision. Have teachers explain their thinking using these terms. Additionally, your team must be vigilant about *not* including every standard that any of you originally marked and that can't easily be resolved as a power or essential standard! We sometimes see teams try to make everyone happy by including anything they find difficult to agree on. Those teams then end up with too many essential standards.

Step Three: Determine Alignment Between Draft Power Standards and Other Relevant Documentation

During this step your team is going to compare your draft list with any released information or clarifying documents that describe what students will be expected to do. These resources could include released assessment items from the CCSS consortia, curriculum frameworks, and assessment blueprints. It's important that your team considers this information and makes adjustments to the draft by adding or deleting standards. This exercise will ensure that your power standards are aligned to the CCSS assessments as well as the primary intent of the standards: preparing students for college and careers. For example, the assessment consortia have written about the importance of students being able to meet the expectations of the first anchor standard in the Reading strand.

> Read closely to determine what the text says explicitly and to make logical inferences from it; cite specific textual evidence when writing or speaking to support conclusions drawn from the text. (CCRA.R.1) (NGA & CCSSO, 2010a, p. 10)

This anchor standard applies to both literature and informational text. In referencing anchor standard one, the SBAC (2012a) states:

> It focuses on students' use of evidence to support their analyses (claims, conclusions, inferences) about text. Hence, whether students are asked to determine the central idea, the point of view, or the meaning of words and phrases and the like, they will be using Standard 1 (making inferences and supporting those inferences with evidence) in addition to one of the other reading standards 2–9. As a result, Standard 1 underlies each Assessment Target. (p. 18)

The grade level for this anchor standard will likely appear on the list of power standards, especially in schools where students haven't been expected to cite evidence to support their understanding. Similarly, the ELA content framework from the PARCC (2012c) states, "The goal of close, analytic reading is to be able to discern and cite evidence from the text to support assertions" (p. 19).

We know that close reading for analysis of text is going to be emphasized on the consortia's summative assessments, so it will be important that students are capable, independent readers (PARCC, 2012c). Students will be required to research a topic, find credible sources, and summarize information. Making the reading and writing connections will also be assessed. Your team will want to review your draft list to make sure you've emphasized these skills.

In mathematics, the consortia acknowledge that in grades K–8 some clusters will take more time and will need greater emphasis than others. They have categorized each cluster into three categories: *major*, *supporting*, and *additional* (SBAC, 2012b; PARCC, 2012e). They describe these designations as:

1. **Major Clusters** make up the majority of the assessment

2. **Supporting Clusters** support the concepts in the major clusters

3. **Additional Clusters** are not tightly connected to the major clusters

These clusters are the same for both consortia (although SBAC doesn't differentiate between *supporting clusters* and *additional clusters*). We recognize that the teams must prioritize standards in the major clusters on their power standards list and use fewer from the other two categories. We don't recommend, however, that a team simply choose only standards from the major clusters. For example, for grade 3, the cluster "represent and interpret data" includes the concepts of bar graphs and pictographs and is considered a "supporting cluster." A team might still want to include this on their essential standards list because it connects to science concepts they teach, which means it meets the filtering criteria "leverage." Your team will want to make sure you've paid similar attention to the clusters in mathematics.

Step Four: Review for Vertical Alignment

During this step, each grade level or course team displays its draft standards on chart paper for the teams from other grade levels or courses to read. For example, an elementary school might display all of the ELA standards in grades K–5 together. A middle school might display the sixth-, seventh-, and eighth-grade mathematics standards together.

Once the teams display the standards, we suggest that each team walks the room and takes some time to read a set of standards across all grade levels. For example, reading just the Literature standards for grades K–5 allows teachers to consider what is being emphasized for all their students at those grade levels. During this step, teachers are encouraged to talk about why their team picked or didn't pick certain standards. A sixth-grade team might share about why it selected standard three in reading literature, which states:

> Describe how a particular story's or drama's plot unfolds in a series of episodes as well as how the characters respond or change as the plot moves toward a resolution. (RL.6.3) (NGA & CCSSO, 2010a, p. 36)

The team might explain that understanding plot development is critical at this grade level to provide the foundation that will enable students to work effectively with more challenging literature at higher grade levels. These discussions might confirm that the vertical alignment of the standards is appropriate or possibly expose some need to eliminate or add standards to a particular course or grade level.

The purpose of this step is two-fold. First, we want to put our emphases where they matter most at each grade level. Making sure that our guaranteed curriculum ensures all essential concepts are being taught and assessed is vital. Second, we want to avoid redundancy in our essentials. If every grade level is teaching and assessing targets around main idea and detail, this will be too much time spent assessing one concept. Instead ask, "Which team 'owns' main idea and detail?"

The second purpose of this step is equally important. This is the opportunity for teachers to talk across grade levels about what students will know and do. For example, seventh-grade teachers will be aware of what sixth-grade teachers have emphasized and guaranteed. This commitment ensures teachers that they don't need to spend a significant amount of time at the beginning of the next grade to reteach important concepts or skills. It is critical for teams to work together across grade levels or courses to create vertical alignment. By feeling confident that their students have mastered the most important content from the prior year or course, teachers can eliminate the review and reteaching they've previously felt obligated to do.

A Planning Decision

What should teams do first—power the standards or unwrap them? (Unwrapping the standards is the focus of chapter 4, page 57.) This question is one we regularly wrestle with as we do this work in schools. Should the teams choose their power standards first and then unwrap those standards as they begin? Or, should they unwrap all the Common Core State Standards to develop a really strong understanding of what these standards mean and then choose the power standards? In our work as consultants, we have tried both of these strategies with different groups under different circumstances. What we've learned is that neither way is superior to the other—they both result in similar products and in similar learning for collaborative teams about what the standards mean.

For many schools and districts, teams have limited time to do this work and need to get started quickly with the process. They might have weekly common planning time but perhaps have little chance for release time for professional development work. For these teams, we recommend choosing their power standards first and then unwrapping them.

If you have the opportunity to provide additional days for professional development for your teams, we suggest that you have your teams unwrap all of the standards first (using the processes and protocols described in chapter 4) and then choose the power standards. In this case, the teams choose their power standards with a deeper understanding of what each standard means.

Powering the standards is invaluable in helping teams address the first critical question, What do we want our students to learn? Similarly, unwrapping the standards provides additional insight into what is involved in responding to that question. As we describe in chapter 4, teams can unwrap the standards to develop a common understanding of what learning targets teams will need to teach and assess. To those two processes, we add a third element. We recommend that teams create scales for these learning targets to help build assessments that guide teams for both corrective instruction and enrichment opportunities for all students (Marzano, 2009). We describe proficiency scales and their development in chapter 5. These two next steps—unwrapping and scaling—ensure what we call *collective clarity* around the standards for your team and what that will mean for your students.

Tips for Teams New to the PLC Process

Even for teams who are not new to the PLC model, the process of determining power standards from the CCSS can be difficult. In fact, identifying power standards is often the first real challenge teams new to the PLC process face as they begin their collaborative work. To make this challenge manageable, make sure that you have successfully worked through identifying norms and roles for team members and that you have written a SMART goal for your team. The term SMART refers to goals which are Strategic, Measurable, Attainable, Results-Oriented, and Timebound (Conzemius & O'Neill, 2002). If you need some support on these steps, protocols are very thoughtfully laid out in chapters 5 and 6 in *Learning by Doing* (DuFour et al., 2010). See also http://allthingsplc.info/tools/print.php for resources to help get started with the PLC process.

Successfully getting started is critical to your implementation of the CCSS; yet, *first-timers* to the PLC process (and possibly even veterans who have been working in PLCs for some time) will likely face some interesting issues. For example, most team members likely believe that they have a common understanding of their grade-level or subject standards. However, the powering process often reveals that this is not the case. Identifying and agreeing to essential or power standards is really about exposing your personal philosophy. What do you really believe is important for students to know and do? This process will challenge you and your teammates' willingness to share your thinking and to build consensus about what's most important. We've seen teams brush past this consensus-building process by *giving in* and by adding too many standards to their lists in order to satisfy everyone. The good news is that even when teams do this, they become quickly aware of their mistake when they try to write and use common formative assessments for all the standards they've identified. Either way, it's important that you and your team recognize that the list you create this year is intended to be in draft form, and the team will review it for possible changes at the end of the year.

With this in mind, as a new team, it is really important to make sure that all team members understand what power or essential standards are—to make sure everyone understands that they must still teach all the standards, but these standards will be the ones that they cover rigorously. Go through the criteria for identifying essential standards, and explain the process before starting so that everyone understands the expected outcome as well as the time needed to complete the process.

Some teams decide to tackle the powering process unit by unit rather than all at once. While we recommend the all-at-once approach because it helps teams see all of the connections, we know that some districts or their states expect their teams to jump right into the work. If your team works unit by unit, it will still be important to find some time to have those vertical conversations across grade levels or departments.

Finally, we encourage you to recognize the value of learning from each other and from your mistakes. In a PLC, teachers commit to continuous improvement. They know that teaching isn't a checklist of tasks that can be completed one at a time until they are finished. Rather, they know the process is ongoing. We learn from what we do and continuously critique and improve our work. The power standards you identify this year will be reviewed and changed for next year. As students move through your system, you will see the need to change the power standards because the students will change as a result of the instruction they receive.

Tips for Principals and Leaders

As you begin powering the standards, it is important to make a few decisions up front. The first is to decide who will facilitate the work and what the timeline for completion will look like. For example, many schools ask the team leaders from each team to be the facilitator for their team. Other schools will have one person who takes that responsibility and works with all of the teachers in a full staff meeting time. Either way, it's important that someone who is comfortable (not necessarily an expert) with the process and the standards lead the process.

Make sure that your leaders understand the purpose for identifying power standards. We are frequently challenged to explain this purpose to groups we're working with because many teachers have the misconception that they don't have to teach all of the standards. You will need to reiterate and explain—with boorish redundancy—that they must teach *all* the standards!

If each team is going to begin the work at its team meetings, lay out a reasonable timeline for completion. For each set of standards, teams will likely need two to three meetings to identify and build consensus for the essential standards. Shortly after that deadline, plan a staff meeting for everyone to come together to discuss the vertical articulation. If you've never facilitated this type of vertical dialogue, it's important to plan ahead of time how the discussion will develop. For example, you may want to ask each team to give a brief explanation about what the members learned for their grade level or subject. Ask team members to pick a couple of ideas that they think are most important for their students. For example, fourth-grade teachers working with mathematics will likely mention the importance of understanding and working with fractions at that grade.

As teachers walk the wall of lists of standards, ask them to think about the following questions: "If a student attends our school, and these standards are the only standards he or she learns, will the student be prepared to move on? If not, what do we need to add?" For ELA, ask questions about the shifts that should occur. For example, "Have we emphasized anchor standard one in the Reading strand? Will our students be able to write all three types of writing when we're done?" In mathematics, have them discuss whether students will have the important prerequisite skills and concepts as they advance to the next grade level or course.

Once you've finalized the draft list of power standards, make sure that all the stakeholders have access to it. Some schools do this by giving parents a copy of the essential standards or having them available on the school's website. Teachers should have copies of the completed list for their team as well as for the other teams in the school.

4

Unwrapping the CCSS

Collaborative Connections

- When teachers examine the standards in isolation, each teacher is likely to interpret the intent and rigor differently. This results in a different level of student expectations and quality of instruction from class to class.

- Unwrapping the standards reveals the smaller learning targets contained within the standards, which aids the design of aligned instruction and assessment.

- The goal of the unwrapping process is collective clarity across the team about the end in mind of the standards.

In our view, the most crucial question collaborative teams address is, What do we want our students to learn? Having a clear focus for student learning aligns all other efforts the team makes; yet as basic as this question may seem, it's actually not a simple one to answer. Initially, many teams thought they answered that question by simply referencing their state standards. However, teams began to realize that unless they built common understanding about the specific skills and concepts embedded in the standards, implementation varied greatly across team members. Collaborating to achieve common understanding, the teachers found that the former state standards could be vague or contain significant gaps in the learning sequence. While the CCSS have provided educators a more complete picture of what students need to know and be able to do when compared to most previous state standards, frequently teachers continue to view the standards on their own. In an initial effort to understand the changes, teachers might quickly scan through the standards on the CCSS website or in the documents their state or district provides. In our practice and work around the United States, we observe that this isolated glance at the standards yields a very different interpretation among teachers—and quite frequently only a surface understanding of the true essence of the CCSS. Teachers working in isolation may apply those standards in very different ways—often with a different end in mind. As a result, their students walk away with different skills and understandings—clearly not our vision for a guaranteed and viable curriculum.

The CCSS reflect the need for teachers to examine the standards with a keen eye and to use their professional filters to see what isn't stated in the standards. As the NGA and CCSSO (2010a) note:

> While the Standards focus on what is most essential, they do not describe all that can or should be taught. A great deal is left to the discretion of teachers and curriculum developers. The aim of the Standards is to articulate the fundamentals, not to set out an exhaustive list or a set of restrictions that limits what can be taught beyond what is specified herein. (p. 6)

So, what process might teams use to establish clarity of the standards and do more than leave it to chance? Let's start by sharing some ineffective or incomplete practices that we have observed.

- **Comparing the CCSS and previous state standards:** As an orientation to the CCSS, grade-level or course teams might examine their standards using a *side-by-side* comparison with their previous state standards. While this can reveal some differences, by and large the activity doesn't necessarily create a deep and shared understanding of what the CCSS are asking students to know and be able to do or the context in which they will be performing. Teams that feel they have a full understanding of the CCSS based solely on a brief side-by-side comparison are likely missing the in-depth conversation necessary to build curriculum coherence across the team.

- **Basing everything on the assessment:** Rather than deeply examining the CCSS and getting clear on what students need to know and do, some teachers are using the wait-and-see approach. They're hoping that simply examining sample assessment items from either the SBAC or the PARCC will enlighten them and provide complete insight into the learning targets established in the CCSS. While having a sample picture of the end in mind is always valuable and will enrich understanding of the implications for the design of instruction and assessment, it doesn't replace the clarifying conversation that can and should be held within grade-level and course teams.

- **Using documents that have it "all figured out":** Undoubtedly, you've been getting some emails or brochures about the next best thing to help teams implement the CCSS. Some of these tools and resources may be coming from publishers, professional organizations, or even other states and districts. Any of these resources have the potential to jumpstart your team's understanding of particular standards and emphases contained within the CCSS. However, in our experience, there is a false sense of security and lack of ownership for their content because the team has not been involved in the analysis and development of the resources. Too often, the tools go unexamined or examined in a fleeting way, unattached to any true dialogue about what they might mean for student learning.

Although there may be some benefits to participating in the preceding activities, we would be remiss in not reiterating our strong belief, which is to really establish a common picture of students' proficiency and the context for demonstrating their learning of the power standards; we strongly advocate that teams engage in the process of unwrapping. (See also *Common Formative Assessment: A Toolkit for Professional Learning Communities at Work* [Bailey & Jakicic, 2012] for more on the unwrapping process.)

Unique Features of Unwrapping the CCSS

We have had the opportunity to unwrap numerous Common Core standards with teams who are new to the unwrapping process and with those who are already familiar with the process using their current state standards. These experiences reveal some generalizations about unwrapping the CCSS.

- The CCSS tend to have a more consistent grain size than many state standards, which makes it easier for teams to understand their meaning. For example, previous state standards frequently reflected a combination of isolated skills or facts that could be acquired in a single lesson with those that required deep conceptual understanding and represented learning across time.

- The standards are coherent from grade level to grade level leading to accomplishing the anchor standards, which helps teachers understand what students coming to them already know. So, as teams unwrap a standard for its meaning, they can check the grade level before and after for more clarity.

- Because of the internal consistency and alignment of the standards for Literature and Informational Text in the Reading strand, teams can do a quick check of meaning between the two sets of standards.

- Because the CCSS are written more consistently than many states' standards, the process of looking at nouns and verbs is an effective guide to identifying learning targets. In fact, simply reading the standard aloud is helpful as teams identify key phrases during the unwrapping process.

- The standards themselves have enough meat to get started with the unwrapping process even if teams are experiencing difficulty seeing the implied learning targets. In fact, many teams add implied learning targets later as they develop unit plans and formative assessments.

The Unwrapping Process

The unwrapping process is a strategy that enables collaborative teams to achieve collective clarity and agreement regarding specific *learning targets* contained within the standards (Bailey & Jakicic, 2012).

Learning targets are the increments of learning—steps of knowledge or concepts and skills—that build on each other and culminate in attainment of the standard. In other words, learning targets are the *knows, understands,* and *able to dos* that a student will demonstrate by the end of instruction.

Why is it important to identify learning targets? Let's consider the scope of the standards as written. Quite often, teaching the content of the standards will take place across a large period of time.

Let's look at a fifth-grade standard in the Reading Standards for Informational Text.

> Explain the relationships or interactions between two or more individuals, events, ideas, or concepts in a historical, scientific, or technical text based on specific information in the text. (RI.5.3) (NGA & CCSSO, 2010a, p. 14)

The complex skills and concepts contained within this standard are *not* ones that learners will acquire all at once. Students don't simply go from not having the skill to having the skill. For example, here's a quick breakdown of some of the smaller learning targets students will need to know and do in order to successfully accomplish the sample standard we've highlighted.

- Read the informational text (depicting historic, scientific, or technical information).

- Identify the key details in the text that inform the reader of key events and scientific or historical ideas, concepts, or processes.

- Analyze the relationships between multiple events and scientific or historical ideas, concepts, or processes.

- Synthesize the connections between the concepts, clearly communicating the influences, relationships, and links among key events, scientific or historical ideas, concepts, or processes.

Breaking down the standard into smaller learning targets provides clarity about the instructional journey students must take in order to accomplish it. Without clearly identifying learning targets, it will be impossible to accurately design instruction and aligned assessments that lead to the end in mind.

Furthermore, teams won't be able to determine which of the steps along the way might be problematic for their learners and point toward the need for focused instruction and common formative assessments. Figure 4.1 illustrates the process for identifying learning targets.

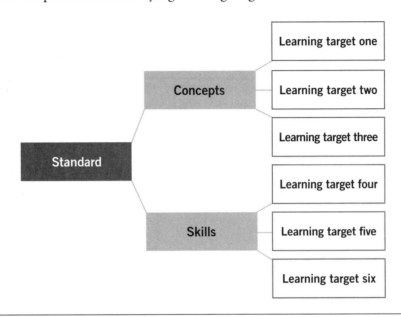

Figure 4.1: Process for defining learning targets.

It's important to note that learning targets should not be confused with instructional activities or strategies. Defining learning targets means that teams are getting clear about what students will know and be able to do by the end of the instructional unit, not about what they will be doing *during* the instructional unit. There may be many instructional strategies that help us do that, but everyone on the team must have the same end in mind, regardless of what strategies or activities they use to get there. We'll illustrate this difference using a grade 5 Reading Foundational Skills standard.

> Use combined knowledge of all letter-sound correspondences, syllabication patterns, and morphology (for example, roots and affixes) to read accurately unfamiliar multi-syllabic words in context and out of context. (RF.5.3a) (NGA & CCSSO, 2010a, p. 17)

A learning target that might emerge from this standard is for students to know the meaning of a common group of affixes to aid in their word knowledge. An activity that teachers might conduct to reinforce or assess this knowledge might be for students to create new words by combining root words, prefixes, and suffixes. While the activity may facilitate students' attainment of the learning target, it is not the learning target.

Unwrapping a Standard

In the unwrapping process, teams huddle around a standard and dig deeply into what's written and not written to reveal specific learning targets. Teams engaged in the unwrapping process share their experiences with the subject matter to inform each other of the specific nuances about how students learn the concepts and skills. These conversations are empowering not only to the teacher who might be new to the team or subject matter but to all who will be teaching to those standards. The goal is *clarity*—and by having that structured conversation that answers the question "What do they really mean by this standard?" every teacher will be enlightened and informed on an equal basis. The result? Their students will receive instruction that is aligned to the intent of the standard. This process also allows teams to talk about what instruction will look like because the learning targets are the building blocks for the standards. They will get clear about what those building blocks are and may have discussions about what instructional practices will work best.

As an example of the need to do more than a surface examination of the standards, let's take a look at this grade 3 Reading Standard for Literature.

> Recount stories, including fables, folktales, and myths from diverse cultures; deter-
> mine the central message, lesson, or moral and explain how it is conveyed through
> key details in the text. (RL.3.2) (NGA & CCSSO, 2010a, p. 12)

When you look at what's involved in guiding students to the level of skill and thinking described within the standard, it's clear that this is a very meaty standard. In fact, as you read this, your mind might already be starting to break this large standard into bite-sized learning targets—ones that you can orga-nize for meaningful instruction and assess in a more cumulative, formative fashion. For example, here's a quick glance at some of the likely learning targets that emerge from the preceding standard:

- Students will know the difference between the terms "central message," "lesson," and "moral" and recognize examples from a variety of stories (including fables, folktales, and myths).

- Students will identify the central message by finding evidence in a specific text.

- Students will identify the key details from the text that support the central message.

- Students will summarize and justify their identification of the central message/lesson/moral they identified within the story with support from details they identified in the text.

Similarly, consider what is involved in unwrapping this mathematics content standard for second grade in the domain Number and Operations in Base Ten (2.NBT).

> Compare two three-digit numbers based on meanings of the hundreds, tens,
> and ones digits, using >, =, and < symbols to record the results of comparisons.
> (2.NBT.4) (NGA & CCSSO, 2010e, p. 19)

Again, let's take a quick look at some of the potential learning targets—the smaller skills and concepts that students would need to know in order to achieve this standard:

- Students can explain the relationship between digits in the ones place, tens place, and hundreds place.

- Students can apply their knowledge of the >, =, and < symbols to compare two three-digit numbers that differ by the hundreds digit (for example, 200 and 300).

- Students can use the appropriate symbols (>, =, and <) to compare two three-digit numbers that differ by the tens digit (for example, 250 and 260).

- Students can use the appropriate symbols (>, =, and <) to compare two three-digit numbers that differ by the ones digit (for example, 524 and 527).

While teachers can independently begin the process of unwrapping the standards to identify learning targets and gain insight on the standards, we assert that it is far more valuable to engage in the pro-cess as a team. The unwrapping process helps move teams from a random or individual understanding and picture of success to a more intentional examination of the standard, one that yields that common picture we want everyone on the team to have. Remember, our goal is to provide a guaranteed and viable curriculum—not a cookie-cutter curriculum but one that guides students to deeper understanding and application of concepts and skills. We want all students to benefit and walk away knowing and doing the things that are most essential.

So how do teams move through the unwrapping process? We outline the steps in the process, using an example standard so that you can follow the process from start to finish.

Step One: Choose a Must-Know Standard

The first step in unwrapping a standard is to focus on what is essential. In chapter 3, you learned about powering the CCSS—a process that assists teams as they identify those standards that are most essential for students to learn, and subsequently, for your team to monitor, however, we also recognize that teams may choose to unwrap their standards first before going through the powering process. Whether you are focusing on a standard identified through the powering process in which your team distinguished the *must-knows* from the *nice-to-knows,* or you are engaging in the process to assist with the design of an upcoming unit, the first step in the unwrapping process is to get agreement on which standards you will be unwrapping. One way to get started is to consider the unit for which you will plan your instruction and assessment. A guiding question might be, What standards will we prioritize in our teaching during this time period or instructional unit? Other questions could include, What standard has been consistently challenging for our student to gain? What standard seems vague or ambiguous, and is worthy of a closer examination? As a team, you will decide which power standards you will address and monitor during that time period. You will most likely select a small cluster of standards, perhaps even choosing ones that cross content areas, such as integrating literacy standards with history and social studies standards. These focus standards will serve as the basis for your instructional plan, which ideally includes common assessments—both formative and summative.

At this time, we also suggest that teams have a discussion of the end in mind. What might it look like if students are successful in attaining this skill or concept? What will they be able to do? We think having a big-picture view of the outcome will assist the process of identifying smaller learning targets through the unwrapping process.

Let's walk through an example of the unwrapping process using a fourth-grade language arts example. The standard we'll unwrap is as follows:

> Compare and contrast a firsthand and secondhand account of the same event or topic; describe the differences in focus and the information provided. (RI.4.6) (NGA & CCSSO, 2010a, p. 14)

Step Two: Highlight Key Terms and Information

Using a team process for highlighting critical information in the standard will help reveal specific knowledge and skills (your learning targets), the context or criteria for learning, and academic language and vocabulary that will be crucial for student learning. To begin the process, we favor identifying key words within the standard. We suggest starting by putting brackets around any information that reveals the context or criteria with which students will demonstrate their learning. We have found this helpful to separate context from skills and concepts in the standards, and it sets the stage for better understanding of their expected rigor and application. Then, using a simple process of circling the verbs, you highlight the skills contained within the standard the students should be able to do. By underlining the nouns, or noun phrases, you bring to light the key concepts or understandings, specific information and processes, and terms the students should know.

Let's walk through an example of this process. Using the sample fourth-grade language arts standard we will first put brackets around any information that tells us about the context or criteria associated with students demonstrating this standard. In this standard, we've bracketed the language that shares the type of text with which students will be required to work (that is, firsthand and secondhand accounts on the same event or topic).

> Compare and contrast a [firsthand and secondhand account of the same event or topic;] describe the differences in focus and the information provided. (RI.4.6) (NGA & CCSSO, 2010a, p. 14)

Next we will highlight the important information by underlining the nouns (which represent knowledge or concepts that the students need to have) and circling the verbs (which represent the skills that students would be able to perform). Through our process, we underlined the words *firsthand, secondhand, account, differences in focus,* and *information provided.* We also identified three verbs (*compare, contrast,* and *describe*).

> Compare and contrast a [firsthand and secondhand account of the same event or topic;] describe the differences in focus and the information provided. (RI.4.6) (NGA & CCSSO, 2010a, p. 14)

By highlighting, we've now placed a common focus on key words in the standards. This quick step ensures that everyone on the team hones in on the highlighted information that's already contained in the standard and uses it to build common clarity.

Step Three: Discuss any Context, Conditions, or Performance Criteria

In contrast to many prior state standards, the CCSS provide more clarity about the context in which students must perform tasks and the level of complexity in the tasks. To gain insight into the intent of the standard, it's important for teams to use any of this information that might be contained in the standard. Some standards are explicit about the level of rigor inherent in the task, the types of text students will be using, or the level of support that will be provided as students perform or demonstrate their knowledge. For example, examine standard nine for reading informational text at the third-grade level. We've bracketed and bolded the portion of the standard that gives us information about the context or expectations:

> Compare and contrast the most important points and key ideas presented in **[two texts on the same topic]**. (RI.3.9) (NGA & CCSSO, 2010a, p. 14)

This standard defines the context of students being presented with two informational texts on the same topic.

Another example is the sixth-grade Writing standard eight. Similar to the preceding example, we've bracketed and bolded the portion of the standard that gives us information about the context or expectations:

> Gather relevant information **[from multiple print and digital sources]**; assess the credibility of each source; and quote or paraphrase the data and conclusions of others **[while avoiding plagiarism]** and providing basic bibliographic information for sources. (W.6.8) (NGA & CCSSO, 2010a, p. 44)

Not only does this standard tell us the type of sources students will be using, it also provides insight into expectations for quality (no plagiarism).

Teams need to ensure that they're on the same page when it comes to the context or criteria contained in the standard. Having a quick conversation on this point is the best approach to getting agreement. For example, in standard six for reading informational text at the fourth-grade level that follows, we highlighted (bracketed) specific information about the type of text with which students would be working.

> Compare and contrast a **[firsthand and secondhand account of the same event or topic;]** describe the differences in focus and the information provided. (RI.4.6) (NGA & CCSSO, 2010a, p. 14)

Since this standard is designed to address informational text, we know that the text students will be working with will be nonfiction and must contain a firsthand and secondhand account. It could be approached within a science unit, using a lab report or firsthand account from an inventor, for example, or in history/social science, using primary documents from an historical event. Again, having this quick conversation aligns everyone's thinking, leading to aligned instructional action.

Step Four: Identify Learning Targets

In this step, identify the learning targets, those smaller pieces of knowledge or skills that students will need to attain in order to reach the standard. When we talk about *knowledge*, we're really asking these questions: What information do students need to know? What concepts should they understand? The knowledge targets are often those that require more direct teacher instruction. We encourage you to look closely at your highlighted standard to jumpstart this conversation. In the highlighting process, the words that were underlined can lead your team to identify the knowledge or concepts that are important to address, including specific terms that they would need to understand.

When identifying *skills*, we're asking these questions: What do we want students to do? How will they apply their knowledge? The skill targets are often those that require students to think and reason. The verbs you circled during the highlighting process can point you to the skills required to attain the standards.

It should be noted, however, that not all learning targets are "right there" in the standard. In fact, you may determine that there are some *implied* learning targets that are critical and lead to the overall accomplishment of the standard. We call this "reading between the lines" of the standard, using professional experience and the collaborative expertise to decide if there are learning targets that must be added to those that are explicit in the standard.

During the process of identifying learning targets, we find that teams benefit from using a template to graphically organize their information. While we've included one example of how your information might be organized (see figure 4.2), as well as other samples that can be found in the appendix (pages 188–190), there are a variety of ways to organize your teams' information. To be clear, this is not about the form, it's about the conversation as you unwrap the standards. However, to jumpstart your process, we suggest starting with something simple, such as the template we'll use throughout the remainder of our process of unwrapping the fourth-grade standard. We'll show how this template is completed as we go through the remaining steps of the unwrapping process. Some teams use document cameras or other projection devices to collectively view the template, and facilitate a common view of the unwrapping process. See page 188 for a reproducible of this figure.

Standard to address: Compare and contrast a [firsthand and secondhand <u>account</u> of the same event or topic;] describe the <u>differences in focus</u> and the <u>information</u> <u>provided</u>. (RI.4.6) (NGA & CCSSO, 2010a, p. 14)	
Context or criteria: Using a firsthand and secondhand account (informational text) of the same event or topic	
Learning Targets	**Knowledge or concepts students need to know:** Know the source of information in a firsthand and secondhand account. Know what is meant by "compare and contrast." Know how a passage of text can have a "focus." Discuss the implications for bias/accuracy depending on the source of information.
	Skills students will do: Recognize the source of text as either firsthand or secondhand. Analyze each text to identify specific information that supports its focus. Compare and contrast the firsthand and secondhand account of the same event or topic (similarities and differences). Describe the difference of information between the two texts. Describe the differences in focus between the two texts. Relate the differences in focus to the different sources (for example, was the firsthand account more biased in its focus?).
Academic language and vocabulary: Will provide this in additive fashion as we go through the steps	

Figure 4.2: Basic unwrapping template depicting context and learning target.

As we shared earlier, when identifying learning targets, it's important to go beyond what the standard explicitly states and look at the implicit knowledge and skills that are necessary for students to acquire. For example, nowhere in our sample standard (page 62) did it state that students would need to *understand* the implications of information that came from a firsthand or secondhand source. We added that as a learning target. Additionally, we looked at the *intent* of the standard, and asked what larger concept would be important for students to have; we recognized that students need to understand why knowing the source of information is important. Therefore we also added that concept as one of the learning targets. Team conversations that focus on the "why" of the standard will often lead to these discoveries and help to ensure that higher-level concepts and skills are included as learning targets.

Step Five: Determine Learning Target Rigor

In this step, teams examine the rigor of each learning target. The verbs in the standard are great indicators of rigor. Teams can use a variety of tools to examine rigor based on the verbs. For purposes of communicating the descriptions of rigor in this process, we reference the three most commonly used models: Bloom's Revised Taxonomy (Anderson & Krathwohl, 2001), the New Taxonomy (Marzano & Kendall, 2007), and Webb's Depth of Knowledge (DOK; Webb, 2002). For a comparison of these taxonomies, see table 5.3, page 82 or the reproducible "Comparison of Taxonomies" (page 193).

Three Taxonomies of Thinking

Bloom's Revised Taxonomy

One of the most common models with which educators categorize levels of thinking is Bloom's Taxonomy (1956). Revised in 2000 (Anderson & Krathwohl, 2000), the taxonomy provides a framework using verbs to describe cognitive processes that progress from simple to complex and concrete to abstract.

- Level One: Remember—Recall, List, Describe, Name, Find
- Level Two: Understand—Interpret, Summarize, Classify, Explain
- Level Three: Apply—Execute, Implement, Carry out
- Level Four: Analyze—Differentiate, Organize, Attribute, Compare
- Level Five: Evaluate—Judge, Critique
- Level Six: Create—Generate, Plan, Produce

Marzano and Kendall's New Taxonomy

Marzano and Kendall (2007) offer educators an alternative way to classify levels of thinking through a two-dimensional taxonomy. The taxonomy examines both the domains of thinking (i.e., information, mental procedures, and psychomotor procedures) and also classifies cognitive processing taking place within those domains into one of four levels.

- Level One: Retrieval—Executing, Recalling, Recognizing
- Level Two: Comprehension—Integrating, Symbolizing
- Level Three: Analysis—Matching, Classifying, Analyzing errors, Generalizing, Specifying
- Level Four: Knowledge Utilization—Decision making, Problem solving, Experimenting, Investigating

Webb's Depth of Knowledge

Depth of Knowledge (DOK) is a scale of cognitive demand (Webb, 2005). It differs from other taxonomies by looking beyond the verb being used and examining the context in which skills are to be performed and the depth of thinking required. This scale has four levels.

- Level One: Recall—Level one requires rote recall of information of facts, definitions, terms, or simple procedures. The student either knows the answer or does not.
- Level Two: Skills and Concepts—Level two requires engagement of mental processing or decision making beyond recall or reproduction. Items falling into this category often have more than one step, such as organizing and comparing data.
- Level Three: Strategic Thinking—Level three requires higher-level thinking than levels one and two and could include activities or contexts, which have more than one possible solution, thereby requiring justification or support for the argument or process.
- Level Four: Extended Thinking—Level four requires high-cognitive demand in which students are synthesizing ideas across content areas or situations and generalizing that information to solve new problems. Many responses falling into this category will require extensive time, as they imply that students will be completing multiple steps, as in a multivariant investigation and analysis.

Let's look at the rigor contained in our unwrapped example (see figure 4.3). Next to each learning target, we've indicated the level of thinking using Webb's Depth of Knowledge (DOK).

Standard to address:	
Compare and contrast a [firsthand and secondhand <u>account</u> of the same event or topic;] describe the <u>differences in focus</u> and the <u>information</u> <u>provided</u>. (RI.4.6) (NGA & CCSSO, 2010a, p. 14)	
Context or criteria: Using a firsthand and secondhand account (informational text) of the same event or topic	
Learning Targets	**Knowledge or concepts students need to know:** The source of information in a "firsthand" and "secondhand" account **DOK1** The process for "compare and contrast" **DOK2** How a passage of text can have a "focus" and how to discover it **DOK2** The implications for bias/accuracy depending on the source of information **DOK3**
	Skills students will do: Recognize the source of text as either firsthand or secondhand. **DOK1** Analyze each text to identify specific information that supports its focus. **DOK2** Compare and contrast the firsthand and secondhand account of the same event or topic (similarities and differences). **DOK2** Describe the difference of information between the two texts. **DOK3** Describe the differences in focus between the two texts. **DOK3** Relate the differences in focus to the different sources (for example, was the firsthand account more biased in its focus?). **DOK3**
Academic language and vocabulary: Will provide this in additive fashion as we go through the steps	

Figure 4.3: Basic unwrapping template depicting context, learning targets, and rigor.

While some of the learning targets are categorized as targeting knowledge and skills at level one rigor (for example, knowing the source of a firsthand or secondhand account), other targets are designated as level three, which engages students in strategic thinking and constructing arguments.

Keeping a consistent eye on rigor allows teams to examine the intent of the standard and ensure that there is a match between that intention and the instruction and assessment provided to students. To support this examination, we've provided an alternative template in the appendix ("Unwrapping Template With Taxonomies," page 194) which assists teams as they compare rigor across the three taxonomies. Later in this chapter, we'll share a *leveled* unwrapping process which assists in the categorization of learning targets into simple and complex concepts and skills based on the team's analysis of rigor. As you'll see, this organization will be instrumental in identifying appropriate assessment items, developing rubrics and scales, and clarifying your sequence of instruction including interventions.

Step Six: Identify Academic and Domain-Specific Language

Knowledge of academic language and vocabulary is critical for students' learning. Why should this language be highlighted? In his book *Building Background Knowledge for Academic Achievement*, Marzano (2004) discusses the power of explicitly teaching subject-specific academic vocabulary. We have found that when teams are intentional about identifying vocabulary and academic language, there is an increased likelihood that they do something with the information. Teams are more likely to ensure student understanding of key words in the unit of instruction by embedding both targeted explicit vocabulary instruction and aligned assessment. Let's look again at our sample standard to see the specific academic language and domain-specific vocabulary that are identified (see figure 4.4, page 68).

Standard to address:	
Compare and contrast a [firsthand and secondhand <u>account</u> of the same event or topic;] describe the <u>differences in focus</u> and the <u>information</u> <u>provided</u>. (RI.4.6) (NGA & CCSSO, 2010a, p. 14)	
Context or criteria: Using a firsthand and secondhand account (informational text) of the same event or topic	
Learning Targets	**Knowledge or concepts students need to know:**
	The source of information in a "firsthand" and "secondhand" account **DOK1**
	The process for "compare and contrast" **DOK2**
	How a passage of text can have a "focus" and how to discover it **DOK2**
	The implications for bias/accuracy depending on the source of information **DOK3**
	Skills students will do:
	Recognize the source of text as either firsthand or secondhand. **DOK1**
	Analyze each text to identify specific information that supports its focus. **DOK2**
	Compare and contrast the firsthand and secondhand account of the same event or topic. **DOK2**
	Describe the differences in information between the two texts. **DOK3**
	Describe the differences in focus between the two texts. **DOK3**
	Relate the differences in focus to the different sources (for example, was the firsthand account more biased in its focus?). **DOK3**
Academic language and vocabulary:	
firsthand	
secondhand	
account	
focus	
compare	
contrast	
bias	
source	

Figure 4.4: Basic unwrapping template depicting context, learning targets, rigor, and academic and domain-specific language.

We just walked through an example standard to illustrate the steps of the unwrapping process. In our example, we examine the context and conditions under which the students would be demonstrating their learning, identify specific learning targets that will need to be taught—those steps leading to proficiency—and pull out specific language that will be targeted in instruction. By engaging in this process with their standards, teams gain a common and more complete picture of what it takes for students to attain mastery of a standard, setting the stage to design high-quality instruction and create aligned formative and summative assessments.

Clarity About the CCSS

The unwrapping process serves as a protocol for teams to closely examine attributes of the standards—intent, content, nuances, and picture of success. Some standards include the use of educational terminology which might not be familiar to teams, but which is explained further within appendix A (NGA & CCSSO, 2010b). For example, consider what is involved in unwrapping this mathematics content standard for fourth grade in the domain Operations and Algebraic Thinking (4.OA).

> Multiply or divide to solve word problems involving multiplicative comparison; for example, by using drawings and equations with a symbol for the unknown number to represent the problem, distinguishing multiplicative comparison from additive comparison. (4.OA.2) (NGA & CCSSO, 2010e, p. 29)

Team members may be unclear on the terms *multiplicative comparison* and *additive comparison*. This standard has a superscript that directs the team to the corresponding footnote, "See Glossary, Table 2" (NGA & CCSSO, 2010e, p. 29). The table clarifies that these terms reference problems in which there are two different sets being compared.

> A blue hat costs $6. A red hat costs 3 times as much as the blue hat. How much does the red hat cost? (NGA & CCSSO, 2010e, p. 89)

Other standards may contain concepts or terms requiring further discussion and exploration to get collective understanding or even agreement. Criteria such as *fluently* or *accurately* can require teams to examine their own thoughts about what the behavior looks like and engage in discussions to build agreement. We encourage teams to dig into the various appendices and notations in the CCSS, as well as other support resources available through SBAC and PARCC to gain further insight about quality or criteria being sought through instruction geared toward meeting the standards (see the listing of resources in chapter 3, page 46).

As teams unwrap their power standards to get clarity about the *what* of the standards, and the specific learning targets to be taught, they will naturally begin to discuss the *how* of the standards—the implications for their instruction and assessment. In particular, teams will engage in decision making about the best instructional sequence for teaching the specific learning targets. Depending upon the standard and the learning targets that are identified, teams may determine that some learning targets will be addressed in clusters throughout a particular unit, or distributed across several units of study.

Consider this first-grade Literature standard:

> Ask and answer questions about key details in a text. (RL.1.1) (NGA & CCSSO, 2010a, p. 11)

You might unwrap this standard into two separate learning targets: (1) Ask questions about key details in a text and (2) Answer questions about key details in a text. However, it is likely that both learning targets will be taught together when instruction about main ideas and details occurs. On the other hand, consider this seventh-grade Literature standard:

> Determine the theme or central idea of a text and analyze the development over the course of the text; provide an objective summary of the text. (RL.7.2) (NGA & CCSSO, 2010a, p. 36)

As a team unwraps this standard, the members find three learning targets: (1) Determine the theme or central idea of a text, (2) Analyze the development of the theme or central idea over the course of the text, and (3) Provide an objective summary using the theme or central idea of the text. In this case, the team may decide to teach the learning targets separately throughout the year, building on students' previous knowledge as each unit of instruction takes place.

The same ideas hold true as teams unwrap the mathematics standards. Consider what is required to unwrap this first-grade mathematics standard in the domain Operations and Algebraic Thinking (1.OA).

> Use addition and subtraction within 20 to solve word problems involving situations of adding to, taking from, putting together, taking apart, and comparing, with unknowns in all positions. (1.OA.1) (NGA & CCSSO, 2010e, p. 15)

The team will likely teach multiple learning targets from this standard over several units of instruction. For example, an initial learning target would involve students applying their knowledge of "adding to" sets of numbers to twenty in the context of word problems, and later progressing to the learning target of "taking from" with sets of numbers to twenty. As a collaborative team, joint unit planning will be crucial to help clarify which targets will be emphasized during each unit of instruction. This process will be discussed further in chapter 6.

A Leveled Approach to Unwrapping the Standards

As teams become more comfortable with the process for unwrapping standards they may want to "raise the bar" and set the stage for designing quality instruction and assessment. In our work, we've added a new dimension to the unwrapping process, we call *leveling the learning targets*. We do this during the examination of rigor, and classify the identified learning targets as either simple or complex concepts or skills. For example, a learning target aimed at having students memorize the definition of a term would be considered a simple concept. However, explaining how that term or concept relates to other concepts would be considered more complex. By leveling the targets, teams are guided to design more accurate assessments that align with the rigor intended in the standards. To illustrate this process, let's follow a team of teachers who will follow the same steps of unwrapping, with the additional layer of leveling the targets.

Across all content areas, the sixth-grade team decides that it wants to be far more intentional about guiding students through the process of writing explanatory texts. Collectively, they prioritize this sixth-grade standard from the Writing strand by following step one (page 62)—choose a must-know standard.

> Introduce a topic; organize ideas, concepts, and information, using strategies such as definition, classification, comparison/contrast, and cause/effect; include formatting (for example, headings), graphics (for example, charts, tables), and multimedia when useful to aiding comprehension. (W.6.2a) (NGA & CCSSO, 2010a, p. 42)

Together, team members highlight key words and phrases in the standard using the same process described in step two (page 62)—bracket any context/criteria information, circle the verbs, and underline the nouns or noun phrases. Figure 4.5 shows the coded version of the standard.

Grade 6 Writing Standard

Standard W.6.2a: Introduce a <u>topic</u>, organize <u>ideas, concepts, and information</u> using <u>strategies</u> such as <u>definition, classification, comparison/contrast, and cause/effect;</u> [include <u>formatting</u> (for example, <u>headings</u>), <u>graphics</u> (for example, <u>charts</u>, tables), and <u>multimedia</u> when useful to aiding <u>comprehension</u>.]

Figure 4.5: Example of key terms highlighted in a sixth-grade Writing standard.

Source: Adapted from NGA & CCSSO, 2010a, p. 42.

The team then considers the context in which students would be required to demonstrate their understanding, cued by the information that they have bracketed. Team members discuss implications for the tools, materials, and activities in which students would participate. In this case, they feel that the learning context is one in which students would be required to integrate a number of strategies to communicate information about a specific topic. They would use an appropriate text structure to define, compare and contrast, or show cause and effect in support of their information, as well as organize and enhance their writing with graphics, formatting, and charts. During the discussion, team members are sure to reference the anchor standards and other support materials that help inform them about the intent of the standards. In this case, they refresh their thinking by looking at standard two and its six parts (a–f) in the Writing strand for sixth grade. This is step three (page 63)—identify any context, conditions, or performance criteria.

> Write informative/explanatory texts to examine a topic and convey ideas, concepts, and information through the selection, organization, and analysis of relevant content. (W.6.2) (NGA & CCSSO, 2010a, p. 42)

After discussing the context in which students would be demonstrating this standard, the team identifies the learning targets (step four, page 64), looking for those that are stated explicitly. Here's what jumps out at the team members.

- **Introduce** a topic.

- **Organize** ideas, concepts, and information.

- **Use** strategies such as definition, classification, compare and contrast, and cause and effect.

- **Include** formatting, graphics, and multimedia to aid comprehension.

They also have a discussion through which they determine that there are additional learning targets that are not explicit, but are also important *know and dos* including:

- Know the importance of clear organization and structure to the reader and target audience

- Gather relevant facts, details, and other information in support of the topic

- Critique the effectiveness of a structure

As part of their conversation, the team examines the learning targets the members identified. They discuss which of these they consider to be simple skills or concepts and those that are more complex in terms of students' ability to understand or perform them. Following the discussion, they organize this information in the template shown in figure 4.4 (page 68). For example, the team identified "Introduce a topic" as the first learning target in its initial glance at the standard. Yet as the discussion evolved, the team realized that students should know the *why* behind clear organization and structure in a piece of writing, including a powerful or compelling introduction. Again, the team places the identified learning targets into the Leveled Unwrapping template, distinguishing them from those skills and concepts that were simple for students to attain and those that were more complex. (See figure 4.6 on page 73.) By adding this dimension to their template they ensure that not only is their instruction designed to target the important concepts and skills in their instruction, but that the assessments they design are aligned with the level of rigor intended (see step five, page 65). This effort of dividing the concepts and skills into simple and complex categories, will also lead to more accurate assessments and development of scales, which will be discussed in chapter 5.

Figure 4.6 has several components starting with guiding questions, which establish the framework for defining the learning targets. The column Depth of Knowledge Level refers to the criteria for depth of knowledge (see page 66 for more about DOK levels).

Finally, the team identifies and discusses the academic language and content-specific vocabulary that would be essential for students to know and be able to use within their instructional experience. Most of the words they identify are found in the actual language of the standard, however, they add additional terms, such as *target audience*, they feel would be important to address within their instruction (see step six, pages 67–68).

The Natural Next Step: Identify Assessment Ideas

As a part of their conversation around the learning targets, team members naturally begin identifying possible assessment ideas which would ensure student understanding. They jot notes using the space provided in the templates so they have a record of their good ideas.

The experience of Leveled Unwrapping engaged this team in a collaborative process that not only yielded clarity about the intent of the standard and learning targets (explicit and implied) but also jumpstarted their understanding of the level of complexity found in their learning targets. We believe that this is a powerful step for teams and brings added value to the conversation. Furthermore, having this information provides the foundation for aligned assessment, as well as for designing a learning progression and a scale for monitoring student attainment. In the next chapter, we will provide additional information on the use of learning progressions and scales as a means to not only answer the second critical question "How will we know if our students are learning?" but also "How well are they progressing in their journey to mastery of the standards?"

"Pre-Packaged" Unwrapped Standards: Good Idea or Not?

By design, the benefits of a team's collaborative efforts to unwrap standards are obvious. Team members build common understanding about what students need to learn, and the steps involved in attaining the standard. Yet, sometimes teams will opt to work with standards that others have unwrapped. Several state departments, such as North Carolina, as well as a number of districts and other educational entities have unwrapped the CCSS. Some teams may find these resources helpful in jumpstarting the process of building shared understanding of what students should know and be able to do (Public Schools of North Carolina, 2012). However, we assert that simply relying on unwrapped standards is comparable to getting the old notebooks of standards when they first came out in the late 1990s. Many of us still have those notebooks lining our shelves. What seems to bring teams clarity is when they actively engage in the *process* of unwrapping—when they grapple with the ambiguous, muddy, and controversial. It's the conversations that come about that help teams arrive at that common picture. One can almost see the lightbulbs burning brighter in the process. Additionally, the unwrapping process reveals a pathway of learning targets, almost like the little lights one finds along a walkway. The learning that the team will target through the design of instruction and assessment is clear to each team member—not randomly interpreted by each

Guiding Questions
- What standards will we prioritize in our teaching during this instructional unit?
- What specific concepts or information do we want students to know? Are they simple or complex?
- What skills do we want them to be able to do? Are they simple or complex?
- What assessment will we use to ensure students successfully learned the concepts and skills?

Standard to address:
W.6.2a. Introduce a topic, organize ideas, concepts, and information, using strategies, such as definition, classification, compare and contrast, and cause and effect; include formatting (for example, headings), graphics (for example, charts and tables), and multimedia when useful to aiding comprehension.

Context or criteria		Students will be required to integrate a number of strategies to communicate information about a specific topic using an appropriate text structure to define, compare and contrast, or show cause and effect. They would need to organize and enhance their writing with graphics, formatting, and charts.		
	Learning Targets	**Depth of Knowledge (DOK) Level**	**Assessment Ideas**	
Knowledge or concepts students need to know	**Simple**			
	Know the importance of clear organization and structure to the reader and target audience.	DOK1	Complete exit ticket—quick write.	
	Complex			
	Know various organizational strategies (like definition, classification, compare and contrast, and cause and effect) and explain the benefit to the reader.	DOK3	Identify examples of organizational strategies from a variety of text.	
Skills students will do	**Simple**			
	Select the structure to be used in a text, including the introduction.	DOK2	Annotate articles that use different text structures.	
	Gather relevant facts, details, and other information in support of the topic.	DOK2		
	Complex			
	Students develop an effective introduction to an argumentative essay or informational report.	DOK3	Use team's writing rubric.	
	Organize the ideas, concepts, and information with an appropriate text structure.	DOK3	Outline rough draft.	
	Create appropriate headings, graphics, and multimedia to communicate key points within an essay or informational report.	DOK4	Use rubrics for quality.	
	Critique the effectiveness of a structure.	DOK4	Group analysis of sample essays or reports with individual reflection.	
Academic language and vocabulary	Organizational strategies, target audience, classification, compare and contrast, cause and effect, and formatting			

Figure 4.6: Unwrapped standard using a Leveled Unwrapping template.

teacher on an individual basis. So how can we work with some of these support tools without sacrificing the power of the process? Two things to consider if teams use unwrapped standards: (1) do so only after building understanding of why and how schools or states unwrapped the standards, and (2) use a protocol that provides a professional filter to guide your examination of the unwrapped standards. The reproducible "Protocol for Team Review of Unwrapped Standards" (page 191) provides guidance for conversations and professional filters teams can use as they examine prepared sets of unwrapped standards.

Tips for Teams New to the PLC Process

The process of unwrapping will be one of the most effective ways for your team to build collective understanding about the Common Core State Standards. If your team is new to the process, you'll want to approach the process in a doable way. We suggest taking one strand in the ELA standards or one domain in the mathematics standards and using the process to clarify a key standard in an upcoming unit of study. Some novice teams may find the process a little scary at first, but remember there is no perfect or right way to unwrap a standard. What is most important is that each team member walks away from the conversation having a greater understanding of the end in mind for student learning. The unwrapping process will move your team from independent practice to a common, collective focus across all of your classrooms. The clarity you build in the process is the linchpin you'll need to build a cohesive and aligned plan for instruction and assessment! Teachers often ask us, "Must we unwrap all the standards before we address the other work that needs to be done?" We know that unwrapping takes time. Here's our thinking: Your context will drive the answer to this question. If your team is just getting started using the CCSS and has limited common planning, you can prioritize and *chunk* your efforts using a unit-by-unit approach. As a team, start by asking the question, "What are the power standards we want to address within this unit?" Those are the standards on which you would focus your initial unwrapping efforts—using the process to get clarity and identify specific learning targets to be addressed within the unit. Over time, unit by unit, you'll have unwrapped all of your power standards. We believe this approach to the unwrapping process is manageable, particularly if you don't have unlimited common planning time.

Many districts, however, do provide professional development time allowing teachers the opportunity to dig in and unwrap all their standards in a content area. We've helped to facilitate schools in this process, and there is a real value in operating in this fashion. For example, an elementary school might have each grade-level team unwrap a specific strand in mathematics, and then post their unwrapped standard on chart paper. As a school, all of the teams walk the walls to examine the nuances of the standard, the language it uses, and its level of rigor.

Tips for Principals and Leaders

We strongly believe that the way to provide all students with a guaranteed and viable curriculum is by engaging teams in a process to build collective clarity about the context, content, and intent of the Common Core State Standards. We know the process of unwrapping the standards is one that gets teams to that clarity. Yet we realize that you may be the recipient of some *push back* in the initial stages when you make clear that teams are expected to move through the process. Teachers may be concerned about the time it might take to dig into the standards in depth, or there may be a *fear factor* about how to move through the process itself. We've found that it helps to jumpstart teams in the process by having them unwrap a vertical strand of standards within a staff meeting and walk the room to examine the continuum of learning that results. By having an entire room engaged in a process, any questions about the process can be addressed, and the experience of revealing a stairstep of learning is exciting and informative for all involved. It's very powerful to begin the process by quickly having teams first examine the context of the standards—doing so will help teams see the *why* of unwrapping—the need to build clarity about the intent and the learning targets contained within the standards.

Because unwrapping the Common Core standards may be a new experience for some (or possibly all) teachers on your staff, your guidance and support will be especially important. Your leadership will be instrumental in helping the teachers gain confidence as they work collaboratively to unwrap the CCSS.

5

Scaling Learning Targets to Define Proficiency

Collaborative Connections

- Teams who develop proficiency scales for the learning targets defined from unwrapping the standards will have better clarity about what each learning target means and what proficiency will look like.

- Proficiency scales will help students know exactly where they are in reaching proficiency on a learning target.

- Teams will be better able to respond after common formative assessments when they have written proficiency scales for their learning targets.

The work that your collaborative team does with powering and unwrapping the Common Core State Standards will help you have a much clearer answer to the question, What do we want students to know and be able to do? However, your team can gain even more clarity by analyzing each learning target further to determine levels of proficiency using a scale process. This process connects the learning targets you identified during the unwrapping process with how teams will assess student learning formatively and summatively. In fact, the learning targets developed during the unwrapping process outlined in chapter 4 can be the starting point for developing scales. The unwrapping and scaling processes both give teams greater clarity about how to respond when students do not reach proficiency. The scaling process takes it a step further, providing clarity regarding what teams can do for the students who demonstrate proficiency quickly and could benefit from additional challenge.

Additionally, proficiency scales set the stage for standards-based reporting, as the proficiency levels can be aligned with the grading scale when reporting by standard or target. For example, if a student demonstrates mastery of the learning target at what will be considered the "proficient" level, they would be meeting the standard on the report card. The process described in this chapter is one we have used with teams who want to establish a more refined description of proficiency.

We want to be clear that while we see the development of proficiency scales as a powerful enhancement of the powering and unwrapping process, we also recognize that not every team is ready for this step. If your team is not ready for this step right now, you can add it in the future once you are comfortable working with one level of proficiency for each learning target. However, you may want to try it out with just a few learning targets at a time. Get comfortable, and see the benefits!

What Is a Proficiency Scale?

Using proficiency scales requires teams to consider what learning looks like when a student is just beginning to demonstrate knowledge of the target, what it looks like when a student is proficient, as well as what it looks like if a student is able to demonstrate knowledge at an even higher level than the target expects (Marzano, 2010).

A proficiency scale is a learning progression that conveys distinct levels of knowledge and skill relative to the specific learning targets teams identify while unwrapping the Common Core State Standards.

Table 5.1 outlines five proficiency levels based on Marzano's (2009) work. We will be using his generic scale but revising it for use with the CCSS and our recommended formative assessment process. It is important to begin by explaining proficiency level 3.0 first as it is considered the mastery level or the level all students are expected to meet. The unwrapped Common Core learning targets—that come directly from the standards—are inserted into this level of the scale. One level up the scale from the 3.0 learning expectation is proficiency level 4.0. This level contains a learning target that describes what learning looks like when students can go beyond the expectations in the 3.0 learning target—this is, when they've demonstrated that they've learned more complex content or gone beyond what was taught in the classroom for all students.

One level below the 3.0 learning expectation is proficiency level 2.0. This level describes what the team considers to be simpler content or beginning concepts for the 3.0 learning target. Proficiency level 2.0 targets may include knowing the vocabulary and facts needed for mastery, but not yet thoroughly understanding the more rigorous concepts. When the team has written the proficiency level 2.0 learning target, they are more likely able to recognize the progress a student is making after initial instruction and will likely make a better choice about how to provide additional instruction to help the student move toward mastery of the 3.0 learning target. If the team used the leveled approach to unwrapping standards outlined in chapter 4, they will have already considered the simpler content and skills and will have a head start on the development of the 2.0 learning targets.

Proficiency levels 1.0 and 0.0 do not include information about the content itself but rather indicate a student's level of competence regarding the content in proficiency levels 2.0 and 3.0. Proficiency level 1.0 indicates that a student could demonstrate partial mastery of the 2.0 learning target and possibly the 3.0 learning target with assistance. Proficiency level 0.0 specifies that the student was not able to demonstrate partial mastery even with assistance.

Table 5.1: Proficiency Scale

Proficiency Level 4.0	Extended Learning Target
Proficiency Level 3.0	Mastery Learning Target
Proficiency Level 2.0	Simpler Learning Target (Simple learning targets from unwrapping may apply.)
Proficiency Level 1.0	With help, partial success at score 2.0 learning target and/or 3.0 learning target
Proficiency Level 0.0	Even with help, no success

Source: Adapted from Marzano, 2009.

When your team begins the work of scaling the learning targets, you will use the template in table 5.1 to insert the learning targets into proficiency levels 4.0, 3.0, and 2.0. If your team did not use the *leveled* approach in the unwrapping process, proficiency level 3.0 will contain the learning targets identified directly from the Common Core standard. This will be the starting point for developing the 4.0 proficiency and the 2.0 proficiency targets. If your team used the leveled approach in unwrapping, you've already identified the simpler (proficiency level 2.0) targets.

Applying the Proficiency Scale Template

Let's first look at a real example of this work in practice. We'll work with a seventh-grade standard for reading literature.

> Determine a theme or central idea of a text and analyze its development over the course of the text; provide an objective summary of the text. (RL.7.2) (NGA & CCSSO, 2010a, p. 36)

The team determines that this is a power standard and unwraps it into three learning targets: (1) determine a theme or central idea of a text, (2) analyze the development of the text's theme or central idea over the course of the text, and (3) provide an objective summary of the text including the theme or central idea. For this example, we will work with the second learning target "analyze the text's theme or central idea over the course of the text." See table 5.2 for the proficiency scale.

Table 5.2: Proficiency Scale for Seventh-Grade Reading Literature Learning Target

Proficiency Level 4.0	Determine a way to change the theme by changing events in the story. (What would happen to the theme if . . . and how would it change?)
Proficiency Level 3.0	Analyze the text's theme or central idea over the course of the text.
Proficiency Level 2.0	Given the theme, the student decides what pieces of evidence from the text best show the theme's development over the course of the text.
Proficiency Level 1.0	With help, partial success at 2.0 content and 3.0 content
Proficiency Level 0.0	Even with help, no success

The team starts with the proficiency level 3.0 and writes it just as it appears in the original unwrapped standard. Then, they tackle writing a learning target for proficiency level 2.0, remembering that this level is a simpler version of the learning target in proficiency level 3.0. It's important to understand that level 2.0 is not a prerequisite skill for the learning target in proficiency level 3.0, but rather an expectation at a lower thinking level. If the leveled approach to unwrapping was used, the team may have done much of this thinking already, and can use the information in the unwrapping document as a starting point for the development of the 2.0 learning target. In this situation, the team discusses what it would look like if the student was not able to perform the skill at the expected level of proficiency—that is, if the student had difficulty analyzing the theme's development over the course of the text. The team decides that a simpler version of the target would be to provide the theme and a list of text evidence, asking students to choose which pieces of evidence from the text best show the theme's development. The team agrees that students who can work with an identified theme and make connections to various places in the text will have mastered some of the simpler content but not the actual target, therefore reaching proficiency level 2.0.

Next, the team discusses what it would look like if students could demonstrate a higher level of thinking (proficiency level 4.0) than that expected in proficiency level 3.0. The team determines that it can be stated as "able to determine how the theme would change if certain events in the story changed," and inserts that information into the proficiency level 4.0 section of the scaling template. The team does not insert learning targets into proficiency levels 1.0 and 0.0 as these levels indicate a student's competence regarding the learning targets in proficiency levels 2.0 and 3.0.

This process allows teams to consider and identify students' learning progression as they become proficient or exceed the learning target. In doing so, they will discuss the level of reasoning they are expecting from students, referencing a taxonomy of thinking levels, such as Bloom's Revised Taxonomy (Anderson & Krathwohl, 2001), the New Taxonomy (Marzano & Kendall, 2007), or Webb's Depth of Knowledge (Webb, 2005). The chart "Comparison of Taxonomies" in table 5.3 (page 82) and a reproducible (page 193) will help teams do this work.

The Importance of Developing Proficiency Scales

Your team might be asking, "Isn't it enough that there is a clear learning target?" As you think about how your team will respond to the data from formative assessments, you'll see that learning targets on their own do not provide the level of specificity regarding student learning that proficiency scales can. The development and implementation of proficiency scales provide teachers with information regarding a student's level of knowledge and reasoning for each learning target that students will be expected to learn. Using proficiency levels 0.0–4.0 on the scale, teachers can determine if a student demonstrates learning at a simpler level than the standard or target expectation, is meeting the expectation, or can demonstrate knowledge at a more complex level of understanding. Having this information allows teachers to design instruction to more specifically meet the needs of individual students or groups of students and to respond more appropriately when they don't learn during initial instruction.

Margaret Heritage (2008) describes how teachers can use formative assessments developed around scales to know what to do next when students need more time and support.

> The purpose of formative assessment is to provide feedback to teachers and students during the course of learning about the gap between students' current and desired performance so that action can be taken to close the gap. To do this effectively, teachers need to have in mind a continuum of how learning develops in any particular knowledge domain so that they are able to locate students' current learning status and decide on pedagogical action to move students' learning forward. Learning progressions that clearly articulate a progression of learning in a domain can provide the big picture of what is to be learned, support instructional planning, and act as a touchstone for formative assessment. (Heritage, 2008, p. 2)

Formative assessment data will also help students know exactly where they are in their own knowledge and understanding of a particular learning target and what they need to do to either meet the level of expectation or exceed it. In one of the middle schools in which we worked through this process, a teacher described the benefits of using proficiency scales with her students. "They can tell you, 'I'm at a 2.0 because I didn't explain my text example and relate it back to my inference.' I love when students can tell me exactly what they can and can't do. It makes them more comfortable with the targets, and it allows me to focus on the areas with which I know they are struggling. No longer do they come in for help on *inferences*. They come in for help to find text support for their inferences or to help them determine how a character is motivated by what they say."

We have seen the power of proficiency scales to transform teaching and learning. Teachers indicate that they know their students better than ever before, and students express that they have a deeper understanding of their learning. Teachers also report that students are more driven to improve, as they are motivated to get to the next level of the scale.

The Process of Developing Proficiency Scales

We suggest that teams develop proficiency scales for the CCSS collaboratively, as they are new to everyone. As teams work through the process of writing scales, they discuss what they believe *proficiency* means, what it will look like when students accomplish the learning target, and what the simpler concepts are that a teacher might address to help scaffold learning for students experiencing difficulty. The deep thinking this requires will provide the team with additional clarity regarding each standard, especially when working with the unfamiliar Common Core standards.

The model we use for the process of developing scales for learning is based on Marzano (2009) with some modifications we've found effective. The process includes four steps:

1.   Insert unwrapped learning targets into the proficiency scale template.

2.   Identify the complexity level of the 3.0 learning target.

3.   Write the 4.0 learning target.

4.   Write the 2.0 learning target.

Before beginning the process, the team should select a familiar taxonomy for describing levels of thinking or complexity. Bloom's Revised Taxonomy (Anderson & Krathwohl, 2001), Webb's Depth of Knowledge (Webb, 2005), and the New Taxonomy (Marzano & Kendall, 2007) are all appropriate for developing proficiency scales and easily apply to the CCSS. Table 5.3 (page 82) shows a comparison of the three taxonomies (also see chapter 4, page 66).

Step One: Insert Unwrapped Learning Targets Into the Proficiency Scale Template

The team begins with one of the unwrapped learning targets as it is written from the power standard. We recommend keeping the Common Core terminology intact for the scaling process, as changing the language can often lead to unintended modifications of the Common Core meaning and rigor expectations. The unwrapped target becomes the proficiency level 3.0 scaled learning target and represents expected proficiency mastery for all students in the class. The team will repeat this process for all learning targets developed from the initial Common Core power standard. For example, if there are three learning targets from one of the power standards, the team will complete three scaling templates for that standard. Consider this fifth-grade mathematics standard.

Recognize volume as an attribute of solid figures and understand concepts of volume measurement. (5.MD.3) (NGA & CCSSO, 2010e, p. 37)

Table 5.3: Comparison of Taxonomies

Bloom's Revised Taxonomy	Marzano and Kendall's New Taxonomy	Webb's Depth of Knowledge
Level Six: Create Generate Plan Produce **Level Five: Evaluate** Judge Critique	**Level Four: Knowledge Utilization** **Decision making** Decide: What is the best way? **Problem solving** Adapt: Figure out a way to … **Experimenting** Generate and test: What would happen if … **Investigating** Research: Take a position on …	**Level Four: Extended Thinking** Design Connect Synthesize Apply concepts Critique Analyze Create
Level Four: Analyze Differentiate Organize Attribute Compare	**Level Three: Analysis** **Matching** Create an analogy, Distinguish **Classifying** Organize, Sort, Identify **Analyzing errors** Identify errors, Critique, Diagnose **Generalizing** Draw conclusions, Create a rule **Specifying** Predict, Judge, Deduce	**Level Three: Strategic Thinking** Revise Construct Compare Hypothesize Cite evidence Formulate Draw conclusions
Level Three: Apply Execute Implement Carry Out	**Level Two: Comprehension** **Integrating** Describe the relationship between, Paraphrase, Summarize **Symbolizing** Depict, Represent, Illustrate	**Level Three: Skills and Concepts** Infer Predict Interpret Use context clues Estimate Compare Organize Graph
Level Two: Understand Interpret Summarize Classify Explain **Level One: Remember** Recall Identify Recognize	**Level One: Retrieval** (These aspects are hierarchical within this level only.) **Executing** Use, Show, Demonstrate **Recalling** Name, Describe, List **Recognizing** Select or identify from (a list) Determine (if statements are true)	**Level One: Recall** Define Identify List Measure Arrange Calculate Recall

Source: Adapted from Anderson & Krathwohl, 2001; Marzano & Kendall, 2007; Webb, 2005.

Let's say the team unwraps this standard into these two learning targets: (1) recognize volume as an attribute of solid figures and (2) understand concepts of volume measurement. The team begins by looking at the first target and lists it as the level 3.0 target (see table 5.4).

Table 5.4: Scaling a Learning Target—Step One

Level of the Scale	Powered Learning Target	Marzano and Kendall's New Taxonomy	Suggested Assessment Strategies and Items
Proficiency Level 4.0			
Proficiency Level 3.0	Recognize volume as an attribute of solid figures.		
Proficiency Level 2.0			
Proficiency Level 1.0	With help, partial success at score 2.0 content and 3.0 content		
Proficiency Level 0.0	Even with help, no success		

Step one is simply an opportunity for the team to prepare the scaling template(s) by inserting the unwrapped learning target into the proficiency level 3.0 section of the template. This prepares the team for the more complex tasks included in steps two through four.

Step Two: Identify the Complexity Level of the 3.0 Learning Target

Step two requires teams to determine the complexity level of the 3.0 learning target using the taxonomy of their choice. It is important to determine the level of thinking required for students to master the 3.0 learning target as it is the basis for developing the 2.0 and 4.0 learning targets, for students to meet proficiency based on the taxonomy they are using. (See also table 5.3 and the reproducible "Comparison of Taxonomies," page 193.) To illustrate the examples in this section, we used the New Taxonomy (Marzano & Kendall, 2007) because it offers more differentiation at the early levels, which is necessary for this particular target. In fact, you should notice also that level one in the New Taxonomy is hierarchical, meaning that *recognizing* is a lower-level skill than *recalling*, and *recalling* is a lower-level skill than *executing*.

Because Marzano uses the term *level* to describe each of the categories of thinking, some teams confuse the thinking level of the taxonomy with the proficiency level of the scale. This is a misunderstanding. The thinking levels of the taxonomy and the proficiency levels of the scale are not connected. For example, proficiency level 3.0 targets do not have to be derived from level three of the taxonomy. It is common to have a proficiency level 3.0 learning target that is at thinking level two in the taxonomy. This step asks the team to consider what thinking level (taxonomy level) the target is asking from students. Because each of the taxonomies has a list of verbs that fit into their categories, teams are often tempted to look for the verb that appears in the learning target and call it a match. However, this doesn't always work because verbs may mean different things when applied to different concepts. The learning target's verb alone does not provide adequate information to determine a thinking level on the taxonomy. It is essential for teams to consider the full context of the learning target, not just the verb, before making a final determination regarding the thinking level (taxonomy level) expected.

Consider the following two learning targets that both begin with the verb *describe*: "Describe the setting of the story." "Describe how the author's bias influences the text." Using the verb only, both of these learning targets would fall into thinking level two based on the Marzano and Kendall (2007) taxonomy. However, when the full context of the learning target is considered, "Describe the setting of the story," it remains at the comprehension level but "Describe how the author's bias influences the text" requires a higher level of thinking, moving it up to thinking Level Three: Analysis on the Marzano and Kendall (2007) taxonomy. It isn't unusual for team members to disagree about where the learning target fits on the taxonomy. They will want to spend some time discussing their ideas until the team feels confident that it has a consensus. While there is frequently more than one right answer about where a target fits on the taxonomy, it is important that teams work together to reach consensus about what they believe.

After deciding on a taxonomy level, teams can add it to their scaling template and discuss possible assessment strategies and items, such as those in table 5.5. (See the "Scaling Form" reproducible in the appendix, page 195.)

Table 5.5: Scaling a Learning Target—Step Two

Level of the Scale	Powered Learning Target	Marzano and Kendall's New Taxonomy	Assessment Strategies and Items
Level 4.0			
Level 3.0	Recognize volume as an attribute of solid figures.	Level One: Retrieval Recognizing	Identify volume as one of the attributes of a solid figure when given a list of attributes.
Level 2.0			
Level 1.0	With help, partial success at score 2.0 content and 3.0 content		
Level 0.0	Even with help, no success		

The team is now ready to move to step three in the process of developing a proficiency scale.

Step Three: Write the 4.0 Target

In this step, the team develops the proficiency level 4.0 learning target, which is more complex than the proficiency level 3.0 learning target. This discussion will require the team to continue using the taxonomy of choice to consider what proficiency will look like with increased rigor. The team begins by considering moving at least one level up the taxonomy from the thinking level expected in the proficiency level 3.0 learning target. Proficiency level 4.0 learning targets require students to extend their thinking and often complete more complex tasks, but it is important that the general content of the learning remain the same.

In our example, the team uses the New Taxonomy (Marzano & Kendall, 2007) to determine the proficiency level 4.0 learning target (see table 5.3 on page 82). It determines that the proficiency level 4.0 learning target should be at Level Two: Comprehension in the category *integrating*. The team feels that to "Describe the relationship between volume and capacity," the student would be demonstrating a deeper understanding of volume. Because the term *capacity* was not explicitly taught in class but referred to generally in discussions, the teachers were convinced that any student who could sufficiently describe the relationship between volume and capacity would be showing extended understanding of volume. The team enters the target into the scaling template for level 4.0 and includes notes about how teachers might assess the target (see table 5.6).

Table 5.6: Scaling a Learning Target—Step Three

Level of the Scale	Powered Learning Target	Marzano and Kendall's New Taxonomy	Assessment Strategies and Items
Level 4.0	Describe the relationship between volume and capacity.	**Level Two: Comprehension** Integrating	**Short Constructed Response** Describe how capacity and volume are related terms. Give an example.
Level 3.0	Recognize volume as an attribute of solid figures.	**Level One: Retrieval** Recalling	**Short Constructed Response** Describe why and how volume is an attribute of solid figures.
Level 2.0	Identify the definition of volume.	**Level One: Retrieval** Recognizing	**Multiple Choice** Identify the definition of volume from a list.
Level 1.0	With help, partial success at score 2.0 content and 3.0 content		
Level 0.0	Even with help, no success		

At this point in the process, the team has now defined the mastery level learning target in proficiency level 3.0, and the extended learning target in proficiency level 4.0. The learning progression is almost complete, and the team is now ready to move to the fourth and final step in the process, development of the simpler learning target in proficiency level 2.0.

Step Four: Write the 2.0 Target

In step four, the collaborative team designs the proficiency level 2.0 learning target, which is subordinate to the proficiency level 3.0 learning target (Marzano, 2009). If the leveled approach was used in the unwrapping process, the simple content and skills from that process can be useful in writing the proficiency level 2.0 learning targets as some of the simpler expectations may have already been defined. If the leveled approach was not used, the starting point for this discussion begins with the taxonomy chart and the team looks to write the proficiency level 2.0 learning target at least one level of thinking below the taxonomy level of the proficiency level 3.0 learning target. However, the concept that was included in the proficiency level 3.0 target remains the same. The team considers what this simpler target might look like and discusses what might happen for students as they begin to learn the target.

In our example, the team considers its proficiency level 3.0 learning target, "Recognize volume as an attribute of solid figures," and the taxonomy category below Level One: Retrieval in the category *recalling*. This means that the proficiency level 2.0 learning target should be written at least one category lower—at Level One: Retrieval in the category *recognizing*. The team members consider how a student might see that volume is an attribute of a solid figure without actually being able to come up with that explanation on their own. Could they ask students from a list of options, which attribute was true about solid figures? If they included *volume* on the list, and students chose that option correctly, the teachers believe it is a step toward the students being able to name the attribute on their own. Assessed this way, the target does not require in-depth knowledge, only the ability to recognize the definition from a list. The team agrees that this places the expected rigor in Level One: Retrieval in the category *recognizing*. The team enters the learning target into the scaling template, completing the scale for this learning target (see table 5.7). The teachers include a note of how they will assess this learning target when they write their actual assessment.

Table 5.7: Scaling a Learning Target—Step Four

Level of the Scale	Powered Learning Target	Marzano and Kendall's New Taxonomy	Assessment Strategies and Items
Level 4.0	Describe the relationship between volume and capacity.	**Level Two: Comprehension** Integrating	**Short Constructed Response** Describe how capacity and volume are related terms. Give an example.
Level 3.0	Recognize volume as an attribute of solid figures.	**Level One: Retrieval** Recalling	**Short Constructed Response** Describe why and how volume is an attribute of solid figures.
Level 2.0	Identify the definition of volume.	**Level One: Retrieval** Recognizing	**Multiple Choice** Identify the definition of volume from a list.
Level 1.0	With help, partial success at score 2.0 content and 3.0 content		
Level 0.0	Even with help, no success		

Are there always four levels prepared for scaling a learning target? Ideally, a proficiency level 3.0 learning target would also have clear proficiency levels 4.0 and 2.0 learning targets, but as teams work through the four-step scale development process, they often find that some proficiency level 3.0 learning targets do not fit this pattern. For example, developing a proficiency level 4.0 target for a procedural skill is sometimes difficult for teams. Typically, proficiency level 4.0 learning targets that include a procedural skill require a more complex demonstration of the skill (Marzano, 2010).

Consider the procedural skill in the Language strand for second grade.

> Capitalize holidays, product names, and geographic names. (L.2.2a) (NGA & CCSSO, 2010a, p. 26)

In this case, as the team works through the scale development process, the members quickly discover that a more complex demonstration of the standard could include asking students to capitalize more difficult or obscure holidays, product names, or geographic names, but this would not require higher-level or more complex thinking. The task of writing the proficiency level 4.0 learning target would be completed, but the purpose of writing a learning target that requires more complex thinking and knowledge would not be. Thus, the team decides not to include a proficiency level 4.0 learning target for this standard.

The development of a proficiency level 2.0 learning target is usually a simpler process, and it is less likely that teams will struggle to write a clear 2.0 learning target. Using the second-grade Language standard (L.2.2a), the proficiency level 2.0 learning target should be a simpler or less complex demonstration of a student's ability to capitalize proper nouns. The team determines that a simpler demonstration might include a student's ability to explain or define a proper noun, or demonstrate the ability to capitalize his or her own name, before moving on to holidays, product names, or geographic names. The guiding questions teams reference during the development of 2.0 levels are: If a student can demonstrate mastery on the proficiency level 2.0 learning target, does it help the teacher and the student determine what to do next? What will it take to move to the 3.0 or 4.0 levels? If the answer to the first question is no, defining the proficiency level 2.0 learning target might not be necessary, with the focus on moving toward mastery of the proficiency level 3.0 expectation. In this example, the team decides to include the proficiency level 2.0 learning target because the teachers want to be sure that students who struggle with the proficiency level 3.0 learning target have a basic understanding of capitalization concepts and could demonstrate proficiency with simple capitalization, as would be required to capitalize their own name.

We have also found that teams struggle to write proficiency levels 4.0 and 2.0 learning targets for some process skills, like many of the standards in the Writing strand. In our experience, the Common Core standards for writing do not require the development of specific levels 4.0 or 2.0 learning targets, but instead can be explained with clearly defined rubric levels. We discuss rubrics in detail in chapter 8.

We encourage teams to take the time to go through the steps of developing proficiency levels 4.0 and 2.0 learning targets by spending time with the taxonomy, thinking through and discussing the possibilities, and then determining the feasibility of proficiency levels 4.0 or 2.0 learning targets.

Applying the Scales in Practice

When teams work with scales, they are able to apply the learning progressions they've laid out in a number of ways. For example, as teams plan their instruction, the scales help them see what the simpler content for the unit includes as well as the more complex content. They can then decide the kinds of scaffolding that might help their students, instructional strategies that might make the progressions clearer for their students, and how they might challenge their most capable learners. Teachers can decide when to include more direct instruction as well as when to provide opportunities for exploration and extension.

The same is true for the students themselves. When learning is clearly laid out as a series of progressive targets, and when students know where they are on that sequence, they are much more likely to feel empowered in their own learning. Many teachers have students keep track of their own learning progression. By allowing some pacing flexibility, students can make progress within their own timeline. When the targets are scaled in this way, peer tutoring can be much more effective than just asking the "smarter" students to help the "struggling" students. For example, students who have reached proficiency level 4.0 could effectively help students who are still at proficiency levels 1.0 or 2.0. Scales will also help teachers write assessments that lead to better diagnoses of student needs. In chapter 7, we'll discuss how teams can include assessment items for proficiency level 2.0 and level 4.0 targets to gather more specific data about next steps after the assessment.

Without question, grading in a scaled system of targets is much more precise and accurate. Teachers can identify which targets have been mastered and where students have learned some of the simpler content but haven't yet reached proficiency. Many of the teachers we've worked with who were reluctant to move to a standards-based (or target-based) reporting system are excited to have the ability to communicate at this precise level. Once you have scaled learning targets with your team, you will have much greater clarity about what they mean and how they set the stage for intentional planning related to assessment and instruction, both of which will be discussed in chapters 7 and 9 of this book. Finally, how teams can use these scales to respond when students need more time or when they are already secure in the mastery of learning targets will be addressed in chapters 10 and 11.

Tips for Teams New to the PLC Process

If your team is new to the PLC process, and this is the first time you are working with essential or power standards, you will likely be focused on designing and implementing instruction, assessment, and intervention aligned to the CCSS. As stated in this chapter, proficiency scales may be something you will want to add later, after your team is more comfortable with one level of proficiency. To get a feel for how the process works, you can scale one standard or unit and develop a related scaled assessment, and using the assessment results, determine the best ways to meet the needs of students who demonstrate varying levels of proficiency.

Other ways your team can begin thinking about levels of proficiency without actually scaling is to engage in planned casual discussions regarding the level of proficiency that is expected for each standard and what it would look like if students could demonstrate proficiency at higher and lower cognitive levels. You may also want to examine student work, looking for examples of students who may already be demonstrating higher levels of proficiency and those who are demonstrating some knowledge of the learning target but are not quite there yet. These discussions will help you begin thinking about how you might use levels of proficiency in the future and will make the process easier once you do engage in the scaling process.

Sometimes, waiting until the team is comfortable is not an option, and new teams will engage in the development of proficiency scales right away as part of a school or districtwide initiative. While this might seem overwhelming at first, the good news is your team will have the opportunity to dig deeper into each power standard as you develop each level of the scale, thus providing even greater clarity regarding what students should know and be able to do. Don't try to accomplish everything at once! Take an upcoming unit, and work with the essential standards in that unit. Get good at the process one step at a time. Feel confident that getting one unit done well will be better than getting multiple units done poorly.

If your team is new to the PLC process but has been working with a clear set of power standards for some time, you may consider beginning the scaling process right away. Not only will your team gain greater clarity regarding what students should know and be able to do but also regarding the power of the collaborative process. When new teams engage in a process like scaling the power standards, they often begin to see that collaboration makes the task more manageable, stimulates new ideas, and promotes coherence in curriculum and instruction. As the team works together, members begin to see that they have the skills and resources to attempt new practices that would exhaust the energy, skills, or resources of an individual teacher (Richardson-Koehler, 1987).

Tips for Principals and Leaders

There are three questions we recommend you tackle as you begin the work of scaling learning targets in your school: (1) How and when will teams complete the work? (2) How will I communicate and monitor team expectations? and (3) How can I support teams in using scales?

How and When Will Teams Complete the Work?

Finding time is often the most challenging part of doing this type of work. It is essential that teams are given ample time to complete the process. Providing released time for the teams is the most efficient way to ensure that time is available for them to complete the work. We have found that most teams can complete the process in one released day as long as the day is focused and expectations are clear. We realize that released time is not always available, and it might require some creativity to find the time. Teams we have worked with have completed the process making use of whatever time they could find within the workday, including scaling a standard or unit at a time during scheduled team meetings or asking certified assistants to supervise students during assemblies so they could work together. If the work of developing proficiency scales is a systemwide expectation, it is likely that a representative team of teachers for each grade level or content area work together to develop the scales for each team. If this is the case, it will be important to give teams time to review the scales and become familiar with them. You may have noticed that the team of teachers is the constant regarding who is doing the work of developing the scales. It is important that as many teachers as possible engage in the process, as discussions during the development work lead to a deeper understanding of the team expectations for student proficiency.

How Will I Communicate and Monitor Team Expectations?

Once teams have created scales, they will then begin considering how to incorporate scales into instruction and assessment. Clear communication regarding implementation expectations is vital, as teams are busy and often have many things they are trying to manage at once. They need to know what your expectations are and then how and when you will be checking in with them regarding their progress. One leader we worked with outlined her initial expectations this way: "I will be checking in with each team every week. Each time I check in, I will want to see how you have incorporated scales into formal and informal assessments and how you have used the data from these assessments to make instructional decisions for students or groups of students. Through this process we will determine next steps. We may find that the scales need to be adjusted or that the assessment questions are not quite showing us what we want to know. Either way, we are in this together, and I am here to support you through it."

This leader set up her expectations and, most importantly, followed through on them. She also supported each team based on where it was. She offered the right amount of pressure and support to help teams see the benefits of a scaled system for meeting the needs of all students.

How Can I Support Teams in Using Scales?

Teams will need a lot of support as they work to implement scaled power standards. Keep the focus on continuous learning and job-embedded professional development. Help them understand that your role will be to support them and challenge them at the same time. Inspirational reminders can help teams understand why you are doing this work. For example, consider the following quote from *Learning by Doing* (DuFour et al., 2010).

Educators work collaboratively in recurring cycles of collective inquiry and action research to achieve better results for the students they serve. Professional learning communities operate under the assumption that the key to improved learning for students is continuous job-embedded learning for educators. (p. 11)

The following list of questions will help you determine where teams are in relation to implementation of scaled power standards and what support they will need. This list of questions is brief—there are certainly several others you can ask. You will want to be strategic regarding the questions you pick based on the team's readiness. One question at a time followed up with opportunities for team learning has worked well in our experiences.

- How are you using the data from formal or informal scaled assessments?

- How does the data help you and students know where they are and where they need to go?

- Have you used a scaled preassessment? If not, how do you know where students are before you begin instruction? If so, how has the preassessment helped you meet the needs of individual students or groups of students?

- How are you currently extending and enriching instruction for students who demonstrate proficiency early or on a preassessment?

- How are you grouping students for corrective teaching or extension and enrichment? Are the groups flexible?

- Are students tracking their own progress using the scales? Do they know where they are and where they need to go?

Part Three

Planning for Learning

6

Determining Pacing and Unit Design

Collaborative Connections

- Pacing guides lead to greater team clarity regarding the skills and concepts students should know and be able to do.

- Collaborative teams benefit from the powerful conversations about student learning that occur during the pacing process.

- The process of developing pacing calendars gives teams the opportunity to think carefully about how assessment, intervention, and extension fit into their daily planning.

The standards are powered, unwrapped, and scaled. How does all of this come together into one cohesive instructional plan? The development of pacing guides and cohesive units of instruction brings the learning targets to life. It is a crucial part of the process that requires your team to think deeply about the most effective and logical progressions of teaching and learning. Instructional time is precious: we need to make the most of the limited instructional minutes we have with students. The ideas, examples, and methods in this chapter will guide your team as you work to develop highly effective cycles of instruction that maximize student learning.

What a Pacing Guide Is

Pacing guides have various meanings in U.S. schools and school systems. Some are very detailed, prescribing exactly what teachers must teach—sometimes down to each lesson. Others loosely define the learning expectations for an entire school year by grade level, subject, or course.

A pacing guide is a thoughtfully planned and designed sequence of teaching and learning that outlines specific learning targets to be addressed within a grading period or unit of instruction.

What a Pacing Guide Is Not

While we believe that pacing guides should provide teachers with guidance regarding when learning targets are to be taught, it is important that they are not so rigid that they diminish the art of teaching. We strongly encourage teachers to place the needs of students above any pacing guide's expectations. In other words, when assessment data indicate that some students need more time to demonstrate proficiency, we feel it's important for your team members to have a system in place to meet their needs, even if the planned amount of time allocated for the grading period or unit has passed. A few ways that teams can ensure that all students have ample opportunities to learn is by intentionally embedding time to differentiate instruction into the pacing guide, allowing for corrective instruction for students who haven't yet met the targets, and implementing extension activities for those who need to go beyond. Alternatively, some schools and school systems have developed a daily intervention period that occurs during the regular school day to meet student needs identified from formative assessment. This ensures that students who need support or extension do not miss regular instruction.

Why Pacing Is Important

Imagine that your team has just finished powering, unwrapping, and scaling the CCSS for English language arts. You now have a clear understanding of what it is students should know and be able to do in English language arts for the entire school year. Ideally, by the end of the year, every student would know the concepts and be able to demonstrate the skills you have carefully identified as the power learning targets. The next step would be to determine a logical progression for the teaching and learning of the targets. It wouldn't make sense for each teacher to simply pick a learning target and begin teaching or start with chapter 1 of the textbook. Remember, the purpose for identifying power standards is to prioritize time to teach essential concepts and skills in depth.

Teachers we work with often feel caught between a rock and a hard place, wondering if they should slow down and risk lack of coverage or speed up and sacrifice depth of learning (David, 2008). So how do pacing guides help solve this problem? A carefully planned pacing guide will provide a common focus for learning within a grading period or unit of instruction that allows time for in-depth instruction and intervention. The skills and concepts teams identify in the pacing guide the instructional focus, as opposed to teachers relying on textbook chapters or other instructional materials. Teams align assessments to these skills and concepts and develop student interventions based on the results from these assessments. In order for meaningful team conversations to occur around assessment data, common team pacing is essential.

Pacing guides provide many other benefits as well. When teams align teaching and learning into clear, logical progressions by grading period or unit, all students in the grade level or course are guaranteed to learn the same material at approximately the same time. What students are learning is not determined by the teacher's favorite units but rather by the learning targets the team designates to be taught within the grading period or unit. When school systems develop common pacing guides by grade level, subject, or course, gaps in learning are less likely to happen when students transfer schools. It is important to note that this does not mean teachers must teach exactly the same way, using the same instructional strategies. They have the flexibility to determine the instructional strategies they will use based on the unique needs of the students in their classroom and also consider their own instructional expertise. However, one of the major values in working together as a collaborative team is the discussions surrounding teaching and learning that happen at the team table. Team members should share successful instructional strategies, learning from each other the best ways to approach instruction related to each learning target.

Pacing guides also provide a unique benefit to special education teachers, English learner (EL) teachers, speech and language pathologists, and other student services staff. A pacing guide's clarity helps such educators know the instructional focus for the grading period, so they can support their students in a more meaningful way. One middle school special education teacher describes it this way, "Before we had pacing guides, I had to find out what each subject-area teacher was focusing on, so I could support the students in each teacher's classroom. It was frustrating because teachers were all in different places. Now, I know that teachers are aligned to the pacing guide and working on the same concepts within a grading period. I know what each of my students needs to be learning, ideally by the end of the trimester. I might approach instruction differently than the regular education teachers do, but I do everything I can to make sure that they meet the expectations outlined in the learning targets."

Novice teachers—or teachers new to a school, grade level, subject, or course—also value the clarity that pacing guides provide. We often hear stories from novice teachers who say that they were given a set of keys, a few teacher editions, and a schedule of their teaching assignments with limited or no information related to what students should know and be able to do. Some have described receiving a three-hundred-page binder of state standards as their focus for instruction. You might have experienced a similar scenario when you first started teaching. The same is true for teachers who transfer to a different grade, subject area, or course. While we do not suggest a highly prescribed plan for teaching each learning target, we do believe that a focused pacing guide of learning targets per grading period or unit with some direction regarding instruction and resources is beneficial to all teachers.

Collaborative Teams Developing Pacing Guides

We believe that teachers should work together to develop pacing guides for the subjects or courses they teach. Teachers will be responsible for teaching the progressions outlined in the pacing guides, so they should be the ones who determine the most logical, coherent pacing of the learning targets. We have witnessed some of the most powerful student learning–centered discussions among teachers during the pacing process. These conversations foster a deeper understanding of the learning targets, including the expected rigor of the targets and the instructional time necessary for in-depth teaching and learning to occur.

If the powering and unwrapping process is done districtwide, meaning teachers from each building in the system collaborate to develop common learning targets by subject or course, it makes sense for full district grade-level teams or representatives from district grade-level teams to work together to develop districtwide pacing guides for each subject or course. We realize that while this might be feasible for a small system to accomplish, it is not likely that a large system could approach the work this way. If a building's grade-level, subject-area, or course teams are responsible for the powering and unwrapping process, the same teams should develop the pacing guides. Additionally, each team should begin the work as soon as that team is ready. Individual teams might accomplish the steps at different times than other teams in the school.

While it might be tempting for district leaders to develop the pacing guides for teachers with the thought that they could finish the process more quickly and efficiently, we don't recommend this approach. Having teachers work collaboratively, using their knowledge and experience, will likely result in a much better product albeit one that takes longer to produce.

Pacing Guide Development

The work of developing pacing guides can be accomplished in a variety of ways. The five-step process outlined below will assist teams and leaders in designing a meaningful approach to this work. The first two steps address who will be participating in the pacing work, when the work will take place, and the pacing process and template that will be used. Steps three and four attend to more specific considerations including gathering the resources necessary to make good pacing decisions and examination of logical, cohesive learning progressions. Step five reminds teams and leaders to reflect on the pacing and refine as necessary which is an often overlooked, but important part of the process.

Step One: Identify Task Participants

The district curriculum staff, building principal, or leadership team should determine who will participate in the development of the pacing guides. This determination, of course, depends on the organizational structures within your system or the origin of the initiative. If this is a district initiative, it is likely that the district curriculum staff will coordinate the team. If this is a building or team initiative, the building principal or collaborative teams will most likely determine the participants. Possible team configurations include grade-level or subject-area teams across the district or within a school.

Step Two: Determine Timeline and Template

The second step of the process is to determine the pacing guide timeline and template. This decision includes whether the team will develop the pacing guide by grading period, unit of instruction, or some other timeline configuration. We recommend that teams develop pacing guides by grading period or unit of instruction. If teams develop a narrower guide, for example, by week or month, teachers are more limited in their ability to adjust instruction to meet the needs of the students in their classrooms. Table 6.1 and table 6.2 (page 98) offer examples of pacing templates that could be used for this process. Table 6.1 is an example of a trimester grading period pacing guide that includes scales.

Table 6.1: Third-Grade English Language Arts Pacing Guide With Scales—Trimester 1

Reading			
Common Core Coding (Adapted for Learning Target Distinction)	Proficiency Level 4.0	Proficiency Level 3.0	Proficiency Level 2.0
RL.3.1a	Ask inferentially based questions to demonstrate understanding of a text referring explicitly to the text as the basis for the answers.	Ask questions to demonstrate understanding of a text referring explicitly to the text as the basis for the answers.	Identify appropriate questions to ask with explicit text references from a list to demonstrate understanding of a text.
RL.3.1b	Answer inferentially based questions to demonstrate understanding of a text referring explicitly to the text as the basis for the answers.	Answer questions to demonstrate understanding of a text referring explicitly to the text as the basis for the answers.	Identify answers from a list of explicit text to demonstrate understanding of a text.

RL.3.3a	Analyze a character's actions in a story, inferring reasons and explanations for their actions.	Describe characters in a story (traits, motivation, or feelings).	Identify character traits, motivations, and feelings from a list.
RL.3.3b	Analyze how a character's actions contribute to events, including how the story would be different if actions were different.	Explain how characters' actions contribute to the sequence of events.	Identify actions, matching them to events in the story.

Instructional strategies and resources: Direct instruction (mini-unit) followed by scaffolded instruction in guided reading groups. Resources include leveled text from the basal textbook and other leveled titles.

Language			
L.3.1.ia	See writing rubric.	Produce simple sentences.	See writing rubric.
L.3.1.ib	See writing rubric.	Produce compound sentences.	See writing rubric.
L.3.1.ic	See writing rubric.	Produce complex sentences.	See writing rubric.

Instructional strategies and resources: Guided practice—teach skills through writing instruction, not in isolation.

Writing: Narrative			
W.3.3aa	See writing rubric.	Establish a situation and introduce a narrator and/or characters.	See writing rubric.
W.3.3ab	See writing rubric.	Organize an event sequence that unfolds naturally.	See writing rubric.
W.3.3ba	See writing rubric.	Use dialogue and descriptions of actions, thoughts, and feelings to develop experiences and events.	See writing rubric.
W.3.3bb	See writing rubric.	Use dialogue and descriptions of actions, thoughts, and feelings to show the response of characters to situations.	See writing rubric.

Instructional strategies and resources: Direct instruction followed by guided writing practice. Resources include *The Write Tools for Common Core State Standards: Narrative—Real or Imagined* (Greiner & Simmons, 2012) and *Units of Study in Opinion, Information, and Narrative Writing* (Calkins, 2013).

The coding used in the pacing template signifies the CCSS original coding to indicate the origin of the learning target. The original coding may be followed by an additional letter or number to distinguish learning targets derived from the original standard. For example, in table 6.1 (page 98) the CCSS Reading standard for grade 3 "Ask and answer questions to demonstrate understanding of a text referring explicitly to the text as the basis for the answers" is coded using the CCSS coding RL.3.1. The CCSS standard was unwrapped into two learning targets and coded with the letter "a" for the first target and the letter "b" for the second target. "Ask questions to demonstrate understanding of a text referring explicitly to the text as the basis for the answers" is coded as RL.3.1a. "Answer questions to demonstrate understanding of a text referring explicitly to the text as the basis for the answers" is coded as RL.3.1b.

Table 6.2 is an example of a trimester grading period pacing guide that does not include scales. Notice that these guides include all of the learning targets to be taught during the trimester but do not prescribe the specific number of days each will be taught.

Table 6.2: Third-Grade English Language Arts Pacing Guide Without Scales—Trimester 1

Common Core Coding	Learning Target
RL.3.1a	Ask questions to demonstrate understanding of a text referring explicitly to the text as the basis for the answers.
RL.3.1b	Answer questions to demonstrate understanding of a text referring explicitly to the text as the basis for the answers.
RL.3.3a	Describe characters in a story (traits, motivation, or feelings).
RL.3.3b	Explain how characters' actions contribute to the sequence of events.
Instructional strategies and resources: Direct instruction (mini-unit) followed by scaffolded instruction in guided reading groups. Resources include leveled text from the basal textbook and other leveled titles.	
Language	
L.3.1.ia	Produce simple sentences.
L.3.1.ib	Produce compound sentences.
L.3.1.ic	Produce complex sentences.
Instructional strategies and resources: Guided practice—teach skills through writing instruction, not in isolation.	
W.3.3aa	Establish a situation, and introduce a narrator or characters.
W.3.3ab	Organize an event sequence that unfolds naturally.
W.3.3ba	Use dialogue and descriptions of actions, thoughts, and feelings to develop experiences and events.
W.3.3bb	Use dialogue and descriptions of actions, thoughts, and feelings to show the response of characters to situations.
Direct instruction followed by guided writing practice. Resources include *The Write Tools for Common Core State Standards: Narrative—Real or Imagined* (Greiner & Simmons, 2012) and *Units of Study in Opinion, Information, and Narrative Writing* (Calkins, 2013).	

Step Three: Collect Resources

During step three, teams gather and prepare the materials they will need to complete the pacing process. The following items should be available as the team begins to develop the guide.

- The standards or learning targets to pace, including the unwrapping templates and scaling templates

- Appropriate curriculum materials, including curriculum guides or maps

- Calendar of grading periods, assessment dates, and days off

- Pacing planning template (see step four)

- Paper or electronic blank pacing guide
- Copy of learning taxonomy, such as Bloom's Revised Taxonomy (Anderson & Krathwohl, 2001), Marzano and Kendall's New Taxonomy (Marzano & Kendall, 2007), or Webb's Depth of Knowledge (Webb, 2005)

Step Four: Examine Learning Progressions

The process of examining targets for viable, logical learning progressions begins in step four. Teams should consider four elements when developing a pacing planning template (see figure 6.1, page 100).

1. **Rigor and time:** Time necessary for in-depth instruction and intervention; time of year issues

2. **Connections to other targets:** Are there targets that should be taught together? If so, why? What is the purpose?

3. **Instructional implications and resources:** Record all conversations related to instruction and resources.

4. **Grading period or unit of instruction:** Is this target a focus for the grading period or a unit of instruction? Should it be taught in more than one grading period or unit? If so, why?

The template (figure 6.1, page 100) provides a manageable tool for teams to use as they develop the pacing guide. The procedure for developing the guide includes these steps.

- The team enters each learning target before the pacing session begins, or as it proceeds through the process. Using electronic programs such as Google Docs (http://docs.google.com) simplifies the task and allows all participants to view and work in one document at the same time.

- The team considers the level of difficulty of each learning target, taking into account the amount of time necessary for in-depth instruction and intervention as well as the time of year to address the target. The beginning of the school year includes many activities that infringe on classroom instructional time. Many teachers spend time clarifying classroom processes and procedures at this time, and often, there are school assemblies and welcome back activities that interfere with instruction. This might not be the best time to schedule a learning target that requires intensive, consecutive, linked days of instruction. The same might be true for months that include many non-attendance days due to holidays, and so on.

- The team considers the learning target's connections to other targets to identify those that might be taught together. For example, targets for CCSS ELA Reading Standards for Informational Text could be taught along with targets for the Writing standards for informational and explanatory text.

- The team uses its pacing scaled targets to decide where it thinks the target or connected targets fit into the pacing guide. Accordingly, the members record the grading period or cycle of instruction for the target. They complete the task by entering the proficiency level 3.0 learning target, discussing the implications of the levels 4.0 and 2.0 targets, and entering those in the guide.

Learning Target or Standard	Rigor and Time	Connections to Other Targets	Instructional Implications and Resources	Grading Period or Unit of Instruction

Figure 6.1: Pacing guide template.

Visit **go.solution-tree.com/commoncore** *for a reproducible version of this figure.*

Step Five: Refine the Pacing Guide

Ideally, after instruction aligned to the pacing guide occurs, teams will refine and make revisions to the pacing guide based on teacher input regarding what worked and what parts of the pacing were challenging or difficult for students or the teacher. Specifically, teams examine the flow within grading periods or units and the flow between grading periods or units.

From Broad Grade-Level or Unit Pacing Guides to Detailed Units of Instruction

The creation of pacing guides is an important first step in the development of more specific, refined units of instruction the collaborative teams develop. In the book *Common Formative Assessment: A Toolkit for Professional Learning Communities at Work* (Bailey & Jakicic, 2012), the authors outline the process for backward planning of specific units of instruction, offering several templates and tools for teams to use in this process. In this chapter, we will emphasize another way teams can use the pacing guide as a starting point for more detailed units of instruction that, like the backward design model, include considerations of time for assessment, intervention, and focused, in-depth instruction.

Figure 6.2 lists the complete set of Common Core ELA learning targets from a third-grade team's pacing guide for the first trimester in a school year and the Common Core mathematics targets from one unit of instruction for that trimester.

A team can then translate a pacing guide into a pacing calendar, which includes the mapped plan for instruction as well as time needed for corrective instruction and enrichment. Figure 6.3 (page 102) shows a sample pacing calendar based on figure 6.2. This team was struggling with how to incorporate common formative assessments (CFA in the calendar), opportunities for reteaching and intervention, and extension into their unit instructional cycles.

Common formative assessments are team-designed, intentional measures used for the purpose of monitoring student attainment of essential learning targets throughout the instructional process. In addition to providing information about which students need additional support or extension, common formative assessments allow teams to examine the effects of their practice, and gain insight as to which instructional strategies yield high levels of learning. Furthermore, the data can be used to provide frequent feedback to students that they can use to adjust their own learning strategies.

Third-Grade English Language Arts Learning Targets for First Trimester

Reading: Literature

RL.3.1a: Ask questions to demonstrate understanding of a text referring explicitly to the text as the basis for the answers.

RL.3.1b: Answer questions to demonstrate understanding of a text referring explicitly to the text as the basis for the answers.

RL.3.3a: Describe characters in a story (traits, motivation, or feelings).

RL.3.3b: Explain how characters' actions contribute to the sequence of events.

Language

L.3.1.ia: Produce simple sentences.

L.3.1.ib: Produce compound sentences.

L.3.1.ic: Produce complex sentences.

Writing: Narrative

W.3.3aa: Establish a situation and introduce a narrator and/or characters.

W.3.3ab: Organize an event sequence that unfolds naturally.

W.3.3ba: Use dialogue and descriptions of actions, thoughts, and feelings to develop experiences and events.

W.3.3bb: Use dialogue and descriptions of actions, thoughts, and feelings to show the response of characters to situations.

Third-Grade Mathematics Learning Targets for Unit Four

3.OA.A.1: Interpret products of whole numbers.

3.OA.A.2: Interpret whole-number quotients of whole numbers.

3.OA.A.3: Use multiplication and division within 100 to solve word problems in situations involving equal groups, arrays, and measurement quantities.

3.OA.C.7: Fluently multiply and divide within 100, using strategies such as the relationship between multiplication and division.

Figure 6.2: Sample third-grade pacing guide.

To prepare for this work, the team gathers instructional materials for English language arts and mathematics and identifies student attendance days and days off. While the plan appears to be tightly prescribed, the team builds in several days for extension, intervention, and reteaching. This allows the team flexibility within the plan to adjust instruction based on the evidence of student learning gathered from the CFAs and informal checks for understanding that take place throughout the unit. The calendar in figure 6.3 (page 102) represents the month of December only and does not show the full instructional cycle for each learning target. For example, students will likely have the benefit of more than two days of instruction on the math and English language arts learning targets prior to administration of the CFA.

The team agrees to check in with each team member after a few weeks to see if the detailed planning is working. At their first check-in, the team members all feel good about the process, feel like the plan is working, and feel students are benefitting. What they really want is evidence that the planning is working. They decide to continue the process throughout the rest of the year, so they can gather evidence and determine how to refine the process based on that data.

December				
Monday	**Tuesday**	**Wednesday**	**Thursday**	**Friday**
			1 **Literacy:** Teach RL.3.1a RL.3.1b W.3.3aa L.3.1.ia **Math:** Teach OA.A.3	2 **Literacy:** Teach RL.3.1a RL.3.1b W.3.3aa L.3.1.ia **Math:** Teach 3.OA.A.1 3.OA.A.2
5 **Literacy:** CFA RL.3.1a RL.3.1b W.3.3aa L.3.1.ia **Math:** Teach 3.OA.A.1 3.OA.A.2	6 **Literacy:** Intervention and Extension RL.3.1a RL.3.1b W.3.3aa L.3.1.ia **Math:** CFA 3.OA.A.1 3.OA.A.2	7 **Literacy:** Teach RL.3.3a W.3.3ab L.3.1.ib **Math:** Intervention and Extension 3.OA.A.1 3.OA.A.2	8 **Reading:** Teach RL.3.3a W.3.3ab L.3.1.ib **Math:** Teach 3.OA.A.3	9 **Reading:** Teach RL.3.3a W.3.3ab L.3.1.ib **Math:** Teach 3.OA.A.3
Notes Instructional focus for all lessons through the month: Miniunits and guided groups for reading, writing, and mathematics				

Figure 6.3: Sample pacing calendar for third-grade team.

Incorporating the Expectations From State Assessment Systems Into Pacing

As noted previously, if your state has adopted the Common Core State Standards, it has also become part of one of two consortia (PARCC and SBAC) that are responsible for the development of Common Core–aligned assessments.

Figure 6.4 displays the PARCC Model Content Framework for eighth-grade English language arts. The framework divides the school year into four quarter-length modules of instruction identifying the broad categories of knowledge and skills students will need to know in order to be prepared for the PARCC assessments. The components of English language arts/literacy are interconnected, and each large box details the amount and type of either writing or reading students should be exposed to throughout the school year.

Table 6.3 (page 104) is one school district's interpretation of the PARCC Model Content Framework. In this version, more information from the text of the framework is included under each topic title. For instance, under "Reading Complex Texts," the team listed literature and informational texts as well as extended texts and short texts that students should read during the course of the grading period. After unwrapping and powering the CCSS English language arts, the team used the pacing guide template in figure 6.1 (page 100) to begin the pacing process, eventually working with the PARCC-aligned pacing guide in figure 6.4 as the final pacing guide. The use of the PARCC-aligned pacing guide helps teams keep the PARCC expectations in mind throughout the pacing process as well as throughout the school year.

	Reading Complex Texts RL/RI.8.10		Writing to Texts W.8.1–6, 9–10, RL/RI.8.1–10			Research Project W.8.1, 2, 4–9, RL/RI.8.1–10
	1 Extended Text	**3–5 Short Texts**	**Routine Writing**	**4–6 Analyses**	**1–2 Narratives**	**1 Research Project**
A	Literature	Literature: 2–3 Informational texts: 1–2	Develop and convey understanding.	Focus on arguments.	Convey experiences, events, or procedures.	Integrate knowledge from sources when composing.
B	Informational	Literature: 2–3 Informational texts: 1–2	Develop and convey understanding.	Focus on informing and explaining.	Convey experiences, events, or procedures.	Integrate knowledge from sources when composing.
C	Literature	Literature: 2–3 Informational texts: 1–2	Develop and convey understanding.	Focus on informing and explaining.	Convey experiences, events, or procedures.	Integrate knowledge from sources when composing.
D	Informational	Literature: 2–3 Informational texts: 1–2	Develop and convey understanding.	Focus on arguments.	Convey experiences, events, or procedures.	Integrate knowledge from sources when composing.
For Reading and Writing in Each Module*						
	Cite evidence RL/RI.8.1	**Analyze content** RL/RI.8.2–9, SL.8.2–3	**Study and apply grammar** L.8.1–3, SL.8.6	**Study and apply vocabulary** L.8.4–6	**Conduct discussions** SL.8.1	**Report findings** SL.8.4–6

*After selecting the standards for instruction, teachers should select texts and writing tasks with clear opportunities for teaching these standards.

Figure 6.4: ELA PARCC Model Content Framework for reading complex texts for grade 8.

Source: Adapted from PARCC, 2012d, p. 6 (see http://parcconline.org/sites/parcc/files/PARCCMCFELALiteracyAugust2012_FINAL.pdf).

Once teams finish the process of developing pacing guides, it is time to celebrate! The work is not over yet; in fact, we are not sure it is ever really over, but the team now has a very clear answer to the first PLC question, What do we want our students to learn? This clarity will be essential when teams begin designing high-quality, target-aligned assessments, interventions, and extensions for students.

Tips for Teams New to the PLC Process

Whether your team is experienced or new to the PLC process, you likely face the same challenge related to pacing and planning with the CCSS—the challenge of how to build time within the school day for teachers to meet students where they are in the learning process for standards that are perhaps more rigorous than ever before. As you begin, remember that identifying power standards allows teams to determine which standards will take up the majority of instructional time, assessment, and intervention. If time is not allocated to address the varying levels of student proficiency related to these standards through the planning and pacing process, it is difficult to guarantee that all students are mastering the power standards or getting what they need for proficiency and beyond.

Table 6.3: Eighth-Grade Instructional Cycle Three in Trimester Two

	Reading Complex Texts	Writing to Texts	Research Project
Instructional Materials	• Four to six short texts per trimester • Three to four literature pieces • One to two informational texts • One to two extended texts (literature or informational text) with two to three weeks of instruction	**70 percent** • Short constructed responses to text-dependent questions • Analytic writing (argumentative, informative, or explanatory) **30 percent** • Narrative writing (real or fictional experiences or events)	• One to two research projects per semester that integrate knowledge from several additional literary or informational texts in various media or formats on a particular topic or question drawn from one or more texts from the module (one to two weeks of instruction per project)
Common Core State Standards	RL.8.2 RL.8.4 RI.8.2 RI.8.4	W.8.2a–c W.8.3a–e	W.8.8 W.8.9a
Language and Vocabulary Targets Embedded Into Routine Reading and Writing Instruction	**Language** L.3.1.ia L.3.1.ib L.3.1.ic L.8.4a L.8.4b L.8.4c		
Instructional Resources	• At-level students: Basal text selections, novels, passages, articles, websites, instructional tools and structures for learning, and so on • Honors students: Basal text selections, novels, passages, articles, websites, instructional tools and structures for learning, and so on		

You will also want to think about how you will record suggested adjustments to the pacing and planning process as teams implement the standards. Who will be responsible for keeping track of needed changes, and where will you document this? For example, you may find that instructing certain targets together did not work as well as you had hoped, or a particular standard took longer to teach and for students to master than you had originally thought. Recording what you find throughout the year will make it easier to refine the pacing and planning later.

Tips for Principals and Leaders

Leading teams through the planning and pacing process centers around two major areas: (1) ensuring that teams approach the planning and pacing process thoughtfully and (2) assisting teams in building in time for corrective teaching and extension. In order to be sure that teams think through pacing carefully, allocate time for teams to consider all factors that can potentially affect pacing. We have found that teams sometimes rush through the pacing and planning, especially as they are getting close to completing the process and are eager to finish.

Leaders will also want to work with teams as they plan more detailed units of instruction and monthly planning calendars, keeping the focus on building in time for intervention and extension. Meet with teams often as they plan out their instructional cycles, asking questions such as:

- What are you currently doing that you can stop doing in order to find more time for intervention and extension?

- How you will address the varying levels of proficiency of your students?

- When will you discuss instructional strategies that you want to try for students at different levels?

- How will you know that the instructional strategies you are trying are working?

- How will you keep track of what has worked so you can replicate it in the future?

7

Defining Rigor and Assessment Practices

Collaborative Connections

- Collaborative teams learn about varied assessment practices when they write assessment items for the Common Core State Standards.
- Writing assessment items at higher levels of rigor supports the work of teaching those students to perform at higher levels of proficiency.
- Writing assessments collaboratively gives ownership of learning for all to the entire team.

Likely, you can recall times where politicians, newspaper editors, or even school leaders used results of your state tests for purposes for which they weren't intended. It's easy to get caught up in the idea that assessment is harmful or that it doesn't really help teachers improve learning. The reality is that when used appropriately assessment can be one of the most powerful tools available to teachers and their students (Black & Wiliam, 1998; Hattie, 2009). Using assessment appropriately means first knowing the purpose of the assessment and then using it and the data it provides for that purpose.

Purpose of Summative Assessment

If we think of summative assessments as those that happen at the end of the learning cycle, these assessments have several important purposes: they tell us whether we are pacing our curriculum well, whether the instructional strategies we are using are working, and whether our curriculum is aligned to the standards we want to teach.

Summative assessment is an assessment that is intended to measure how well students have learned the concepts *after* the teacher has finished teaching.

If the assessments are well-designed, they also tell us whether our students have learned multiple learning targets, and if they can see the connections among those targets and use them in a meaningful way. For example, consider a seventh-grade teacher who has been teaching two Reading Standards for Informational Text concurrently: "Determine an author's point of view or purpose in a text and analyze how the author distinguishes his or her position from that of others" (RI.7.6) and "Determine the meaning of words or phrases as they are used in a text, including figurative, connotative, and technical meanings; analyze the impact of a specific word choice on the meaning and tone" (RI.7.4; NGA & CCSSO, 2010a, p. 39). At the end of the unit, the teacher may ask students to read a piece of informational text and explain what the author's purpose is in writing the piece and then to look at the words the author uses in the text to describe how those words impact the tone of the text.

The CCSS have at their heart a goal to make sure students are prepared for college and careers. Being able to understand not just the specific content being taught at a given time but also the connections to other content is part of this preparation. The standards have a higher level of rigor than many typical state standards, which is evident in an analysis of the verbs used for these standards. However, the CCSS also refer to the importance of relevance. In looking at the Rigor/Relevance Framework (Daggett, 2012), one sees that learning has more relevance when students can use new concepts and learning across many different disciplines. This framework suggests that there are two continua for teams to think about when considering how to develop more complex curriculum, instruction, and assessments. The first continuum is related to the idea of increasing demand on thinking and the second on increasing the demand for students to apply their thinking in various disciplines (see figure 7.1).

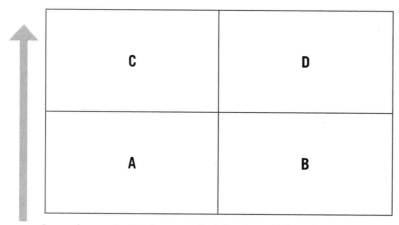

Increasing application from one discipline to multiple real-world situations

Figure 7.1: Rigor/Relevance Framework.
Source: Adapted from Rigor/Relevance Framework® © International Center for Leadership in Education, Daggett, 2012.

The developers of the CCSS had two goals: (1) to increase the cognitive demand for students, and (2) to simultaneously increase the application of standards into multiple disciplines connected to real-world situations. In the context of figure 7.1, the developers were asking for curriculum, instruction, and assessments opportunities that would fall into Quadrant D.

Purpose of Formative Assessment

Collaborative planning teams focus on making sure that all of the students have mastered the learning targets from the power standards they've identified as the guaranteed curriculum. They rely on team-developed common formative assessments to frequently check the learning of their students. Teams write these assessments around specific learning targets they've identified as those that are important for all students to master, those that could likely lead to misconceptions, and those that may be prerequisites to future learning or instruction.

Common formative assessments identify students who need more time and support as well as what kind of time and support will be beneficial. In addition, these formative assessments also allow teams to identify those students who can benefit from more challenging work because they have already demonstrated that they've learned the targets. Well-written formative assessments provide teams with data that are much easier to respond to than that from poorly written formative items.

The Rigor of the CCSS

One activity we often ask teams to do as they are transitioning to the Common Core is to circle every verb in each standard, such as those on the list of their grade-level Informational Text standards or one domain for their grade-level mathematics standards. The teachers will quickly see that the verb (or the thinking level of these standards) requires much more cognitive demand than the traditional state standards. Verbs like *analyze, trace, justify,* and *interpret* used in the CCSS may be different than verbs like *identify, compare, name,* and *describe* found in the state standards. This activity is an important first step as teachers begin to think about how their curriculum, pacing, and instructional strategies will change as they teach the CCSS. This level of rigor will also change the way they assess their students if they really want to know whether students are mastering these standards.

As teachers become more familiar with the CCSS, they will realize how important it is for students to show their reasoning skills on assessments. For example, the ELA standards expect students to cite textual evidence, and the mathematics standards expect them to justify their answers. Rather than solving problems provided in isolation, students will be asked to examine information from a number of sources and identify problems and potential solutions—tasks that require students to apply reasoning in a meaningful context.

The PARCC sample items demonstrate the importance of reasoning skills. For example, the items may include a multiple-choice question, which asks students to choose the sentence that states the theme of a story they've read. The follow-up multiple-choice question asks students to choose three pieces of evidence (quotes directly from the story) that support their choice in the first question (Advances in the PARCC [2012d] ELA/literacy assessment. See the PowerPoint presentation at www.parcconline.org/samples /item-task-prototypes).

Another example of the increased expectations for higher-level reasoning with the ELA standards concerns the expectations for using close reading. Instead of scaffolding complex text with lots of preteaching activities, teachers are using close reading strategies to support students in independent reading of more difficult text. Fisher and Frey (2012) explain how teachers allow students to discover information and make sense out of it in an inquiry-based lesson. They stress that, "Sometimes it's better to let students struggle a little" (p. 86). Close reading is a strategy that has students reading the same piece of complex text multiple times for multiple purposes. Students practice and become confident readers of appropriate texts without the significant scaffolding of prereading experiences teachers used in more traditional reading programs. This prepares students for the expectations of the Common Core State Standards.

In mathematics, students will be required to solve problems with real-world applications, some with multiple ways to get to the correct answer. They will be expected to show and justify their reasoning as they solve these problems.

Aligning Common Formative Assessments to Rigor

Common Formative Assessment: A Toolkit for Professional Learning Communities at Work (Bailey & Jakicic, 2012) walks through the big ideas and processes for designing and implementing team-developed shared formative assessments. Let's quickly review some of those concepts. The purpose of formative assessment is to gather information regarding student learning of targets that are currently being taught. By using formative assessment, and in our opinion assessments that are common across a team, teachers check student learning along the way so that those who haven't yet learned the concepts are provided additional time and support while instruction is ongoing. The notion that the targets must be clear to both the teachers and the students remains paramount. Just as crucial, however, is the importance of connecting the rigor of the learning target to the type of assessment. For example, when a teacher believes he or she has taught students to think analytically and then assesses only basic content knowledge, the mismatch means that the information from the assessment is not valid—it doesn't measure whether the student has actually learned the learning target.

Formative assessments should measure a small number of learning targets so teachers can respond quickly. With the CCSS, we recommend teams use only one or two learning targets for common formative assessments. This allows teachers to respond immediately after initial instruction when students are experiencing difficulty or showing proficiency beyond the expectation of the learning target.

Previewing the End in Mind

Figure 7.2 shows how integrating common formative assessments into instruction might look. This is an example of a sixth-grade ELA unit for reading informational text and writing arguments based on the following standards.

Standards for Reading Informational Text

Cite textual evidence to support analysis of what the text says explicitly as well as inferences drawn from the text. (RI.6.1)

Determine an author's point of view or purpose in a text and explain how it is conveyed in the text. (RI.6.2)

Trace and evaluate the argument and specific claims in a text, distinguishing claims that are supported by reasons and evidence from those that are not. (RI.6.8) (NGA & CCSSO, 2010a, p. 39)

Writing Standard

Write arguments to support claims with clear reasons and relevant evidence. (W.6.1) (NGA & CCSSO, 2010a, p. 42)

The instructional plan lists eleven learning targets the team unwrapped during its planning of this unit.

This team intentionally allocated time after each CFA to provide a differentiated response for their students ("Response day" in figure 7.2). However, it's important to note that not every CFA will require a full day to respond, and it's also possible that some will need more than one day. The key is that the team consider this response time as they are creating their pacing guides. We'll discuss further how the team responds during this time in chapters 10 and 11. Responding might mean that students are shared

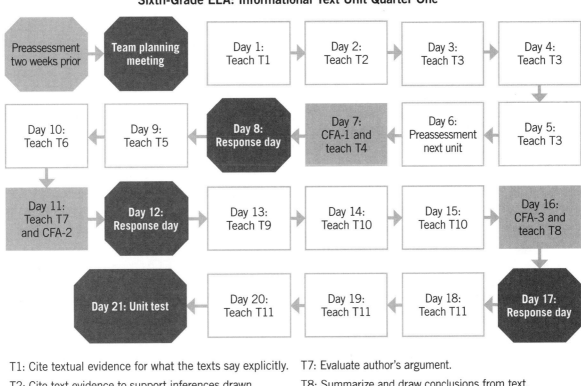

Sixth-Grade ELA: Informational Text Unit Quarter One

T1: Cite textual evidence for what the texts say explicitly.

T2: Cite text evidence to support inferences drawn.

T3: Determine author's point of view and purpose.

T4: Trace author's argument.

T5: Identify claims.

T6: Distinguish supported and not supported items.

T7: Evaluate author's argument.

T8: Summarize and draw conclusions from text.

T9: Writing—Introduce claims.

T10: Writing—Organize claims and evidence.

T11: Writing—Support claims and evidence from research.

Figure 7.2: Sample sixth-grade Informational Text unit.

among different teachers on the team, or it might mean that each teacher keeps his or her class of students but provides multiple activities to fit the various needs of the students.

Deciding on the Most Appropriate Type of Assessment

Deciding on the most appropriate type of assessment is a very important team decision. This will ensure the data results are truly reliable—that you can feel confident that you are identifying the right students for more time and support as well as those who can benefit from challenge. Let's consider the different types of assessments and how collaborative teams can make good decisions about which type will be best used in any given CFA. Selected-response items, constructed-response items, performance tasks, and technology-enhanced items may have a place in your assessment system; however, your team must consider the strengths and weaknesses of each when writing your own assessments.

Selected-Response Items

These items are those in which the answer to the question is on the page, and students must choose the correct answer. For example, forms of selected response are multiple-choice items, true or false items, and matching items.

Selected-response questions are quick for students to take and easy for teachers to grade. When your collaborative team wants to respond immediately to students who haven't learned a particular learning target, this is certainly one type of question you will want to consider. These questions have right or wrong answers that allow your team to know that no matter who grades the assessment the score will be the same. Because the tests only take a short amount of time for students to take, each assessment can have a sufficient number of items written for any one learning target to ensure that the students didn't guess the right answer. This will increase the reliability of your results. Knowing that high-stakes tests often rely heavily on multiple-choice questions, your team will want to make sure your students have experience with this type of item.

The most common selected-response question is multiple choice. Multiple-choice questions consist of an item stem (the statement or question that precedes the choices) and a varying number of answer choices that students select the correct answer from. It is important that there only be one correct answer choice and that all of the distractors—incorrect choices—be reasonable.

In writing and using multiple-choice questions, you'll need to consider two things to make your assessment reliable. The first is that you must have enough questions to make sure a student can't simply guess the correct answer and appear to have learned a target. For multiple-choice questions, we recommend at least four questions per learning target to ensure this reliability. We will now consider how to write items that enhance reliability by writing quality items that don't confuse students who *do* know the concepts.

The first thing teams can do to increase the reliability of their results with multiple-choice questions is to write the questions at the lowest possible reading level by avoiding difficult vocabulary that is not being assessed and complex sentence structure that might get in the way (Stiggins, Arter, Chappuis, & Chappuis, 2004). Unless the item is intended to assess reading comprehension, reading level shouldn't get in the way of students demonstrating what they've learned.

In considering how to write good item stems, one recommendation is to make sure the stem includes an entire statement or question. This allows students to read through the entire question before trying to determine the answer or solve the problem (Gareis & Grant, 2008). Your team will also want to make sure you don't confuse your students by using the word *not* in the stem. When asking, "Which one of the following does *not* fit" or "Which of these is *not* an example of," we could confuse students who know the answer if it's asked in a straightforward way (Gareis & Grant, 2008). You'll also want to highlight adjectives like *most likely* and *best* in the stem.

When thinking about answer choices, there are several guidelines your team should consider. The first is to make sure there is only one correct answer and that all of the answer choices are reasonable. Also, make sure to put the answer choices in a logical order (for example, alphabetical) so that students don't try to guess the correct answer by its position. Keep answer choices similar in length and parallel in grammar (Gareis & Grant, 2008; Popham, 2003; Stiggins et al., 2004). These recommendations make sure that students don't see the items as "games" that they can use strategy to solve rather than demonstrating their knowledge of the learning targets.

Many high-stakes assessments rely heavily on multiple-choice questions, and not all of those questions will follow the guidelines we recommend. However, for teacher-created formative assessments, we want to make sure that students get the help they need around the learning targets we're assessing. We want to eliminate the possibility that a student misses a question because it was too difficult to read or because the expectations for the answer were unclear. We also want to eliminate, as much as possible, students being seen as proficient because they guessed the correct answer.

An important consideration for formative assessments is that the results provide information that will direct us to what to do next when students haven't learned a particular target. To be able to do this, each question must only assess one learning target at a time. Consider this example of a mathematics problem that includes two targets.

Which of the following numbers is a factor of 250 and a multiple of 5?

    a. 50   c. 92

    b. 80   d. 120

This problem asks students to be able to use two concepts—*factor* and *multiple*. While this problem might appear on a summative assessment, it doesn't work as an item for a formative assessment because students who answer incorrectly might not know how to find multiples, they might not know how to find factors, or they might not know how to find either.

Savvy item writers can create multiple-choice items that use the incorrect responses to understand the students' misconceptions. For example, when mathematics teachers know that there are some incorrect strategies a student might use to solve a problem, the test item would include a distractor for the answer a student would likely give using that incorrect procedure.

If, on the other hand, your team is looking to understand a student's reasoning or to evaluate in more depth any misconceptions he or she may have, selected response will not provide that information for you. For those targets that expect more cognitive demand, selected-response questions will not be a good match.

Multiple-choice items can be used to provide options for struggling students to show what they know. For example, some teams use multiple-choice items as a scaffold means of assessment when students are unable to correctly answer a constructed-response question designed to assess knowledge of a complex target. If a student reads a piece of text and is unable to identify the main idea, the teacher may follow up with a list of possible responses for those students who can't generate the main idea independently. The multiple-choice question assesses the simpler knowledge (being able to identify the main idea).

Constructed-Response Items

Students must provide an answer—either short or long—to a constructed-responses question to show their understanding. Sometimes constructed-response items require students to fill in a graphic organizer.

Constructed-response items can be written to demand either short or long responses from the students. These items include both the question itself and often some additional stimulus information. Stimulus information is some kind of text or data that the student needs to read and reason through in order to answer the question. For example, many reading questions provide a piece or pieces of text that the student must first read in order to answer the question. In mathematics, the students may be given some background data (perhaps a graph or chart) or information (website about a topic) that helps them solve the problem. For questions written to the ELA standards in history and social studies, the stimulus information may consist of a political cartoon or a well-known speech. Often the stimulus information increases the level of cognitive demand of the question because students are asked to think about the content of the stimulus and make some decisions about how to use the information it contains.

When writing constructed-response items, it's important to give the student as much information in the question itself about what you are expecting in their response. For example, if you want text examples (want students to cite evidence), how many do you want? Do you want quotes? Page numbers? This specific detail helps students to not only provide what you want but also helps them frame their answers. For example, by asking for quotes, the student knows he or she must provide a text-dependent answer (Fisher, Frey, & Lapp, 2012).

What you include in the stimulus information will also be an important consideration. While some mathematics problems should contain information not needed in the solution to the problem so that the answer is not so obvious, too much extraneous information will make the problem unclear. What Stiggins et al. (2004) call *point the way* asks us to be specific enough so that students who know and understand the target being assessed can actually demonstrate that understanding in their answer. On the other hand, we don't want to provide so much information that students are guided to the correct answer when they don't know and understand the target. The question itself should be easy enough to read and easy enough to understand that the reading process doesn't get in the way of the student being able to answer the question correctly.

One mistake we've sometimes seen teams make is to offer students a choice in which constructed-response questions they want to answer. Teachers provide this option in an effort to get their students more engaged in the assessment. However, this practice when applied to formative assessment is not likely to provide the information about what kind of additional time and support a student needs. Consider the situation in which a teacher asks students to read a story and answer either a question about what happened in the plot or about the characters. If the student chooses the first question, the teacher doesn't know if the student understood the characters. Instead, the teacher should either only assess one target at a time or assess both targets using the same piece of text but include questions for both of the targets.

When designing constructed-response questions collaboratively, it is important that your team creates a rubric describing both the correct response (what proficiency will look like) and what it will look like when students can go beyond proficiency, as well as what it will look like if they have only learned some of the simpler content. Chapter 8 (pages 129–133) goes into more detail about how to construct these rubrics.

Constructed-response items have the advantage of allowing you to see and understand the student's thinking about a particular question. When students are required to show their thinking or justify their response, you can immediately see where the student went wrong in an incorrect response. These assessment items also are easier to write around some of the higher levels of thinking that the Common Core State Standards require. Consider, for example, this fifth-grade Informational Text standard: "Analyze multiple accounts of the same event or topic, noting important similarities and differences in the point of view they represent" (RI.5.6; NGA & CCSSO, 2010a, p. 14).

Looking at the learning target based on this standard, "Analyze multiple accounts of the same event or topic," you can see that writing multiple-choice questions that require students to analyze the accounts would be very difficult. On the other hand, writing a constructed-response question, which provided some content and expectations, would make assessing this target much easier.

However, when using constructed-response items, your collaborative team must be very specific about how responses will be scored in order to get common data. In fact, you will likely need to practice collaborative scoring in order to make sure teachers are all scoring answers the same way. When using these protocols, your team does not have to score all student responses together but rather score enough of them collaboratively to be confident that teachers are scoring student work in the same way. For example, each teacher on your team might randomly select one or two pieces of student work to bring to the table. Each team member scores the pieces and discusses how they should be scored so that eventually everyone gives the same score. Or, each teacher might bring three samples of work: one high, one average, and one low. Your team can score all of the pieces collaboratively to get a consensus on what the appropriate score should be. More information about collaborative scoring is provided in chapter 8.

Another difficulty your team must consider in using constructed-response items is the time it takes to score student answers. This is especially true in middle and high school in which teachers may have 100 or more students in their classes throughout the day. To facilitate scoring large numbers of constructed-response questions, we recommend that your team considers using graphic organizers for student responses. This will help you see the specific parts of each student response in an easy-to-score way. For example, if students are asked to compare and contrast how the settings of two stories changed the outcome of the story, a Venn diagram could be used to show how the settings were alike and how they were different. Additionally, students can write a follow-up explanation to explain how the events affected the outcome.

Performance Tasks

PARCC and SBAC use performance tasks in addition to the more traditional selected-response and constructed-response questions. SBAC (2012b) defines performance tasks in this way:

> Performance tasks challenge students to apply their knowledge and skills to respond to complex real-world problems. They can best be described as collections of questions and activities that are coherently connected to a single theme or scenario. These activities are meant to measure capacities such as depth of understanding, writing and research skills and complex analysis, which cannot be adequately assessed with traditional assessment questions. The performance tasks will be taken on a computer (but will not be computer adaptive) and will take one or two class periods to complete. (p. 1)

Your collaborative team may consider writing performance tasks or using some sample released tasks from the consortia in a formative way to provide students experience with answering these more lengthy and integrated tasks. (See www.smarterbalanced.org/sample-items-and-performance-tasks/ and www.parcconline.org /samples/item-task-prototypes for more information.) Your team will likely want to consider writing performance tasks when seeking information about how well students can connect multiple learning targets. You can use summative performance tasks after you have assessed students formatively on the specific learning targets. We recommend having end-of-unit or grading period assessments similar to the item types students will encounter on the high-stakes, end-of-year PARCC or SBAC assessments. You will want to consider and plan for the amount of time these tasks will take for students to complete as well as the amount of time it will take for you to score them.

Technology-Enhanced Items

PARCC and SBAC use technology-enhanced assessment items. These items "are computer-delivered items that include specialized interactions for collecting data" (SBAC, 2012c). These items will assess whether students can categorize objects in mathematics, create graphs and charts, select a range of numbers, reorder sentences in writing, and highlight a concept in reading. Their purpose is to overcome the inability of selected-response questions in assessing higher-order thinking by creating a response on the computer that can be quickly scored. The response requires more than just selecting an answer from a list, but doesn't require student writing which might be subjectively scored.

Whether or not your team decides to try its hand at writing technology-enhanced items, it is important that you consider the thinking and reasoning behind these questions to ensure that your students will be able to do this work. For example, grouping objects in mathematics requires students to be able to sort items by a variety of characteristics. Using manipulatives in team-developed assessments could easily simulate this work. In writing, students might be asked to edit samples of writing that are similar to those they might see on these items. Students could reorder sentences with numbers rather than the computer mouse. Teams should be careful to ensure that their formative assessments have a similar level of rigor and high levels of thinking required.

Planning the Common Formative Assessment

As noted previously, in order for your team to be able to respond quickly and accurately when a student needs help on an essential skill, such as those in the CCSS, we recommend limiting your CFAs to no more than two learning targets at a time. The process for planning and writing these assessments has two steps.

Step One: Choose Learning Targets and Determine Level of Thinking

After unwrapping the standards and scaling the learning targets, you will quickly see that you likely still have too many learning targets to formatively assess. You will want to consider which, of all the learning targets you have listed, will be the most important targets for you to gather formative information. Deciding which learning targets to assess is more about professional judgment than it is about following a particular protocol. What targets does the team feel will likely provide the best information about student learning? To this end, we suggest you consider the following questions.

- Is the learning target a prerequisite skill for something students will be learning later in this unit of instruction or school year? Your team might choose one learning target to assess that will require students to incorporate knowledge of other targets as well. Consider this sixth-grade standard for reading informational text: "Determine an author's point of view or purpose in a text, and consider how it is conveyed in the text" (RI.6.2; NGA & CCSSO, 2010a, p. 39). The team unwraps the standard into the following learning targets.

    + Determine an author's point of view or purpose.

    + Explain point of view (implied target).

    + Consider how the author's point of view is conveyed in a text.

- In order to be able to master the last learning target, the student would likely have to be proficient on the first two learning targets; therefore, the team only has to assess the third learning target.

- Is the learning target something that students need to know now and forever? Consider mathematics concepts like understanding place value or understanding equivalent fractions or ELA concepts like understanding two authors' points of view and how they might provide information on the same topic in a different way.

- Is the learning target something that is particularly difficult, or is it one that often leads to misconceptions? For example, *area* and *perimeter* are two concepts that students often confuse. It would be important that students understand conceptually the difference between the two.

Once your team chooses the learning targets to assess, you can then determine the level of thinking or cognitive demand the target requires from students. This action clarifies the level of proficiency for meeting the learning target.

Bloom's Revised Taxonomy (Anderson & Krathwohl, 2001), Marzano and Kendall's (2007) New Taxonomy, or Webb's (2005) Depth of Knowledge will be helpful to copy during this step. However, we recommend that you don't just look at the verb in the learning target and find it on the taxonomy list to complete this step (see discussion on this point in chapter 5, page 83). For example, consider the verb *compare*. On Bloom's Revised Taxonomy, this verb is listed under the category *Remember/Understand*, which is the second level. On Webb's Depth of Knowledge it is a level three in the category *Strategic Thinking*. As we discussed in chapter 4 during the unwrapping process, your team must discuss the specific target you will be assessing and decide what you really expect from students who have reached proficiency to be able to do.

If your team follows our process for unwrapping standards into learning targets, you will likely have already had this discussion. If so, this step is just a confirmation of your previous work. However, sometimes teams revisit their thinking from their earlier discussions and change their mind about the level of cognitive demand as they talk about how the target will be assessed. In PLCs, teams are very open to changing their thinking as they learn more: here is continuous improvement at its finest!

Using the planning template in figure 7.3, the team enters the learning targets to assess. See page 196 for the reproducible "Planning Common Formative Assessments."

Learning Target	Bloom: Remember/ Understand Marzano: Retrieval DOK: Recall	Bloom: Apply Marzano: Comprehension DOK: Skills and Concepts	Bloom: Analyze Marzano: Analysis DOK: Strategic Thinking	Bloom: Evaluate/Create Marzano: Knowledge Utilization DOK: Extended Thinking	Total Number of Questions
Learning target one					
Learning target two					

Figure 7.3: **Template for planning common formative assessments.**

Step Two: Choose Type of Assessment Item

Your team now decides what type of assessment item to write and how many items you need to adequately assess each of the targets. During this step your team must consider the advantages and disadvantages of each of the types of assessment items (see page 111). Will the type of assessment item provide valid information about student learning? To do so, the item must be able to assess the target at the level of cognitive demand expected. For targets that have verbs at the thinking level of analysis and above, you will likely want to use constructed-response questions rather than selected-response items. You will also want to use the most efficient assessment strategy that can still provide accurate information for each target. For example, you'll want to use selected-response questions over constructed response to make scoring quicker if the learning target is an appropriate match.

Many teachers we've worked with want to know if they should be concerned about how they can make their assessments valid and reliable. Reeves (2007) reminds us that we don't have to be held to the same standards of *psychometric perfection* as the writers of high-stakes tests. Test designers (psychometricians) use statistical analysis to ensure the quality of their items over large numbers of students. Because your team is working with fewer numbers of students, you don't need to reach that same level of precision. However, we still want to have confidence in the decisions we're making about student needs.

There are certain practices teams can use to make sure their assessments are valid—meaning that the items are tightly related to the content being taught (Gareis & Grant, 2008). First, the team identifies the learning targets that are being assessed and second, the team determines the thinking levels those targets are asking of students.

Reliability is about the confidence a team has that the information from the assessment accurately measures student learning. To ensure reliability, teams should write a sufficient number of questions so that the chances of guessing are eliminated. We recommend that you have at least four well-written selected-response questions or one well-written constructed-response item around each learning target. While using more items is probably always better than fewer items when considering reliability, the purpose of these formative assessments is to gather information quickly so that corrective instruction occurs as soon as possible. Well-written questions that ensure a student's reading level doesn't get in the way also increase reliability (Gareis & Grant, 2008).

Examples of the Completed CFA Planning Process

Consider the following example of a team creating a common formative assessment for a fourth-grade standard for reading informational text, the same standard we unwrapped in chapter 4.

> Compare and contrast a firsthand and secondhand account of the same event or topic; describe the differences in focus and the information provided. (RI.4.6) (NGA & CCSSO, 2010a, p. 14)

After the fourth-grade English language arts team unwraps the entire standard, the members choose the following targets to teach at the beginning of their unit:

1. Recognize the source of text as either firsthand or secondhand.

2. Compare and contrast a firsthand and secondhand account of the same event.

3. Describe the difference in focus between the two.

4. Describe the difference in information provided between the two.

The teachers choose the second learning target to assess, as they believe it is an important skill for all of their students to be able to meet and believing that if students can compare and contrast the two accounts, they would be able to recognize the source for them. They also choose the fourth learning target because they are teaching a unit on informational text with how to write a quality informational essay, and they feel they have been emphasizing the use of supportive details.

They determine that the target "Compare and contrast a firsthand and secondhand account of the same event" has a cognitive demand that fits into Bloom's Revised Taxonomy in the *Apply* level. They determine the learning target "Describe the differences in information provided between the two" has an *Analyze* level in Bloom's Revised Taxonomy.

They use the assessment planning template in figure 7.4 to get started with writing their CFA. The lightly shaded boxes in the first row on the template are there to remind your team that learning targets with high cognitive demand usually require constructed-response questions. The darker shading highlights the thinking level for each of the targets being assessed.

Learning Target	Bloom: Remember/ Understand Marzano: Retrieval DOK: Recall	Bloom: Apply Marzano: Comprehension DOK: Skills and Concepts	Bloom: Analyze Marzano: Analysis DOK: Strategic Thinking	Bloom: Evaluate/Create Marzano: Knowledge Utilization DOK: Extended Thinking	Total Number of Questions
1. Compare and contrast a firsthand and secondhand account of the same event.					
2. Describe the differences in information provided between the two.					

Figure 7.4: Sample fourth-grade learning targets identified for CFA.

Their next step is to decide what type of assessment items to use and how many items they will write. In this example, the team decides to use four multiple-choice questions for target one and one constructed-response item for target two.

Their completed formative assessment plan is shown in figure 7.5 (page 120).

Learning Target	Bloom: Remember/ Understand Marzano: Retrieval DOK: Recall	Bloom: Apply Marzano: Comprehension DOK: Skills and Concepts	Bloom: Analyze Marzano: Analysis DOK: Strategic Thinking	Bloom: Evaluate/Create Marzano: Knowledge Utilization DOK: Extended Thinking	Total Number of Questions
1. Compare and contrast a firsthand and secondhand account of the same event.		Four multiple-choice items			
2. Describe the differences in information provided between the two.			One constructed-response item		

Figure 7.5: Sample completed formative assessment plan for fourth-grade reading Informational Text standard.

Your CFA might have a combination of selected-response and constructed-response items or only one type of item. The key is making sure that the target you're assessing matches the rigor of the item type.

In this second example, a seventh-grade mathematics team unwraps a standard in the domain Ratios and Proportional Relationships (7.RP). (See figure 7.6.)

Use proportional relationships to solve multistep ratio and percent problems. (7.RP.3) (NGA & CCSSO, 2010e, p. 48)

The team decides that the targets should include:

1. Use proportional relationships to solve multistep ratio problems.

2. Use proportional relationships to solve multistep percent problems.

They recognize that both targets are DOK Level Three: Strategic Thinking.

The team has already assessed several other learning targets related to the cluster. Therefore, the team focuses on the real-world application of proportional relationships in this CFA (see figure 7.7, page 122).

The students will be solving two constructed-response problems that have multiple steps to solve. They will be required to show each step they use to solve the problem and to explain their thinking about the solution. The team will use a rubric to score the answers (see page 130).

Planning Scaled Assessments

If your team has created scales for each of your learning targets, your CFA will be designed in a slightly different fashion, and you will use a variation of the assessment planning chart (see the reproducible "Assessment Plan for Scaled Assessments" in the appendix, page 197). Your team will design an assessment with items for each of the scaled learning targets. That is, items that assess proficiency on the target

Learning Target	Bloom: Remember/ Understand Marzano: Retrieval DOK: Recall	Bloom: Apply Marzano: Comprehension DOK: Skills and Concepts	Bloom: Analyze Marzano: Analysis DOK: Strategic Thinking	Bloom: Evaluate/Create Marzano: Knowledge Utilization DOK: Extended Thinking	Total Number of Questions
1. Use proportional relationships to solve multistep ratio problems			One constructed response		1
2. Use proportional relationships to solve multistep percent problems			One constructed response		1

Figure 7.6: Sample common formative assessment plan for 7.RP.3.

written at level 3.0, items to see if the student can go beyond and reach the target written at 4.0, or items that assess a simpler 2.0 target to see if the student has learned that target.

When planning the assessment, your team decides how many assessment items will be written for each target level and what kinds of assessment items to write to help differentiate the way you will respond after the assessment. To do this, the first step is the same as discussed previously in this chapter (page 116): To determine the level of cognitive demand for the proficiency level 3.0 target, as well as the level of cognitive demand for the proficiency level 4.0 and proficiency level 2.0 targets (see page 120). This step is important as it helps you decide what types of assessment items and how many questions you will need to write for each of the scaled targets.

In practice, this might mean that a teacher can assess the proficiency level for a learning target with a constructed-response question. The teacher might assess the simpler content for that same target using several selected-response items. The proficiency level 4.0 target may also need a constructed-response question. Thus, the assessment for that one learning target may consist of four selected-response items and two constructed-response items.

Table 7.1 shows how this might look for one of the targets we scaled in chapter 5 (see page 79).

Table 7.1: Proficiency Scale for a Learning Target Based on a Seventh-Grade Literature Standard

Level 4.0	Determine a way to change the theme by changing events in the story. (What would happen to the theme if . . . and how would it change?)
Level 3.0	Analyze the theme's development over the course of the text.
Level 2.0	Given the theme and a list of evidence from the text, choose what pieces of evidence from the text best show the theme's development over the course of the text.
Level 1.0	With help, partial success at score 2.0 content and 3.0 content
Level 0.0	Even with help, no success

Your team will want to develop assessment items for levels 2.0, 3.0, and 4.0 for this target.

As you look at the three levels for this scaled target, your team decides that the levels of cognitive demand are the following: Marzano's New Taxonomy Level Three: Analysis or Depth of Knowledge Level Two: Skills and Concepts (level 3.0 learning target), Marzano's New Taxonomy Level Four: Knowledge Utilization and Depth of Knowledge Level Four: Extended Thinking (level 4.0 learning target), and New Taxonomy Level Two: Comprehension or Depth of Knowledge Level Two: Skills and Concepts (level 2.0 learning target). As a result, you decide to complete the assessment plan (see figure 7.7).

Learning Target	Bloom: Remember/ Understand Marzano: Retrieval DOK: Recall	Bloom: Apply Marzano: Comprehension DOK: Skills and Concepts	Bloom: Analyze Marzano: Analysis DOK: Strategic Thinking	Bloom: Evaluate/Create Marzano: Knowledge Utilization DOK: Extended Thinking	Total Number of Questions
Level 4.0: Determine a way to change the theme by changing events in the story.		Four multiple-choice items		One constructed-response item	5
Level 3.0: Analyze the theme's development over the course of the text.			One constructed-response item		1
Level 2.0: Given the theme and a list of evidence from the text, choose what pieces of evidence from the text best show the theme's development over the course of the text.		Four multiple-choice items			4

Figure 7.7: Sample common formative assessment plan for scaled learning target for seventh-grade Literature standard.

As you write and use this assessment, you will want to consider how much time it will take for administration and scoring. You'll also want to consider whether all students will be given all of the items. Some teams provide the proficiency level 4.0 questions as challenge questions. Students are asked to try them out—students know that not everyone is expected to be able to do these items.

Since teams use their proficiency level 2.0 questions to help determine how to respond to the students who didn't master the target, they may ask all students to answer these questions knowing that students who can answer the proficiency level 3.0 and 4.0 targets will easily get these questions correct. However, the information will help you to know if those students who couldn't answer the proficiency level 3.0 target correctly did understand some of the simpler content.

Gathering the Data From Common Formative Assessments

When your team uses the process we recommend to write their CFAs, you will find that the data you gather are very easy to use. If the assessment has only one target, the data will tell you which students have or have not mastered that target. If you've written the assessment based on scales, you can easily sort the results by proficiency levels 1.0, 2.0, 3.0, or 4.0 according to student responses.

With two learning targets, it's important to sort the students for each learning target as some students will demonstrate proficiency on one target, both targets, or neither target. The corrective instruction your team plans must be specific for each of these targets.

For example, for the two learning targets in figure 7.4 (page 119), your team could easily sort out the students who reached proficiency on "Compare and contrast a firsthand and secondhand account of the same event" from those that didn't show proficiency. You could then respond to each of these groups. Then, you could look at the second target and sort the students who were proficient on "Describe the differences in information provided between the two." You would provide a separate response to this target.

In chapters 10 and 11 we'll discuss in more detail how a team might plan its response and structure its groups. The key is to have the right data to tell you *which* students need help or challenge and *what kind of* help or challenge they will benefit from.

Planning Summative Assessments

In addition to common formative assessments, your team may also want to write your summative assessments together. These might include end-of-unit assessments or benchmark and interim assessments. We consider these types of assessments more summative than formative because teachers have finished the instruction, and any additional intervention for students will likely occur sometime after Tier 1 instruction.

The biggest difference between planning formative and summative assessments will be the number of learning targets to assess. For summative assessments, you will want to consider assessing more learning targets on the same assessment. These learning targets will likely come from multiple different standards. The questions may ask students to put together multiple learning targets to come up with the correct answer. We discussed previously that when designing formative assessments, it's best to include only one or two targets at a time in order to provide specific targeted corrective instruction. This guideline is altered when designing a summative assessment. Summative assessments will likely have more than two learning targets, and while there is no optimal number, teachers will want to consider the amount of time it will take for students to respond when making this decision. Once you are confident that students have learned these targets in your CFA, you may still want to make sure that students can explain connections between learning targets, since this is what we know students will need to be able to do in the real world—and on the high-stakes tests!

As you plan the summative assessment, your team must be specific about the learning targets that you'll assess and must determine the level of cognitive demand required in the same way you planned the formative assessments. You will still need enough selected-response, constructed-response, or performance task items to make the data reliable.

Tips for Teams New to the PLC Process

When teams are new to the PLC process, they often ask for a list of tasks to complete at their meetings. They want to have a big picture about how to lay out the expected products from their work. One particularly helpful source we recommend is "Critical Issues for Team Consideration" from *Learning by Doing* (DuFour et al., 2010). This list is a good place to start. Visit **go.solution-tree.com/commoncore** for the reproducible. The process, however, can start anywhere and at any time. We recommend teams begin writing CFAs by picking the next unit they will be teaching. Don't expect perfection, but be willing to learn as you work together. Sometimes the magnitude of the project of writing CFAs overwhelms teams. Be aware that you will never get everything accomplished in one year. Be willing to take this process a step at a time because each small step will make the next step easier, and each small step will improve student learning.

Be aware that writing and using common formative assessments is often the most "threatening" step in the PLC process. Teachers are often worried that their scores will be the worst scores for anyone on the team; some teachers are even worried that their scores might be better than everyone else's scores. Therefore, it's very important to discuss from the beginning how you will handle data on your team. Teams often add data norms. For example, "We will use data to judge instructional strategies, not each other" or "We will only use data to decide what to do next." Our experience is that when teams keep their conversations focused on how to improve student learning, this fear of data being used inappropriately goes away quickly.

As you get started with the process, you will likely uncover some interesting information about how teachers on your team interpret *proficiency* at different levels. Teachers set different expectations about reasoning, writing, and, especially, completing tasks. Your team should expect to spend some time wrestling with what proficiency should look like. Writing questions and prompts together will help you see how to build consensus on this important topic. One way to get started is to bring samples of student work to the table to look at together. What is proficient? What is beyond? Most importantly, discuss why you believe what you believe.

As you write the CFA, make sure to ask yourselves whether the information (data) you get back will guide your next steps for instruction. Is the CFA written around specific learning targets at the level of cognitive demand you expect to teach them at? Remember that you can't assess everything you teach, even if you only assess your power standards. Your team will use its *collaborative* professional judgment about what to assess. Keep your assessments short and focused on a few learning targets at a time.

Make sure to keep in mind that the quality of the assessments written is far more important than the quantity of assessments written. In your first year, you will begin the process but will be able to create additional assessments each year. Don't forget to keep copies of each assessment to be used again next year as well as information about what worked and what didn't work. Next year, you start from where you left off this year.

Tips for Principals and Leaders

We see three common mistakes that teams make when they write CFAs together, whether around the CCSS or around their own state standards. Be careful to make your teams aware of these mistakes and to provide feedback about these issues on the actual assessments teams produce.

The first mistake teams make is that they write their assessments around standards rather than around learning targets. In chapter 4, we discussed the importance of unwrapping standards into learning targets. In order to get information that will tell a team how to respond to students experiencing difficulty, it is really important to make sure their formative assessments are written around the more specific learning targets.

Secondly, teams often include too many targets on their assessments. In order to effectively respond when students haven't learned, it's important to select targets that have the most bang for the buck. By this we mean that these are the most critical targets for student learning; those that are foundational to the unit of instruction. Short, frequent assessments that provide just enough information are the desired outcome.

Finally, we often see that teams use a type of assessment or write questions that are not at the expected level of cognitive demand. For example, if we're asking students to analyze information using a multiple-choice question, there is a possible disconnect in the cognitive demand of the assessment. We want to be able to see the students' thinking in the response and will likely need a constructed-response question for that to happen.

In our experience, one important topic any principal should address about common formative assessments is how the data will (or hopefully *will not*) be used to evaluate teachers. If the information from formative assessments is used to plan next steps for students, it certainly should *not* be used to evaluate teacher performance as its purpose is to help teachers know what to do next for their students. If it's misused for evaluating teachers, they will likely not be willing to share their results to use for planning purposes. When principals communicate that they won't use this information in an evaluative way, it allows teams to confidently share and use the data appropriately.

Using Rubrics to Provide Feedback

8

Collaborative Connections

- Collaborative teams use rubrics to ensure consistent scoring of constructed-response items and performance tasks in common assessments.
- Students use rubrics to know exactly what they have to do to reach proficiency and beyond for specific learning targets.
- Common formative assessments include analytic rubrics, which help collaborative teams and individual students know what to do next in their learning.

We've already established that the CCSS require students to think and reason more abstractly—more rigorously—than perhaps they have had to do previously in programs based on state standards. Your collaborative team will likely find that, in parallel fashion, your assessments will also need to adjust to that rigor, ultimately resulting in the use of more constructed-response and performance tasks rather than relying on multiple-choice items. Most high-stakes tests have relied heavily on multiple-choice items, and teachers tried to use similar items in their own assessments so that students were prepared for items they would likely encounter on the standardized tests. Now, given the depth of thinking that we are examining based on the CCSS, it will be difficult, if not impossible, to assess with multiple-choice questions. Your team must, therefore, rely more heavily on constructed-response questions and performance tasks to assess student learning at these higher levels. If you've had prior experience in using constructed responses or performance tasks, you know that they are clearly more subjective. This means, of course, that in order to ensure your team scores student responses to these questions and tasks in the same way, rubrics will be important.

As suggested in chapter 7, we highly recommend teams practice collaboratively scoring student responses to common formative assessment items to ensure that they are scoring answers the same way. The questions you've written are likely very new questions based on these new learning targets, and your team may find that there are unexpected student responses that they will need to discuss.

There are many different ways to collaboratively score student work, but they all rely on teachers individually scoring an anonymous piece of the student work using a rubric and then comparing the resulting scores. Teams must then work together discussing their different points of view to come to a common agreement on the actual score for the work. We include two reproducible protocols in the appendix for doing this type of scoring: "Collaborative Scoring Protocol" (page 199) and "Variation on Collaborative Scoring Protocol" (page 200).

The Purpose of Rubrics

Your team creates rubrics, or scoring guides, to establish the expectations about what learning targets will look like when your students have succeeded in learning them. The rubrics need to provide a specific enough description for both your students and your team about what that target looks like when accomplished and so that everyone understands exactly what the expectations are for proficiency.

A rubric is the written description of levels of proficiency or quality a team has developed for learning targets or criteria for student work.

In previous chapters, we've recommended that your teams develop collective clarity around the expectations you have for student proficiency and have advised you to select your power or essential standards, unwrap those standards, and scale each of the learning targets to assess. Each of these steps makes the collective understanding of what proficiency will look like much clearer for everyone on the team. The rubric puts those expectations into writing for both you and your students.

We know that students benefit when teams use common assessments. When your team writes common assessments, you are increasing the likelihood that all students on that team have a guaranteed and viable curriculum, you learn together about good instructional practices, you create equity for all of the students on your team because each teacher has the same expectations for learning, you increase your collective knowledge about assessment practices, and you increase the power of your response for both students who need more time and students who can benefit from challenge (DuFour et al., 2010). However, to ensure these benefits, teachers must give and score common assessments in a collaborative and consistent way. This means that if each teacher on your team scores a student response without some important collaborative scoring practices in place, the resulting information or data won't have much value because the scores will be dependent on the person scoring rather than on the answer or performance itself. In chapter 7, we recommended some protocols your team can use to apply collaborative scoring practices (pages 116–118). However, the first step in collaborative scoring is writing a rubric together that explains what the specific expectations are for students to do in response to each assessment item.

A second, and equally important, purpose for developing a rubric is to involve your students in the assessment by making sure you are crystal clear about what they need to do to show that they have mastered a learning target. When students thoroughly understand a rubric, they are much more likely to be able to show what they know about the target being assessed.

Finally, the rubric is a key factor in helping students use feedback to know what to do next in their own learning. Being aware of what they need to do to advance their learning helps to build students' confidence and sustain their motivation.

The Value of Feedback

Feedback is unquestionably one of the most important things you can use to affect student learning in a positive way. Hattie (2009) lists it as one of the most important innovations teachers can use with students and, in fact, ranks it tenth out of the 138 instructional strategies he examined while analyzing the research on educational practices. In this chapter, we'll relate how feedback connects to the types of rubrics and their uses for collaborative teams.

Royce Sadler (1998) suggests that feedback to students must provide three things: (1) it must clearly communicate the expectations for learning to students, (2) it must provide *multicriterion* feedback about the student's current learning, and (3) it must provide enough information that students know how to get from where they are to the final expectation. These expectations are Sadler's (1998) three questions posed from the student's point of view: Where am I going? Where am I now? How can I close the gap? (as cited in Chappuis, 2009). Rubrics can provide the information that students need to answer these three questions.

Hattie and Timperley (2007) connect the three Sadler (1998) questions with the effectiveness of feedback to student learning. They suggest that there are four levels of feedback teachers can provide.

1. Task feedback (FT)

2. Process feedback (FP)

3. Feedback about self-regulation (FR)

4. Feedback about self as a person (FS)

They look specifically at how effective each of these types of feedback is based on the research they've studied. FP and FR provide the most significant difference in student learning. We believe that using rubrics effectively provides effective feedback to students about the process they are using to answer questions and solve problems (FP) and about their own thinking about a learning target (FR); thus, they are likely to support increased student achievement. In fact, Hattie and Timperley (2007) suggest that the effectiveness of improving learning lies in:

> devising assessment tasks that provide information and interpretations about the discrepancy between current status and the learning goals at any of the three levels: about tasks, about the process or strategies to understand the tasks, and about the regulation, engagement, and confidence to become more committed to learn. (p. 101)

In order to apply these findings in the context of common formative assessments, let's examine how your team might connect these important practices to your own work.

Types of Rubrics

Rubrics are powerful tools that you can use to help students answer Sadler's (1998) first question in regard to their learning, Where am I going? As we discussed in chapter 7, your collaborative team will begin by developing short, common formative assessments for the learning targets you've identified as being most important for your students to learn. These formative assessments are built on a small number of learning targets and are given frequently to know what to do next. In addition to these questions, your team will want to provide opportunities for students to put together several learning targets, often from multiple standards, in a summative assessment periodically throughout the year. These assessments will likely include performance tasks similar to the items from the SBAC (2012b) and PARCC (2012a) consortia. For both of these types of assessment items, any constructed responses will require a collaboratively developed rubric to score. For students to be involved in the process—and, therefore, more motivated to do well—they must understand what learning targets are important to learn and what those learning targets look like. Rubrics help communicate the answer to both of these topics.

When carefully constructed, a rubric provides a clear understanding to your team and students about specific learning targets and assessment types, such as constructed-response items, research or essays (written products), or performance tasks. Additionally, an effective rubric provides teams with the criteria for assessing student performance on learning targets as well as scoring their levels of proficiency.

There is no right number of criteria or proficiency levels to assess student performance. Many teams use four levels: (1) beyond proficient, (2) proficient, (3) partially proficient, and (4) not proficient. Having these multiple levels allows students to see their progress over time when looking at certain learning targets. However, for some learning targets there could be only two levels: *proficient* and *not proficient*. Your team will make the decision about how many levels to use when examining the learning target you're assessing and how to respond. Also, note that although we use the word *level* in our description, many teams assign points to the levels (such as 3 points, 2 points, 1 point, and 0 points), as is the case for SBAC (2012b) rubrics.

Figure 8.1 shows a sample rubric for scoring constructed-response questions. Notice the rubric lists each target separately and the descriptions of the levels of proficiency are specific to the target.

Learning Target or Criteria to Assess	Beyond Proficient	Proficient	Partially Proficient	Not Proficient
Target one				
Target two				

Figure 8.1: Sample rubric for scoring constructed-response questions.

For products and performance tasks, rubrics must list the scoring criteria for the assessment item. For example, if a student is producing an argument in writing, and the piece will be scored on two criteria—(1) the use of clear reasons and evidence supporting the claims and (2) the use of credible sources—each criterion is a learning target for this unit of instruction. Therefore, it's important that the rubric explains each criterion. Figure 8.2 illustrates this point.

Learning Target or Criteria to Assess	Beyond Proficient	Proficient	Partially Proficient	Not Proficient
Student provided clear reasons and evidence.				
Student used credible sources.				

Figure 8.2: Sample rubric for scoring individual learning targets.

As noted previously, we recommend using only one or two learning targets for common formative assessments of the CCSS. If the criteria are assessing writing, teachers should only score the piece based on the targets in the CFA. For summative assessments, lengthier or more complex products, and performance tasks, the number of criteria will likely be more than two.

Once you've developed the rubric, it will be important to share it with your students. Showing samples of student work for each of the targets at the varying levels is one way to ensure students understand the rubric. Students should know how to use a rubric to determine what level of learning they are currently at and to be able to read about the expectations on the next level to see what it is that they have to do to move ahead.

When developing a rubric for student use, it is important that the learning targets or criteria are written in student-friendly language that students can understand. For example, phrasing learning targets as "I can" statements is a great start. However, if what follows the words "I can" is not language that students understand, they will not be able to reach the expected result. Consider this example of an "I can" statement based on the CCSS for teachers to use with kindergarten students: "I can actively engage in group reading activities with purpose and understanding." We would argue that although written from a student's perspective, this statement is not written in student-friendly terms, and kindergarten students are unlikely to understand it. We recommend that teams instead write these targets in language students would understand. For example, "I can read books and tell if they are stories or about facts."

Holistic Versus Analytic Rubrics

A holistic rubric considers the entire product or performance and uses one total score rather than looking at each criterion separately. These rubrics are often used in summative assessments to score writing prompts. For example, SBAC uses a four-point rubric to assess argumentative writing in a holistic way. The combination of many criteria (focus, organization, elaboration of evidence, language and vocabulary, and conventions) is all combined into one score (for example, see www.smarterbalanced.org/wordpress /wp-content/uploads/2012/05/TaskItemSpecifications/EnglishLanguageArtsLiteracy/ELARubrics.pdf).

The example of a holistic rubric for mathematics problem solving in figure 8.3 shows how multiple criteria are scored at once. This rubric could be used to score various summative assessment items throughout the year.

3	The solution is thorough and accurate. The diagram or drawing supports the thinking done to solve the problem.
2	The solution is not complete although the answer may be accurate. The diagram or drawing does not provide enough information to support the thinking done to solve the problem.
1	The solution is not thorough or accurate. If a diagram or drawing is present, it does not provide enough information to support the thinking done to solve the problem.

Figure 8.3: Sample holistic rubric for mathematics problem solving.

For common formative assessments, however, these rubrics generally don't help teams know what to do next for their students. Because holistic rubrics consider the product as a whole, teams cannot respond to each criteria or learning target—one of the main purposes of formative assessments.

Instead, we recommend your team uses an analytic rubric that considers each of the learning targets separately so teachers can respond in a more focused way. Figure 8.4 (page 132) provides a template your team might use to write an analytic rubric. See the reproducible "Analytic Rubric Template" (page 198). Figure 8.4 is an analytic rubric because it considers each of the learning targets separately.

Using holistic rubrics helps teachers and their students know exactly where a student is in his or her learning at a given time, but often doesn't provide the specific information a team needs to know about students to be able to respond to the next steps of learning. Later in this chapter we'll discuss how students can use both types of rubrics to know what to do next.

Analytic Rubrics

Analytic rubrics are used to describe proficiency expectations in detail so that your collaborative team can more easily score student responses in an equitable way and use the results in your classrooms. The rubric has to be specific enough that each teacher can clearly score a student response at the same level as the other teachers on your team. It's important that as your team is learning to write and use rubrics together, each teacher bring student work to the meetings and practice applying the rubric together so everyone understands the levels for each criterion on the rubric in the same way.

This understanding begins when your team works together to write the proficiency level for the response or product. Consider the way your team might develop a four-level rubric. You will start by agreeing on what *proficiency* will look like: when a student meets the target the way it was taught and at the expected mastery level. During this discussion, your team must be as specific as you can in your description. For example, if you want the students to provide details from the text, how many details will they need to provide? Do you want text quotes or page numbers? Then, after deciding on proficiency, your team can discuss the other levels. Figure 8.4 shows a four-level rubric with proficiency descriptors. The first step in the process—describing "proficiency"—is shaded to show where the team started its work in writing this rubric.

Learning Target or Criteria to Assess	Beyond Proficient	Proficient	Partially Proficient	Not Proficient
Describe the difference in information provided from firsthand and secondhand accounts.	The response explains thoroughly and accurately the difference in information from the two types of accounts, provides at least three specific details from the text to support the differences, and generalizes how and why the accounts are different.	The response explains the difference in information from the firsthand and secondhand account in this text and provides at least three specific details from the text about the differences.	The response demonstrates only an understanding of the definitions of *firsthand account* and *secondhand account*.	The response doesn't demonstrate an understanding of the difference between a firsthand and secondhand account.

Figure 8.4: Sample four-level analytic rubric.

Once you have written the proficiency level expectations, you can move on to writing the other levels. The highest level (Beyond Proficient) will lay out exactly what it will look like if students go beyond the expectations. Level two (Partially Proficient) will provide a description of the expectation for partial meeting of proficiency, either a partial answer or perhaps only the information that is the simpler content needed for full mastery. As your team writes these various levels collaboratively, you will find that you will more thoroughly understand exactly what you are expecting students to do to demonstrate they've learned this target. You will also have a better understanding of some of the instructional strategies that might be used while teaching the target.

Generic Versus Task-Specific Rubrics

The rubrics described in the previous section all describe those written for a specific task. Your team might also want to consider using generic rubrics for certain assessment items. Generic rubrics are those that define student expectations with more general terms and can be applied over a variety of products and tasks. They are often used with student writing, mathematics problem solving, and other skills that develop over a longer period of time.

Figure 8.5 is an example of a generic rubric for a mathematical explanation that might be used by a team throughout the year with any CFA that asks for students to explain how to solve a problem.

Learning Target or Criteria to Assess	Beyond Proficient	Proficient	Partially Proficient	Not Proficient
Mathematical Explanation	Answer includes a complete and thorough explanation of how the student solved the problem and why he or she took each step. There is also explanation of an alternate way to solve the problem or how this might apply in other situations.	Answer includes a complete and thorough explanation of how the problem was solved and why each step was taken. It may include a diagram to help explain the solution.	Answer doesn't thoroughly explain the solution or why the student took certain steps. It may be vague or difficult to understand in some places.	Answer doesn't explain how the student solved the problem or provides incorrect mathematical reasoning.

Figure 8.5: Sample generic rubric for mathematical reasoning.

Generic rubrics have a purpose in our work in that they capture, in writing, what collaborative teams, and their students, must be able to do with a particular skill over a period of time and in a variety of circumstances.

Checklists and Rubrics

Are checklists and rubrics the same? Although both provide information about student learning on selected tasks, they are different in other ways. From the previous descriptions of analytic rubrics, you can appreciate the depth and scope of information that these scoring tools can provide. Checklists provide less-extensive information; nonetheless, they are practical tools for some situations.

Many teams use checklists with their students for both formative and summative assessments. Typically, teams use a checklist with specific targets or skills the team is looking for students to be able to do or be able to use in practice. For example, a team is assessing a target from a fourth-grade standard from the Speaking and Listening strand.

Engage effectively in a range of collaborative discussions (one-on-one, in groups, and teacher-led) with diverse partners on *grade 4 topics and texts*, building on others' ideas and expressing their own. (SL.4.1) (NGA & CCSSO, 2010a, p. 24)

The team assesses the target "The student can carry out assigned roles in a group"—a criterion that the teacher looks for while students are working in a group. When the teacher sees a particular student complete that target, he or she adds a check on the student's checklist to record mastery of the target.

Typically, checklists have only two levels—*proficient* and *not yet proficient*. Teams may also use checklists to assess a product that is more summative. For example, in a piece of student writing, the team may create a checklist that includes multiple learning targets including items like "well-written argument statement," "supporting claims that are logical and relevant," or "words that bring cohesion to the claims, reasons, and evidence." Each of these can then be checked off if they are present in the piece of writing.

When teams work collaboratively to create the lists of skills to be assessed with a checklist and agree together what those skills look like when the students demonstrate them, the checklist becomes an effective assessment tool.

Feedback to Support Student Learning

Feedback is critical in providing information that answers Sadler's (1998) second and third questions: Where am I now? How can I close the gap? Carefully written rubrics provide information that enables students to answer these questions. The rubric should describe exactly what the product or answer or performance will look like for that target or criterion at that specific level. Consider the rubric described in figure 8.4 (page 132). If a student scores a "2" "Partially Proficient" on his or her first attempt, he or she should look at the description for a "Proficient" response to see how to change the first response and move forward. The student sees that he or she needs to more thoroughly explain the solution and perhaps even include a diagram to help the explanation. If the student has learned how to use a rubric to create a better response, he or she will know what to do to improve the answer the next time. If the student can't do this, the teacher will have to work more closely with the student to understand whether the student is having difficulty solving the problem or explaining his/her solution.

When students are using generic rubrics (for example, see figure 8.5, page 133) that are the same over time, they can keep track of their progress by watching the proficiency levels attained each time. As they become more proficient, for example, on providing mathematical explanations or support in their writing, they should see their scores move further ahead. Students use the rubrics to keep track of their progress and also set goals for their future products or performances.

When students are asked to produce writing or other products, it helps them to see samples of what the teachers are expecting. What does the student's writing look like when it meets the target? However, it's also important that they see what it will look like if they go beyond the target or if they only partially meet the target. We recommend that students be given samples of work at each of the levels. Of course, the team won't give them samples on the exact question that is on the assessment but would provide examples from similar products or questions.

Using Rubrics for Scaled Questions

When your team writes questions for targets you have scaled, those questions will be designed to sort the student's levels of proficiency in a different way. With a scaled assessment, your team has created questions to assess *proficient* (level 3.0 questions) separately from questions that assess *beyond proficient* (level 4.0 questions) and *partially proficient* (level 2.0 questions). For each set of questions, the rubric may identify only what it will look like if the student meets that level or not.

For example, let's say your team is working on the seventh grade reading target "Trace and evaluate the argument and specific claims in a text, assessing whether the reasoning is sound and the evidence is relevant and sufficient to support the claims" (proficiency level 3.0). You add a proficiency level 4.0 target "Identify and defend which piece of evidence best supports the argument," and 2.0 target "Identify the key argument in a text."

You develop constructed-response questions for each of these targets and use the rubrics in figure 8.6 to score student work.

For the 4.0 target question:

4.0 Mastered	4.0 Not Yet Mastered
Identifies and clearly defends the strongest piece of textual evidence to support the author's claim	Does not identify and/or clearly defend the strongest piece of textual evidence to support the author's claim

For the 3.0 and 2.0 target questions:

Mastery (3.0)	Partial Mastery (2.5)	Below Mastery (2.0)	Well Below Mastery (1.0)
Correctly identifies and traces the claim (argument) and accurately evaluates whether reasoning is sound, relevant, and sufficient to support the argument	Correctly identifies and traces the claim (argument) and attempts to accurately evaluate whether reasoning is sound, relevant, and sufficient to support the argument	Correctly identifies and traces the claim (argument), but does not provide accurate evaluation of whether the reasoning is sound, relevant, and sufficient to support the argument	Does not correctly identify and trace the claim (argument), and does not provide accurate evaluation of whether the reasoning is sound, relevant, and sufficient to support the argument

Figure 8.6: Rubrics for scoring student work on constructed-response questions.

These rubrics allow the student to know exactly where he or she is in learning that target and exactly what they have to do the next time. The student can accurately say, "I've learned the level 2.0 target, but I still have to work on knowing when the reasoning in a piece of text is relevant and sufficient."

Next Steps

When your team has carefully laid out the rubrics with answers to your common formative assessment questions, and when you've gathered the data from the student responses, the next steps are to provide more time and support for students experiencing difficulty or provide enrichment opportunities for students who have met proficiency. With well-designed rubrics, these steps are much clearer and much easier. Rubrics that are well-designed can help your team—and your students—recognize what they need to do next to advance learning. We'll explore how your team responds to its assessments in chapters 10 and 11.

Tips for Teams New to the PLC Process

Chapter 8 of *Common Formative Assessment: A Toolkit for Professional Learning Communities at Work* (Bailey & Jakicic, 2012) provides ways teams can approach student feedback. If your team has not discussed the importance of student involvement in the assessment process, this is an important discussion to start with. Students need to be able to answer Sadler's (1998) three questions in order to effectively be a part of the process. Otherwise, assessment is something teachers do *to* students rather than something they do *with* students.

Remember that rubrics are the written descriptions for you and your students about expectations for student work. The more precise you can be with your rubrics, the greater the likelihood is that students will be able to meet your expectations. However, be cautious that you don't get so involved with choosing the words themselves that you lose sight of the purpose. Sometimes it helps to give the rubric to students to let them tell you what's unclear. At the same time, your team will want to write the learning targets on the rubric in student-friendly form. Many teams start the target with "I can" (see page 131). This helps you and your students see what they have to be able to do.

We highly recommend that you build a repertoire of student-work samples—both strong and weak examples—that you can use to show what each level of your rubric looks like. The more you work with these examples as a team, the more common your expectations for student performance will be.

Tips for Principals and Leaders

Probably the most difficult aspect for teams who will use rubrics in their assessments is making sure that each member applies the rubric in the same way. We've included in the appendix several protocols ("Collaborative Scoring Protocol" on page 199 and "Variation on Collaborative Scoring Protocol" on page 200) for teams to use for collaborative scoring of student work. It is critical that teams understand why they must score student work the same way. If they don't, the assessment can't be used to work collaboratively on the response because a *proficient* for one teacher doesn't mean the same thing as a *proficient* from another teacher. As principal, you may want to visit team meetings to have this discussion.

Making this happen also means that teams will need some extended time, especially at the beginning, to get familiar with and practice collaborative scoring practices. You may want to consider providing some released time for each team to work together for a half or full day after teachers give an assessment scored with a rubric. During this time, the teachers bring student work to the table and score it together to make sure they have common expectations. This embedded professional development may be some of the best staff development that occurs for your teachers. They will see clearly how each of them teaches and assesses students.

Part Four:
Working on the Work

9

Using Quality Instructional Practices

Collaborative Connections

- The CCSS require that teams examine their instructional practices and adjust those practices in order to better prepare their students.

- Teams should examine their practices to ensure that they sufficiently address the need for rigor and relevance, that they promote the four Cs (creativity, communication, collaboration, and critical thinking), and that they scaffold student learning of new concepts and skills.

- Teams must make these shifts in doable fashion. They should prioritize their focus as a team to manage the information and implement new practices.

We begin this chapter by highlighting a statement from the CCSS ELA:

> By emphasizing required achievements, the Standards leave room for teachers, curriculum developers, and states to determine how those goals should be reached and what additional topics should be addressed. Thus, the Standards do not mandate such things as a particular writing process or the full range of meta-cognitive strategies that students may need to monitor and direct their thinking and learning. Teachers are thus free to provide students with whatever tools and knowledge their professional judgment and experience identify as most helpful for meeting the goals set out in the Standards. (NGA & CCSSO, 2010a, p. 4)

Some teams might view this statement as a double-edged sword. On one hand, as professionals, it's comforting to know that we're not faced with a limited viewpoint of what works or a lockstep direction for how to teach. In fact, this statement reveals that we're given professional latitude to design instruction that is highly effective—the ability to use our experience and unique strengths and context considerations without dictated hoops through which everyone must jump. On the other hand, the statement also reveals the huge responsibility we have as professionals. Clearly, it's not the standards that make the difference, it's what *we* do to engage and empower our students to attain those standards.

What end do we have in mind? It's certainly not "Stepford Teachers"—everyone teaching exactly the same way on exactly the same day. While we *do* want to ensure that all students are learning the things that are essential—the guaranteed and viable curriculum—we're not asking teachers to standardize their teaching; we cannot take away the unique style and art that each teacher brings to the classroom. Yet we do want to share what works, and if there's a powerful strategy that results in high levels of learning, wouldn't you want that for all of our students? Furthermore, if one of the strategies you used *wasn't* effective, wouldn't you want to replace it with one that was? Wouldn't you all want our own children to receive the best possible instruction that builds his or her knowledge and skill in an engaging and effective way? Our charge as professionals working within professional learning communities is to work together to figure out what that best instructional practice looks like based on what we know right now and what we might strengthen in our teaching toolkits. This chapter focuses on what teams do to make decisions about effective practices in the context of the CCSS. It's not designed to give the reader specific strategies for teaching the Common Core—in other words, we're not giving you the "fish." Frankly, that would be an impossible task to complete. Rather, our hope is that the strategies in this chapter will help your team learn to fish. Let's look at what your team can do to work collaboratively and successfully while making instructional design decisions.

Responding to the CCSS Shifts

In chapters 1 and 2, we summarized some of the shifts that were evident in the CCSS. We shared that the guiding questions of a PLC are the ultimate framework to rely on when making the transition to the new standards. To re-examine the process collaborative teams use to address these guiding questions, we present figure 9.1, which you will likely recall from its appearance in chapter 1.

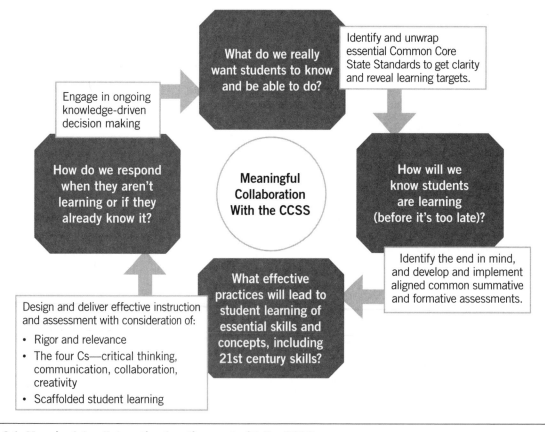

Figure 9.1: Meaningful collaboration for alignment with the CCSS.

We believe that an additional question is needed between steps two and three of the familiar set of four PLC guiding questions. We like to call this question 2.5: "What effective practices will lead to student learning of essential skills and concepts, including 21st century skills?" We are not alone in making this observation. Bradley Ermeling (2013) observes, "What's missing between 2 and 3 is the critical question that involves instruction: How will we teach this well so that all students learn?" (p. 2)

In this third step of the backward planning process, teams answer this question by proactively and collaboratively designing their instruction so that it embeds the types of instructional strategies and practices they know are effective in yielding high levels of student learning. Picture the team of scientists in the movie *Apollo 13* (Grazer & Howard, 1995). Remember the scene in which one of them dumps a box of supplies and tools onto a table and asks the team to construct the carbon monoxide filter that will aid the stranded astronauts? This is the same process. As a team, we're asking each other to bring our best tools to the table before instruction begins so that we can design a unit of instruction in a way that is most likely going to lead to high levels of student learning. Using this backward planning model allows teachers to share expertise, experience, and ideas up front—which, as a result, will increase the chance that more students will learn the skills and concepts that are most essential. By collaboratively planning their instruction, they will ensure that all students at that grade level or within that course will receive quality-first instruction. No longer does it depend on the individual teacher to figure things out or continue to use ineffective strategies because these are within his or her comfort zone. We're looking for strategies that have evidence of effectiveness.

Lesson Planning Versus Learning Planning

We feel compelled to invite you to recall some of the concepts discussed in chapter 6 (pages 93–95). When we describe teams coming together to share practices as part of their planning, we are not implying that they are simply coming in with their favorite worksheets or activities and offering them to other team members if they wish to accept them. The process isn't focused merely on what the *teachers* are doing, as often is the case in typical lesson planning. Rather, it is constantly focused on what the students will be learning—as we shared previously, we call this *learning planning*. The process of learning planning reflects teams being intentional about how they construct their instructional design based on the things they want students to know. The process reflects a *dot-to-dot* line of thinking (see figure 9.2). As a team, teachers first get absolutely clear about the knowledge and skills that are targeted in the unit of instruction (dot one). They then design summative and formative items to provide meaningful and timely data as to whether students are actually attaining that knowledge and skill (dot two). So here we are on to dot three—how are we designing our instruction?

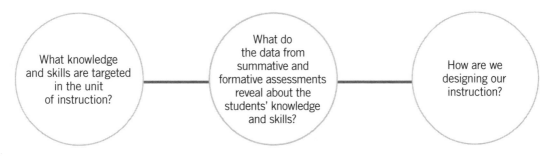

Figure 9.2: Dot-to-dot line of thinking.

As teams identify effective practices that will propel their students' learning forward, they may need to rethink their business-as-usual practices. They may find that asking questions such as, "What should we keep? What should we let go?" will begin creeping into their team's conversations. These are definitely the right questions! Doing things the same old way without examining their effectiveness is counter to the notion of continuous improvement in student learning—the foundational value within PLCs. Effective collaborative teams in a PLC look at evidence of effective practices and are open to letting go of things that support high levels of student learning. To ignore evidence of ineffectiveness is simply educational malpractice.

Shifts in the CCSS: Implications for Instructional Design

When deciding how to best organize this chapter, we began looking at the big ideas behind the CCSS—a big-picture view of how teaching to the CCSS might differ from previous standards. In doing so, we discovered that the considerations that teams make when designing instruction seemed to fall into three major areas: clarifying rigor and relevance, considering the four Cs, and scaffolding student learning (see figure 9.3). Let's walk through these considerations.

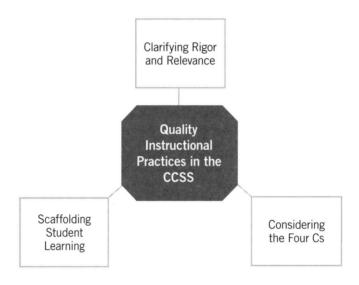

Figure 9.3: Elements of quality instructional practices for implementing the CCSS.

Clarifying Rigor and Relevance

In their article "What Do You Mean by Rigor?" Elliot Washor and Charles Mojkowski (2007) examine the issue of rigorous learning relative to the CCSS. They state, "Truly rigorous learning—both academic and nonacademic—involves deep immersion in a subject over time, with learners using sophisticated texts, tools, and language in real-world settings and often working with expert practitioners who serve as mentors" (p. 85). In other words, they don't define rigor as *difficult* work, but rather as *work in depth*. Rigorous tasks may be challenging and will stretch students' thinking, but they're not out of reach for students.

What is implied in Washor and Mojkowski's (2007) definition of rigor is the active learning on the part of the students and a strong connection between students and the *why* of the task. In other words, a driving problem or context helps to focus the students to not only become more knowledgeable about content but to apply and reflect on the result of that application. When we look at the pattern of rigor inherent in the CCSS, one thing stands out—the silver platter is gone. The message that the CCSS resoundingly communicate is that students must be placed in situations in which they struggle with *relevant* problems so that they can apply their knowledge and skills. They must read challenging text and use that text to support an argument being made either by an author or a thesis that they are asserting. They are expected to make sense of multiple sources of information, whether that information comes from a traditional textbook, an online resource, a primary document, or a technical report. This context is a very different scenario for some students. No longer are we pointing to the answers for students and saying, "Look right here for the answer!" We're not frontloading students in order to engage them in error-free or even struggle-free learning. This is a different mindset for those of us who have tended to take away the struggle students might encounter in learning. Trying to keep kids from feeling frustrated or *stretched* when encountering challenging work has an unfortunate result. They never get the opportunity to build those cognitive muscles and experience *efficacy* when their hard work pays off. What we are hearing from the world of work is that successful employees don't seek the easy way out—rather, they roll up their sleeves, hunker down, and persist with challenging issues and problems. We hope to build those mindsets with our students—that's what the Common Core State Standards are asking us to do.

When we use the term *relevance*, we're talking about the level of connection students will have to the content they are learning. It doesn't imply that they have personal experience, although relevance is more readily established when students have prior instruction or exposure to related or familiar concepts. A task is considered relevant when students have a purpose for knowing. The information they will be seeking will serve to answer a key question that the teacher has posed in the context of something that is meaningful, such as a real-life problem. When a task is relevant, students know the *why* behind their quest for information, and the task engages them in that quest to answer a meaningful question or solve a problem connected to their lives, either personally or generally. Learning that is relevant goes beyond learning something simply to be able to recite it back. Relevant learning implies application and connection to a larger context including real-world situations that are predictable and unpredictable (Daggett, 2012). Webb's Depth of Knowledge, as we discussed in chapter 4, offers teams a progression of relevance, a framework for examining the level of application or for processing knowledge. We feel Webb's taxonomy can help teams consider the types of learning experiences they are providing their students, particularly as they look at the relevance of their work. We cannot and should not simply amplify the difficulty of tasks and expect students to respond accordingly. When we make sure that rigor is connected to relevance and that the learning experience engages students as active participants rather than passive recipients, they will be more likely to move forward and meet the challenges they are presented with.

Let's take a look at this example of instruction that is rigorous and relevant based on a fourth-grade mathematics standard.

> Add and subtract mixed numbers with like denominators, for example, by replacing each mixed number with an equivalent fraction, and/or by using properties of operations and the relationship between addition and subtraction. (4.NF.3c) (NGA & CCSSO, 2010e, p. 30)

In a traditional approach, students might be taken through instruction that guides them through an algorithm with opportunities for modeling and practice and an assessment that gives them a number of mixed-fraction problems that are designed to determine whether they learned to whatever level of mastery is deemed appropriate. The focus is on the algorithm.

Let's look at another way of approaching this same standard. In an approach that reflects both rigor and relevance, students might be presented with a real-life problem, such as the need to organize and plan a party in which students had to prepare enough cookies for seventy-five students. However, their recipe, which contains many fractions, only serves twenty-five. Students will work together to determine how they will rewrite the recipe to make sure they will have enough cookies at their party. In this example, students have a *reason* for finding a solution to the problem. They need to make sure there are enough cookies for the party. Not only do they need to find a solution but also design their question and develop an appropriate equation. This is an example of rigor *and* relevance. Students are problem solving with a purpose. They're challenged and stretched but with a connection to something that is real and meaningful.

In chapter 4, we unwrapped standards to ensure that teams reached collective clarity about the end in mind of the standards. Through our description of the unwrapping process, we suggested some tools that help teams examine the rigor implied within those standards, including Webb's Depth of Knowledge (Webb, 2005), Bloom's Revised Taxonomy (Anderson & Krathwohl, 2001), and Marzano and Kendall's New Taxonomy (Marzano & Kendall, 2007). Remember, our purpose for examining the rigor implied within the standards was to ensure that your instruction and assessments were appropriately aligned to lead to that level of thinking and application. Our big idea is this: Teams must constantly reference the end in mind as they design their instruction and determine how they will guide their students' learning. The journey to high levels of learning is one that must be aligned and intentional. Let's move on to our next area of consideration when examining instructional practice.

Considering the Four Cs

The CCSS illuminate the instructional shifts needed not only to help students master the increased academic rigor found in the content of their K–12 education but also to truly prepare students for a success in a more rigorous *context*—the world of college and careers. This world of college and careers isn't a fixed context—in fact, we know that it will be difficult to predict the actual challenges that students will face a mere five years from now! To that end, we know that the CCSS integrate many of the 21st century skills and dispositions that students must possess as a result of their education. These skills and dispositions are not a means to an end but are reflective of the cognitive, academic, emotional, and physical competencies that individuals will need to succeed in 21st century life (Partnership for 21st Century Skills, n.d.a.). The Partnership for 21st Century Skills' Framework for 21st Century Learning focuses on outcomes and support systems for fostering life and career skills; information, media, and technology skills; and learning and innovation skills, also known as the four Cs: critical thinking, communication, collaboration, and creativity. Schools can address these outcomes through a focus on core subjects using the 21st century themes. See figure 9.4.

To further the alignment of the CCSS and the 21st Century Skills Framework, the Partnership for 21st Century Skills has created a Common Core Toolkit (see www.p21.org/tools-and-resources/publications /p21-common-core-toolkit) which may assist teams as they examine this integration. In this toolkit, the Partnership for 21st Century Skills recommends the following for moving forward.

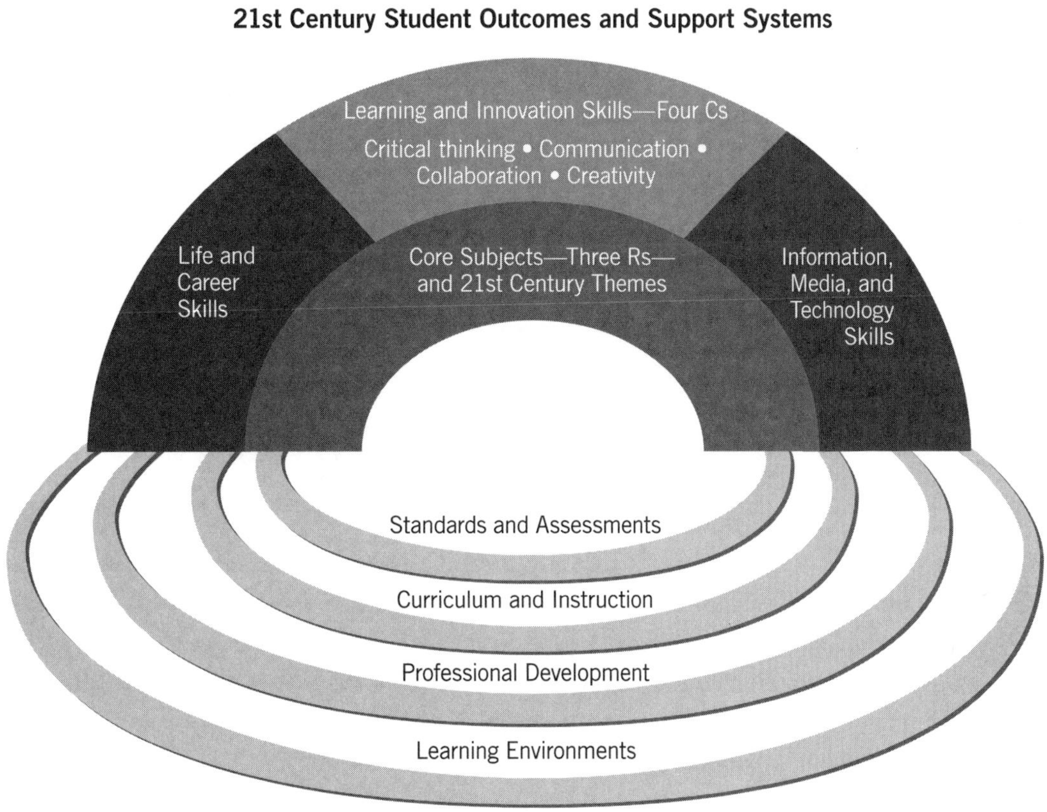

21st Century Student Outcomes and Support Systems

Figure 9.4: The Partnership for 21st Century Skills Framework for 21st Century Learning.

Source: Partnership for 21st Century Skills, n.d.a. www.p21.org. Used with permission.

- Ensure educators understand the importance of 21st century skills and how to integrate them into daily instruction.

- Enable collaboration among all participants.

- Allow teachers and principals to construct their own learning communities.

- Tap the expertise within a school or school district through coaching, mentoring, and team teaching.

- Support educators in their role of facilitators of learning.

- Use 21st century tools, such as digital media and social networking.

We feel that the parallels in focus and purpose between these recommendations and the tenets of PLCs are evident. This section will focus on the first recommendation: Understand the importance of 21st century skills and how to integrate them into daily instruction. This is a significant shift from a focus that traditionally emphasizes academics, yet we know it's a crucial one if we want to prepare our students for success in learning and life. Let's examine the skills being discussed, consider them in the context of the shifts contained within the CCSS, and discuss potential strategies for supporting their development.

When teams intentionally address strategies for embedding the four Cs into their daily instruction, they are empowering their students to be responsive to the ever- and quickly changing contexts they will face on entering college and careers. We feel that by examining the why of these four Cs and having a picture in mind of what practice could look like, teams will be able to examine the instructional activities they design for students and refine or rethink how they can construct their learning plans. While we'll discuss each of the four Cs in isolation, we want to remind you that they are naturally integrated with each other. In other words, we don't work on creating and then work on collaborating. Fostering these skills and dispositions is infused throughout instructional activities.

Creativity

When we look at this first C, we benefit from examining it through two questions. First, what opportunities do students have to *think* creatively? Are we structuring every learning event to have the correct answer, or are we providing opportunities for students to create new and worthwhile ideas? Are we letting students brainstorm new ways of tackling a problem, or are we merely pointing to the right way of doing something?

Second, what opportunities do students have to create in collaboration with others? While the question might seem redundant, it's actually emphasizing the need to engage students in a very different skill set—working and communicating with others, including the ideas and opinions of others, to develop a new idea or product. Feedback from the workforce reminds us that this skill set is crucial to the workplace. Have you ever experienced an individual who *wasn't* in possession of this skill set? Even though an individual student might have great ideas, we need to make sure that he or she is empowered to communicate those ideas and work with others to make them a reality.

During a TED conference presentation, Sir Ken Robinson (2006) passionately points out the importance of nurturing creativity in *all* students across all subject matters, not simply the arts. In a humorous yet pointed fashion, he poses that we stigmatize mistakes through our traditional approach to learning and that students are educated out of creativity when the environment fails to foster learning through making mistakes, innovating, and approaching problems in multiple ways. This is a bold statement, and one we feel is worthy of considering as we redesign our instruction.

Here are some potential strategies that foster creativity and innovation. Mind you, this list is not exhaustive. We encourage teams to examine these ideas and use them as starting points to bring in strategies and opportunities designed to encourage and foster creativity and innovation in students. As you read this list, think about how integral the items are to the CCSS. We've added a few sample references to the standards to help illustrate the connections.

- Use group brainstorming to identify potential research questions or solutions to a problem. For example, groups of students can be presented with a real-life mathematics problem and generate potential strategies with which it could be solved. In this activity, students could apply Mathematical Practice 1: "Make sense of problems and persevere in solving them" (NGA & CCSSO, 2010e, p. 6).

- Incorporate options for choice in creative work, such as designing informational brochures, writing poetry, or creating illustrations. These activities are emphasized frequently within the literacy standards. For example, consider this fourth-grade Reading Standard for Literature: "Make connections between the text of a story or drama and a visual or oral presentation of the text, identifying where each version reflects specific descriptions and directions in the text" (RL.4.6; NGA & CCSSO, 2010a, p. 11).

- Have students create alternative endings for stories or replace words with more elegant and engaging synonyms. This is particularly good when students are learning to create quality introductions or apply their knowledge of figurative language such as that required in this sixth-grade Language standard: "Distinguish among the connotations (associations) of words with similar denotations (definitions) (for example, stingy, scrimping, economical, unwasteful, thrifty)" (L.6.5c; NGA & CCSSO, 2010a, p. 53).

- Have students create media presentations to communicate concepts or information, something frequently referenced in the CCSS. An example is this ninth-grade Reading Standard for Informational Text: "Analyze various accounts of a subject told in different mediums (for example, a person's life story in both print and multimedia), determining which details are emphasized in each account" (RI.9.7; NGA & CCSSO, 2010a, p. 40).

- Use role playing to support development of perspectives or concepts, including the development of arguments presented to support a position on a topic. The CCSS Speaking and Listening standards facilitate this kind of activity. Consider for example this tenth-grade standard: "Respond thoughtfully to diverse perspectives, summarize points of agreement and disagreement, and, when warranted, qualify or justify their own views and understanding and make new connections in light of the evidence and reasoning presented" (SL.10.1.d; NGA & CCSSO, 2010a, p. 40).

- Provide an opportunity for students to create a movement-based demonstration to communicate their understanding of new concepts. For example, students can design a group movement in mathematics to depict the concept of place value as a way of showing their understanding of this first-grade mathematics standard: "Understand that the two digits of a two-digit number represent amounts of tens and ones" (1.NBT.2; NGA & CCSSO, 2010a, p. 15).

Classroom Example: Fostering Creativity

As part of their study of the effects of pollution on the environment, students in the second-grade class are given the option to self-select and work with one of four creative teams. Each team has the same purpose: to impact the community's awareness and behaviors related to pollution. One team's focus is creating a song that could be an antipollution anthem. Another team's task is to design and create a meaningful brochure. The third team focuses on creating a videotaped public service announcement, and the fourth team's task is to design an invention that would help consumers recycle.

Two things are at work here. First, this is clearly an intentional design to not only foster creativity but also to engage students in deeper thinking about the big ideas they are studying. Students, by being able to self-select, are able to engage in a creative area that taps into their interest and potentially their strengths. The teams have parameters for working together and rubrics to use in examining the quality of their work. However, they are not limited in *how* they approach the task.

Communication

Although traditional classrooms have focused on communication for as long as we can remember, the demands of our current and future contexts will require individuals to possess a much wider and deeper repertoire of communication skills that impact their learning and their lives. There's no doubt that your team might already be experiencing some of these shifts in your personal lives. Since 2000, you may have expanded your own experiences and vocabulary to include words like *blogging*, *Web 2.0*, and *wikis*. If you're like many teachers experiencing these digital shifts, your students may be even more adept at using these new tools than we are!

To realistically prepare our students for the future, we must ensure that they're able to communicate clearly—articulating their thoughts and ideas effectively through oral, written, and nonverbal communication skills in a variety of forms and contexts. They also need to communicate for a range of purposes and judge the effectiveness of those communications based on their audience. Finally, communication includes effective listening—being able to not only repeat what they hear but also to decipher the intentions, knowledge, and meaning behind the speaker's words (Trilling & Fadel, 2009). When we think of this area of instructional need, it's clear that simply expecting students to participate in communication activities won't be enough. Our goal as educators is to help students identify effective and ineffective practices for communicating, the needs of various audiences, the role that communication can play in persuading and informing others, and the tools that are most appropriate.

Developing students' communication capabilities is central to the purposes of standards within the Speaking and Listening strand of the Common Core ELA. Consider the impact of these anchor standards on building students' ability to communicate effectively.

> Prepare for and participate effectively in a range of conversations and collaborations with diverse partners, building on others' ideas and expressing their own clearly and persuasively. (CCRA.SL.1)
>
> Evaluate a speaker's point of view, reasoning, and use of evidence and rhetoric. (CCRA.SL.3) (NGA & CCSSO, 2010a, p. 22)

Teams should consider this focus on communication as a call to action to rethink their current practices and begin to look ahead to how their students will be expected to communicate in the very near future. Our prediction is that when you start to integrate practices that foster more student communication in a variety of formats and contexts, you will reap multiple benefits in both engagement and learning. Following are some examples of practices your team may want to consider.

- Have students write blogs related to specific content. Require responses from classmates. There are a number of student-appropriate blog tools available for educators, such as WordPress (http://wordpress.org), PBworks (http://pbworks.com/education), and Penzu (http://penzu.com).

- Engage students in digital storytelling, focusing on a specific topic but also embedding video clips and other media into the story.

- Ask students to explain a concept to others in a number of ways, including working with other students, providing live presentations, creating or engaging in asynchronous conversations (such as a discussion thread), or engaging in synchronous conversations (such as videoconferencing).

Collaboration

When we examine the concept of *collaboration* within the context of what success looks like in the real world, three specific skill sets are evident (Partnership for 21st Century Skills, n.d.).

1. To work effectively and respectfully with others

2. To exercise flexibility, compromise, and willingness to assist others so that a common goal can be met

3. To assume shared responsibility for collaborative work, including valuing each team member's contributions

While the notion of having students work together within a classroom is not a new one, our awareness of its importance has definitely increased. In addition, our definition of what collaboration *could* look like is expanded to include others outside of the classroom, such as professionals within a particular field of study or other students around the world. Students will be expected to collaborate with others in a number of contexts, including face-to-face or virtually.

As teams begin to examine how they build in opportunities for collaboration, they must also consider how they teach skills of effective collaboration. What does it look like when collaboration is effective? What might result in ineffective collaborations? Just like teachers, every student needs to develop these skills. We can't simply throw students into the deep end of the pool and expect them to swim without adequate preparation and support.

Critical Thinking

Let's look at how the Partnership for 21st Century Skills (n.d.) defines the skills needed in critical thinking and problem solving. Students should be able to do the following.

Reason effectively: Use various types of reasoning (inductive, deductive, and so on) as appropriate to the situation.

Use systems thinking: Analyze how parts of a whole interact with each other to produce overall outcomes in complex systems.

Make judgments and decisions: Analyze and evaluate evidence, arguments, claims, and beliefs; analyze and evaluate major alternative points of view; synthesize and make connections between information and arguments; interpret information and draw conclusions based on the best analysis; and reflect critically on learning experiences and processes.

Solve problems: Solve different kinds of unfamiliar problems in both conventional and innovative ways; identify and ask significant questions that clarify various points of view and lead to better solutions. (www.p21.org/overview/skills-framework/260)

Here's the good news: in our examination of the CCSS, we've discovered significant emphasis on the level of critical thinking and problem solving these outcomes describe. In literacy, for example, the standards place significant emphasis on analyzing information, evaluating the quality of information, and building arguments supported by evidence. Likewise, the Mathematical Practices focus on students' abstract reasoning, constructing viable arguments using logical progressions, and solving complex problems. Here's the reminder: as teams, we must ensure that we embrace this heightened emphasis on critical thinking and problem solving so that our students are given the opportunity to think. We can strengthen these skills by engaging students in a variety of activities, such as research, inquiry, and other problem-solving activities.

By purposefully embedding and integrating the four Cs into your instruction and providing students with ongoing experiences through which the four Cs are strengthened, you will be helping your students build skills and confidence they will benefit from throughout their life. Later in this chapter, we highlight project-based learning as a vehicle to support all of the four Cs as well as all of the other shifts in the CCSS (see page 151).

Scaffolding Student Learning

Inherent in the CCSS is the notion that students will be facing more challenge—challenging problems, challenging texts, and challenging contexts. However, students will not simply rise to the occasion by mere presentation of these challenges alone. We must design our instruction to systematically support and build those skills that enable students to meet those challenges. That systematic support is referred to as *scaffolding*. The goal of scaffolding is to provide support and gradually release the supports so that students are empowered with new skill sets that enable them to function independently. Think of how babies learn to walk. First, it doesn't happen overnight. Babies practice. They stumble and fall. They may get frustrated. Second, there is a natural sequence to and expectation of needed support. We would never let a baby sit in the middle of the room without the support of a walker, a piece of furniture, or a parent's nurturing hand and let him or her figure it out alone.

As a team, we must ask two questions: (1) What is the *appropriate* support for our students as they face the challenges in learning, and (2) Are we *organizing* our instruction to systematically provide that support?

It's important to note that there are appropriate times during which we *want* students to struggle, and these are definitely foundational principles guiding the CCSS. One such example is how, at one time, we might have approached a learning activity in which students were encountering new and challenging text. In our well-intended efforts to ensure that students had the best likelihood of success while reading a tough passage, we would frontload them with a great deal of background information, ensuring that they knew what the passage was going to be about, the challenging words contained in the text and what they meant, and any insights about the author's thinking. This approach resulted in students who might have had a modicum of success reading the passage, but who didn't walk away having developed the skills required to read complex text. In other words, we inadvertently provided too much support. We created a dependency on frontloading of challenging text, which didn't empower students.

As teams design units of instruction, they should ensure that across the unit and across the year, they are intentionally scaffolding the skills they are trying to develop. The gradual release of responsibility model of instruction is a structured method that embeds the concepts of creating a learning process through which the responsibility and ownership of new concepts and skills are eventually transferred to the learner (Pearson & Gallagher, 1983). While many educational theorists and practitioners have operationalized this model, we like the simplicity of the "I do it, We do it, You do it" model Douglas Fisher and Nancy Frey (2008) describe. This model embeds the sequence that transitions from teacher demonstration and modeling, to group processing and practice, and finally, to independent practice and mastery. Table 9.1 describes guiding questions and resources applicable to selected instructional and practice considerations—clarifying rigor and relevance, considering the four Cs, and scaffolding student learning.

Table 9.1: Considerations for Effective Instructional Practices

Considerations for Instruction and Practice	Guiding Questions	Sample Tools and Digital Resources
Clarifying Rigor and Relevance	Are we building sufficient background knowledge and hooking students with the *why* of learning in this unit? Have we created a compelling reason to learn this information? Who is driving the inquiry? Are we designing our instruction to provide appropriate depth and application of students' knowledge in this unit?	Cognitive Rigor Matrix (Hess, 2009) Rigor/Relevance Framework (Daggett, 2012)
Considering the Four Cs	Are we embedding opportunities that ask students to brainstorm and develop original ideas toward solving a problem? Designing something? What and how are students expected to communicate within this unit? Are we supporting and integrating the effective use of digital tools as a means to communicate in a variety of ways and to a variety of audiences? What is our expectation for students to collaborate with their peers or other relevant individuals during this learning? Have we provided support and guidance for their ability to do this effectively? Are we asking students to solve problems and tackle challenging concepts? Are we asking them to think in terms of systems beyond their immediate context? What type of decisions are we asking them to make based on information they are seeking? Are we challenging them by having them conduct meaningful research and inquiry?	Partnership for 21st Century Skills (www.p21.org) Buck Institute for Education (www.bie.org) http://pbl-online.org www.edutopia.org www.teachingchannel.org
Scaffolding Student Learning	What is the appropriate type of scaffolding for this area of learning? Are we systematically building skills that transfer ownership for learning to the student? Are we employing an "I do it, We do it, You do it" structure to ensure that students are receiving sufficient modeling, practice, and engagement with these new concepts and skills?	Fisher & Frey, 2008

Project-Based Learning

Project-based learning (PBL) is an approach for engaging students in relevant and rigorous learning activities that are authentic in nature and have as the outcome some solution or answer to a real-life problem or question. The model of instruction involves providing students with complex tasks based on challenging questions or problems and often involves students working in collaboration with others to problem solve, research, investigate, and communicate their findings. Variations of project-based learning exist and include problem-based learning and enriched learning projects (Bellanca, 2010).

According to the Buck Institute for Education (n.d.), rigorous and meaningful effective project-based learning is intended to teach significant content, and requires critical thinking, problem solving, collaboration, and various forms of communication. Inherent in PBL is the requirement that students conduct inquiry and create something new, whether it is an idea or a product. The projects are always based in *need-to-know* relevancy for students, and there is an underlying purpose for their work. As teams examine this option for structuring their instruction, they must also consider the implications for teacher practice. Teachers must be versed in developing student inquiry, managing a project-based classroom, and building facilitation skills that guide students rather than simply presenting them with knowledge to memorize.

The Journey of Changing Instructional Practice

We hope that this chapter provides teams with a sense of hope about how they might approach their instructional practice with the CCSS. It's an exciting time, yet we realize the challenges may seem overwhelming. As you embark on the journey of clarifying rigor and relevance, considering the four Cs, and scaffolding student learning, start with the notion of *refinement*, not complete *redo*. Your initial efforts will likely bring positive results which serve to fuel your future efforts. We suggest beginning with an area that you all agree to study and implement. As a team, conduct an honest assessment of your collective practice. Collectively, ask significant questions such as:

- Are we harnessing the power of instruction to truly prepare our students?

- Are we giving students the opportunity to work with others to solve authentic problems?

- Do we facilitate and foster students' creativity and innovative solutions and give them a chance to try things out?

- Are we expecting students to communicate to a variety of audiences in a variety of ways?

We suggest you initially focus your efforts on one or two elements you identify in this assessment so that the end result is a team *empowered* versus a team *paralyzed* by too much input at once. Prioritize your first efforts. For example, you may decide as a team that your initial focus will be placed on building in strategies to scaffold students' ability to read complex text, and conduct activities all centered on that focus. As a team, you might study strategies for engaging students in reading complex text, such as conducting *close reading* (Fisher et al., 2012). After building shared knowledge in the area, you might all agree to embed close-reading opportunities for your students at least once per week, and you might strategize a common assessment around the students' ability to read complex text. Finally, after reviewing the results and the impact on student learning, the team would then reflect on their next steps for deeper implementation. Within the area of mathematics, your team may decide to first adjust their instructional approach by utilizing the phrase "explain your reasoning" on a regular basis during daily checks for understanding.

Stay in Touch With Effective Practices

Just as we want our students to be responsive to a quickly and ever-changing world, so must our instructional practice. We strongly encourage teams to keep abreast of successful instructional research and guidance. This is an ongoing proposition; we're never done learning. As a result, you need to tap into a constant spring of resources so you don't stagnate. Here are some ideas to consider as a team.

- Follow a blog or Twitter.
- Focus with your colleagues.
- Join an online community.
- Participate in webinars.
- Read books that can provide practical information to your team.
- Participate in action research to study the impact of your practices on student learning.

Another way to stay in touch with effective practices is to keep abreast of professional literature. While this chapter focuses primarily on the areas requiring a shift of thinking from our prior standards, we by no means want to ignore the tremendous amount of information available on effective teaching practices. A number of key works are available to prompt teams' use of effective practices that yield high levels of learning. While the resources available are endless, we've listed a few of our favorites and have categorized them by topic so that teams can quickly reference them as needed.

Resources for Effective Practice

General Instructional Strategies

- *Classroom Instruction That Works: Research-Based Strategies for Increasing Student Achievement* (Marzano, Pickering, & Pollock, 2001)
- *Understanding by Design* (Wiggins & McTighe, 2005)
- *The Art and Science of Teaching: A Comprehensive Framework for Effective Instruction* (Marzano, 2007)
- *Visible Learning: A Synthesis of Over 800 Meta-Analyses Relating to Achievement* (Hattie, 2009)
- *Better Learning Through Structured Teaching: A Framework for the Gradual Release of Responsibility* (Fisher & Frey, 2008)
- *Productive Group Work: How to Engage Students, Build Teamwork, and Promote Understanding* (Frey, Fisher, & Everlove, 2009)

Literacy

- *Common Core English Language Arts in a PLC at Work*™ series (Fisher & Frey, 2013a, 2013b, 2013c, 2013d; Fisher, Frey, & Uline, 2013)
- *Teaching Students to Read Like Detectives: Comprehending, Analyzing, and Discussing Text* (Fisher, Frey, & Lapp, 2012)

Mathematics

- *Common Core Mathematics in a PLC at Work*™ series (Kanold, 2012a, 2012b, 2012c, 2012d, 2013)

Project-Based Learning

- *Enriched Learning Projects: A Practical Pathway to 21st Century Skills* (Bellanca, 2010)

Digital Learning

- *Teaching the iGeneration: 5 Easy Ways to Introduce Essential Skills With Web 2.0 Tools* (Ferriter & Garry, 2010)

Tips for Teams New to the PLC Process

Talking about best instructional practices is something that feels pretty natural for most teachers. The difference between typical conversations about instructional strategies and those collaborative teams hold within a professional learning community, however, is that in a PLC, there is a continuous focus on what works—in other words, what instructional strategies have the best chance to result in high levels of learning. Rather than simply sharing preferred activities or projects, collaborative teams make the most of backward planning, taking a close look at the end in mind of the standards and designing an instructional experience that embeds practices that research supports. We encourage teams to use the processes of brainstorming and consensus building when making decisions about how best to approach instruction when planning common units.

Tips for Principals and Leaders

It's common for teams to want to jump into conversations about instructional strategies and engaging activities without first being clear about what students need to know and do. As a result, conversations may fall back on favorite practices rather than a true plan for learning that aligns to the learning targets. To avoid this pattern, remind teams that this phase is part of the backward planning process, and they should spend time discussing instructional practices only *after* they've built common understanding about the specific learning targets and intent of the standards.

That said, as a site, you may examine some common instructional practices that need emphasis across all disciplines or courses. For example, structuring student participation in collaborative conversations is one instructional practice that you might examine as a staff, with a focus on determining some collective commitments about how those structures could be embedded across teams, grade levels, or departments. Other strategies that could serve as a schoolwide or departmentwide focus include the close reading of informational text, citations of evidence within informational writing, digital learning, and opportunities for innovation. We suggest prioritizing one or two areas per year so that teams can build their knowledge of the practices, practice implementing them, and share the results of their practices through reflective activities. Of course, it's important to celebrate the differences seen in student engagement and learning, which reinforces the implementation of these powerful practices.

10

Responding When Students Need More Time and Support

Collaborative Connections

- Collaborative teams have a greater capacity to respond to student needs than individual teachers have.

- Collaborative teams that clearly answer the first two critical questions of PLCs will have an easier time providing time and support for students in need than those who don't.

- Understanding the coherence of the Common Core State Standards will aid teams in responding to identified student needs.

We've often preached that giving a formative assessment and not responding to the results in your classroom is really equivalent to not giving the assessment at all. Unfortunately, we've seen teams go through the hard work of writing, giving, and scoring assessments and then not knowing what to do next with the results. The CCSS may change the actual response teams will use, but many other structures and practices will remain the same. Let's first examine what stays the same.

Observing What the Data Show

If your team has written your common formative assessments as we've described, by choosing a small number of learning targets and writing questions specifically for those targets, you will be set up to respond to the data quickly and easily. Teams should organize assessment data by *learning target* and *student*.

Take for example, a fifth-grade team who gives a mathematics assessment around two learning targets: (1) when adding fractions with unlike denominators, find equivalent fractions with the same denominator, and (2) use the equivalent fractions to solve problems. The team writes four multiple-choice questions to assess the first target and one constructed-response question to assess the second. When creating the assessment, the team decides that a student must answer three out of four multiple-choice questions to be considered proficient on the first target. For the second target, team members develop a rubric with four levels: *beyond proficient*, *proficient*, *partially proficient*, and *not proficient*. Students must meet the criteria listed for either beyond proficient or proficient in order to pass this target. After scoring the answers, each teacher creates a list of students who did not reach proficiency on the first target and a second list of those students who didn't reach proficiency on the second target. Some students will be on one or the other list, and some students will be on both.

If the team scaled each of the two learning targets, the teachers will have questions written for proficiency level 4.0, proficiency level 3.0, and proficiency level 2.0 for both targets. Students who score either a level 2.0 or level 1.0 will be listed as those students who need more time and support on that particular target. Again, a student might need help on one or both of the targets.

Creating Time for Response

Quality core instruction must include time for teaching students as well as time for assessment and corrective instruction when teachers identify students as having difficulty with a particular learning target. We are purposely using the term *corrective instruction* rather than *intervention* to differentiate the response that we believe must be a part of quality core instruction and what many now call their Tier 1 response (Buffum, Mattos, & Weber, 2012). We also believe your team should create pacing guides to allow for time—during the regular instructional period—for response (corrective instruction) to common formative assessments as we suggested in chapter 6.

Tier 1 responses are those that happen for all students and are considered part of core instruction.

Tier 2 responses are considered supplementary to the core instructional program and happen for only some students who need more time and/or support.

Tier 3 responses are considered more intensive and happen for those students who require much more time as well as more individualized support.

Take for example, a fifth-grade team with three teachers who plan to adjust instruction based on the assessment results. This team may decide to reassign all students the day after the assessment based on the results: one teacher takes all of the students who were proficient, one teacher takes all of the students who were partially proficient, and the third teacher takes all of the students who were not proficient. The team plans a different activity or lesson for each of these groups based on what it believes will help the group to make progress forward. The corrective instruction occurs during the regular class period. The team assigns students to the new teacher for only that class period, and they are not grouped together for the future.

In another example, a high school creates a master schedule so that in any period core instruction occurs; teachers make sure there are two sections meeting during that period. That is, they might assign two sections of algebra 1 during periods one, four, and six. In this case, the teachers can exchange students between the two teachers: one teacher takes the proficient students, and the other takes the students who aren't proficient.

Finally, there will be times when teachers decide to keep all of their own students and respond in their classrooms. For this situation, the team plans the different activities or lessons to respond to each group of students, but the classroom teacher must conduct the lessons at the same time as he or she would in a typical differentiated lesson.

No matter how your team creates time for the response, the response to the common formative assessment occurs as part of the regular instructional time and not as a separate intervention or separate class. Because all students and all teachers are involved in this response time, it will be important that no new instruction occurs during this response time.

For students who aren't proficient on the common formative assessment, teachers need to give another assessment after the corrective instruction to ensure the student has achieved proficiency on the learning target. If the student is still not proficient after corrective instruction, your team will continue to move forward with its new instruction and ensure students have more time and support through a Tier 2 or Tier 3 intervention program schedule at another time. The classroom teacher may provide this additional support (Buffum, et al., 2012) but it will not occur during direct classroom instruction. For example, Tier 2 interventions might have identified students receiving more instruction around a specific topic such as adding fractions. This instruction occurs in a smaller group for a period of time until the student has demonstrated understanding about this concept. Tier 3 intervention might occur for students who are having difficulty with math operations in general and need more individualized support over more than a short period of time.

The assessment teachers use after the corrective instruction might be the same assessment that they used as the CFA taken previously or it may be an alternate version of that assessment. Your team will want to make this decision based on the grade level of your students as well as the type of questions you use in the assessments. If it's likely for students to remember the questions from the first assessment, you will likely want to use alternate questions for this reassessment.

How your team structures time for supporting students may vary by grade level, subject area, and even team size. Table 10.1 (page 158) has a summary of ideas for finding time.

Transitioning From Your State Standards to the CCSS

What *will* change for most classrooms and teams across the United States is the actual response to assessment results that will be required to meet the greater demands for rigor in the CCSS. In the past, schools and teams developed their response plans using their state standards—standards that were in place for a number of years. Now, your team is developing a plan to help students who might not have been taught the prerequisite skills for these new standards—especially if this is the first year of implementation of the CCSS. You must consider what will be taught for all students and what will be taught for smaller groups of students. We know that the rigor of the CCSS increases demands on students' learning. This means that the expectations have increased for most students, and these expectations won't necessarily wait for students to catch up during this transition time. Therefore, your team will need to be reactive to the new data to move your students beyond where they currently are to where they need to be. Your team may find that the gap between your current students' learning and the new level of proficiency is wider than it was under your former state standards.

In fact, for science and technical subjects and history and social studies classes, your team will now have standards in ELA that never before existed. For example, seventh grade social studies teachers might be teaching this Reading standard: "Cite specific textual evidence to support analysis of primary and secondary sources" (RH6-8.1). In the future, incoming students who have been taught the CCSS ELA will bring more knowledge into your courses about such things as referring to primary- and secondary-source documents, reading and writing arguments, and looking for reasoning that is reliable. In the meantime, you must be prepared to provide instruction, for all your students, that helps to close this gap in student learning.

Table 10.1: Finding Time for Support

Team	Ways to Find Time for Response
Elementary Grade-Level Team	In these schools, the master schedule provides a block (literacy or mathematics) for the teams at the same time. They may also have some additional support staff available to them during this block—either certified staff (special educators, EL teachers, and so on) or noncertified instructional assistants. The teachers may group together students by data from the CFA and assign them to different teachers for response.
Elementary Grade-Level Team	If the teachers choose not to move students from their homerooms or if the master schedule doesn't support common teaching time, the team can still *plan* the response together, developing different activities for each group of students. The teachers then keep their own students and respond during the regular instructional period.
Middle School Content-Area Team	In some middle schools, teams plan the master schedule so that there are always two sections of a course meeting during an instructional period. For example, two sections of eighth-grade mathematics meet during first period. These teachers can then share their students between the two teachers for a day of response. One teacher takes the students who aren't proficient, and the other takes those who are.
Middle School Content-Area Team	When the master schedule doesn't support sharing students between teachers, the team can still develop its plans collaboratively so that all of the teachers have a response for those students who didn't reach proficiency, as well as for those who did reach proficiency.
High School Course Team	In high schools, teams must plan time for teachers who teach the same course to work together to design responses for students. Just as in the middle school scenario, some high schools will develop their master schedules so that when any section of a core course meets during a certain period, there is a second section of that same course that meets at the same time. When this happens, the teachers can group together students across classes by who met and didn't meet proficiency.
High School Course Team	For noncore courses, or in schools unable to schedule classes at the same time, teams of teachers who teach the same course can plan ways to respond to students in a collaborative way. Each teacher keeps his or her students but plans for a differentiated response. This ensures that all students have access to the same response when they need additional time and support.

To ensure that there are no gaps, you will likely want to review the previous grade level or course to see how a particular standard is written; this will allow you to scaffold student learning to include information that wasn't previously taught. The Institute for Mathematics and Education (http://math.arizona .edu/~ime/progressions) has created progressions documents for the Common Core mathematics to support this work for selected skills and concepts. These progressions can help you see any content and skills that you need to scaffold as you help students (Common Core Standards Writing Team, 2012). For example, for students learning about fractions in grades 3–5, teachers can use the progression document on the domain Number and Operations—Fractions to review what previous learning their students will be expected to have. As your team plans to respond to those students having difficulty on a particular learning target, it will be important for you to consider whether the student has been exposed to the expected prerequisite skills. If not, teachers must provide explicit instruction in the prerequisite skills and concepts for students who are experiencing difficulty.

For the ELA standards, prerequisite knowledge plays an important role in that each standard relies on the grade-level standard before it. For example, consider the Informational Text standard for sixth grade, "Trace and evaluate the argument and specific claims in a text, distinguishing claims that are supported by reasons and evidence from claims that are not" (RI.6.8; NGA & CCSSO, 2010a, p. 39). In seventh grade, the standard reads, "Trace and evaluate the argument and specific claims in a text, assessing whether the reasoning is sound and the evidence is relevant and sufficient to support the claims" (RI.7.8; NGA & CCSSO, 2010a, p. 39). For the first year of implementation, the seventh-grade teacher will likely have to explicitly teach how an author supports claims with reasoning and evidence before he or she can teach about sound reasoning and relevant evidence. After the first year of implementation, students will enter seventh grade with stronger prerequisite knowledge.

Designing the Right Response

When your team plans its response for students who haven't learned a target the first time, it becomes imperative that you consider the cognitive demands of the learning target. If your team uses our protocol for unwrapping standards, you've likely done this already. By considering the proficiency level for a target on a taxonomy list, you are identifying the cognitive demand or thinking what proficiency requires from students. By considering this, you can *back up* the concept to examine where a student's learning is interrupted. That is, after identifying the level of thinking on a taxonomy list, consider what the thinking levels or learning targets are that precede the expected learning. This process is spelled out in chapter 4 (see pages 70–72).

For example, when a team unwraps the fourth-grade Informational Text standard "Refer to details and examples in a text when explaining what the text says explicitly and when drawing inferences from the text" (RI.4.1; NGA & CCSSO, 2010a, p. 14), it finds the following targets written explicitly in the standard.

1.   Refer to details and examples in a text when explaining what the text says explicitly.

2.   Refer to details and examples in a text when drawing inferences.

The team members begin completing the unwrapping template by listing these two targets; the first one, they believe is a simpler skill, and the second is a more complex skill. See figure 10.1 (page 160), which illustrates the details included in the unwrapping template.

During the unwrapping process, the teachers also discuss that students need to know what an inference is in order to be able to draw inferences as they read and so they list "Know an inference is a conclusion or judgment a reader makes from the information the author provides" as a simple knowledge learning target. They also include a simple skill "Comprehend and generalize informational text" as an implicit target for this standard.

This team administers a CFA on the learning target "Refer to details and examples in a text when drawing inferences from the text" by giving the students a piece of informational text to read and asking them to make some inferences. After scoring the responses, the teachers see that some students aren't proficient on that target.

	Learning Targets	Taxonomy Level	Assessment Type
Knowledge or concepts students need to know	**Simple** • Know that an inference is a conclusion or judgment a reader makes from the information the author provides.	Level One: Retrieval	Multiple-choice questions after students read a piece of text
	N/A	N/A	N/A
Skills students will do	**Simple** • Comprehend and generalize information from informational text. • Refer to details and examples in a text when explaining what the text says explicitly.	Level Two: Comprehension	Multiple-choice questions on the same piece of text
	Complex • Refer to details and examples in a text when drawing inferences.	Level Three: Analysis	Constructed-response questions from the same piece of text
Context or criteria			
Academic language and vocabulary	Inference	Level One: Retrieval	Multiple-choice questions on the same piece of text

Figure 10.1: Sample unwrapping template for fourth-grade Reading Informational Text standard RI.4.1.

Developing a Hypothesis to Guide Your Work

Marzano (2007) discusses how important it is for good teachers to rely on both the art and the science of teaching. He describes the research around specific strategies that teachers know are effective as the *science* of teaching. He also makes the case, however, that good teachers don't just routinely employ those strategies without considering specific students' needs. Instead, they rely on their knowledge and experience to try out a variety of approaches—they use the *art* of teaching in their work.

We believe that high-performing teams capitalize on both the art and science of their work as well. Teams come together to discuss how to respond to the data they have about students who have and haven't learned the learning targets. They create a hypothesis about why this has happened. Their hypothesis includes professional judgment, experience with students at that age or grade level, and understanding of quality instructional strategies.

In the example in figure 10.1, the team decides to group all of these students who haven't learned the target "Refer to details and examples in a text when drawing inferences" together for corrective instruction. As the team plans the response, it makes a hypothesis—an educated guess—about why these students aren't proficient or where their learning of the target breaks down. In other words, did the student not have the prerequisite skills to learn this new concept, or did their thinking break down sometime during the learning process?

We believe that it's important to use the work you did during the unwrapping process to help you develop this plan. In figure 10.1, the team identifies the learning target "Refer to details and examples in a text when drawing inferences" as being at Level Three: Analysis in the New Taxonomy (Marzano & Kendall, 2007; see chapter 5, page 82). In creating a hypothesis about why these students experienced difficulty in learning this target, the team works backward on the taxonomy list to see what content or skills might be giving the student difficulty. The fourth-grade team knows that this particular learning target is built on the idea that students, who have reached proficiency on it, can also comprehend the text itself, know the meaning of an inference, and can understand the details and examples the author provides in the text. The team then must decide whether the student is having difficulty drawing the inference or citing the examples from the text to support the inference.

Let's say the team members make the hypothesis that the student's difficulty comes in seeing the direct connection from the information in the text to the inference the reader makes. The plan they develop for corrective instruction is based on this hypothesis. The team decides that to help students see this connection, the teacher must make this connection more explicit. To do so, the teacher creates sentence strips for each sentence in a paragraph from a new piece of informational text and posts them in the front of the room. The teacher then provides the students with an inference that a reader would make from that paragraph and asks the students to select the sentence that supports the inference. After several practice trials, and once the teacher feels students have gotten that concept, he or she reverses the work by selecting one sentence from another paragraph and asks students to make an inference from that sentence. For many students, this direct connection between the details or examples and the inferences a reader makes is all they need to be able to demonstrate this understanding in their own reading.

Similarly, for mathematics, consider the first-grade standard from the domain Number and Operations in Base Ten (1.NBT).

> Understand that the two digits of a two-digit number represent amounts of tens and ones. Understand the following as special cases:
>
> a. 10 can be thought of as a bundle of ten ones—called a "ten."
>
> b. The numbers from 11 to 19 are composed of a ten and one, two, three, four, five, six, seven, eight, or nine ones.
>
> c. The numbers 10, 20, 30, 40, 50, 60, 70, 80, 90 refer to one, two, three, four, five, six, seven, eight, or nine tens (and 0 ones). (1.NBT.2) (NGA & CCSSO, 2010e, p. 15)

When the team unwraps this standard, it agrees to assess the target "Understand that 10 can be thought of as a bundle of ten ones—called a 'ten.'" For this example, the team uses Webb's (2005) Depth of Knowledge taxonomy (see chapter 5, page 82) to plan for corrective instruction. The team works backward from the level of thinking of the actual target to see what other thinking the student must do. In discussing this target, the team decides that proficiency will expect student thinking to be Level Two: Skills and Concepts because the student has to go beyond recognition to organizing or classifying. As they plan their response for students who aren't proficient on this target, team members look at the DOK taxonomy to see what the simpler concept to this complex learning target is. They decide that students need to understand the simpler learning target they put on their unwrapping template—"know the concepts 'one' and 'ten.'" Figure 10.2 (page 162) presents the details of the unwrapping process.

	Learning Targets	Taxonomy Level	Assessment Type
Knowledge or concepts students need to know	**Simple** • Know one and ten. • Know that the far right number in a two-digit number is the number of ones. • Know that the first number in a two-digit number is the number of tens.	Level One: Recall	N/A
	Complex • Understand that 10 can be thought of as a bundle of ten ones—called a ten. • Understand that any objects left over when bundling tens are ones.	Level Two: Skills and Concepts	Constructed-response questions
Skills students will do	**Simple** • Count by ones. • Count by tens.	Level One: Recall	N/A
	Complex	N/A	N/A
Context or criteria			
Academic language and vocabulary	one ten	Level One: Recall	N/A

Figure 10.2: Sample unwrapping template for first-grade mathematics standard 1.NBT.2.

The team's hypothesis is that students are having difficulty seeing the connection between a *one* and a *ten*. The team develops a plan to have students work with place-value mats building double-digit numbers with their place-value manipulatives. Students actually "bundle" together their ones cubes whenever they have ten of them and move them to the tens column on their place-value mat. Figure 10.3 shows the team's plan. (See the reproducible "Developing a Response to a Learning Target," page 201.)

Learning Target	Planned Response
Proficiency Target Understand that 10 can be thought of as a bundle of ten ones—called a ten.	Students who have demonstrated mastery of the proficiency target may benefit from additional challenge. These students may work with some tasks that use the "ten" and "one" concepts to solve realistic real-world problems.
Simpler Content for Target Understand "one" and "ten."	Have students work with place-value mats grouping the ones blocks into tens blocks.

Figure 10.3: Sample response to a learning target.

In another example, a high school algebra 2 team is working on the learning target "Simplifies rational expressions" from the standard A-APR.D.6 (NGA & CCSSO, 2010e, p. 65). The teachers have given a short CFA on this learning target. When the team examines the data collaboratively, the teachers identify a group of students who got nearly everything incorrect. Because they asked the students to justify their answers on the assessment, they hypothesize that these students are weak in the prerequisite skills of reducing whole-number fractions. They realize that the next steps need to help students see the connections to the skills they learned several years earlier to being able to simplify expressions. They plan a lesson that helps students review the process with whole numbers and then builds in specific connections to expressions.

Using Scales to Develop the Response

The scales your team develops for each of your learning targets and assessment items to determine whether students have learned each level for that target make developing the response much easier. Take the example in table 10.2. The team develops the following scaled targets.

Table 10.2: Proficiency Scales for Learning Targets Based on Fourth-Grade Reading Informational Text Standard RI.4.1

Level 4.0	Evaluates an inference by the quality of the facts and examples
Level 3.0	**Refers to details and examples when drawing inferences from text**
Level 2.0	**Knows that inferences are based on the facts and details from the text**
Level 1.0	With help, partial success at score 2.0 content and 3.0 content
Level 0.0	Even with help, no success

This team created assessment items to determine whether students have learned the proficiency level 2.0 (simpler) target "Knows that inferences are based on the facts and details from the text" as well as whether they learned the proficiency level 3.0 target "Refers to details and examples when drawing inferences from text." After scoring the assessment, the teachers can identify more specifically where in the learning progression a student's understanding breaks down. If, for example, the student passes the 2.0 simpler target but not the 3.0 target, the misunderstanding happens at that step. In this example, the team knows that students understand that the inference and the details or examples from the text are connected to each other, but the student isn't able to be specific where the inference came from in the text. The team may want to focus its corrective instruction on helping students see where in a piece of text a particular inference comes from. In this case, the teacher might use a document camera to project a paragraph on the screen. He or she will then orally give the students an inference and ask the students to find the information in the text that supports that inference. Over time, the teacher makes the task more difficult by making the inferences more subtle. Figure 10.4 (page 164) summarizes the team's actions. (See the reproducible "Developing a Response to Scaled Learning Targets," page 202.)

Scale	Learning Target	Planned Response
4.0		
3.0	Refers to details and examples when drawing inferences from text	
2.0	Knows that inferences are based on the facts and details from the text	Use a document camera to project a piece of new text for the students to read. Provide an inference and ask the students to show—in the text—where the inference came from.

Figure 10.4: Sample response to a scaled learning target.

Developing Good Hypotheses

Developing a strong response for students having difficulty means making a good hypothesis about why students didn't understand the learning target in the first place. Using actual student work samples to see typical student mistakes often helps teams create a good hypothesis. For example, a third-grade team may see students select the first sentence in a multi-paragraph text as the main idea. The team recognizes that some students inaccurately believe that the topic sentence or main idea is always the first sentence. Teachers who work in high-performing collaborative teams are more likely to create good hypotheses than those who either work independently or who function more as a group than as a collaborative team. Some groups of teachers only share ideas but don't work together to judge and improve each new idea. Thus, they aren't really functioning as collaborative teams.

A good hypothesis is based on a number of factors, including the following.

- The team understands the learning target and the learning progression it takes to reach proficiency.
- The team has a wide repertoire of instructional strategies to use to teach concepts and skills.
- The team picks the best response strategy for students based on the data and information available.

The *art* of teaching supports this work.

Choosing the Best Strategy for a Response

We've discussed the way a team develops an understanding of the learning progression previously in this chapter as well as in detail in chapter 5 (pages 81–87) when we discussed building scales. We discussed the importance of choosing the best instructional strategy and having a wide repertoire of strategies in chapter 9. However, we haven't yet discussed ways high-performing teams choose the best response strategy. Teams who work well together value the data (information) their assessments provide. They are willing to share their results and to discuss whether certain strategies are better than others at helping students reach proficiency. One of the first steps we recommend your team takes when looking at your results is to examine the data to see whether one teacher or classroom has better results than the others. The purpose of this step is to judge the effectiveness of specific instructional strategies, *not* each other. For example, if one teacher gets better results than the rest of his or her colleagues, you will want to know what strategy he or she uses. Likely the team will decide to use that same strategy when helping the students who didn't meet proficiency.

To do this effectively, we encourage your team to make sure that you have team norms in place and to make sure those norms will help you share and evaluate data in a nonjudgmental way. (Use the reproducible "Survey on Team Norms," page 203, to reflect on your experiences as a member of a collaborative team.) For many teachers, having classroom data on the table for everyone to see can be somewhat threatening. When teams build norms to ensure that they are using data the right way, the threat is diminished. For example, your team may create the following norm, "We will use data to judge the effectiveness of instructional strategies, not to judge each other." Norms make developing effective hypotheses and responses much more likely. In addition to writing these data norms, it's important to regularly review them together at the beginning of your meetings and follow up when a team member doesn't follow one.

Another team consideration when developing a hypothesis to drive your corrective response is to look at which students will be involved in the response. Is there anything that you know about these students that can help your team develop a good hypothesis? For example, if the students are ELs, the team might want to consider whether some basic or academic vocabulary words are getting in the way. If these are students who tend to have difficulty making abstractions about content, the team will want to create a response that makes the abstract connection as explicit as possible.

Using Re-Engagement Lessons to Respond in Mathematics

Some teams we are working with are using a strategy in their mathematics classes to respond after a common formative assessment around a math task called a re-engagement lesson. This strategy comes from the Silicon Valley Mathematics Initiative (Foster & Poppers, 2009). This strategy is a way for teachers to respond to all of the various levels of understanding in the class in a whole group after the assessment is given. The idea of whole-group response is built on the belief that even students who were "correct" on the assessment task can learn more by exploring other ways the task was answered by other students. Students who didn't complete the task accurately will benefit from hearing from other students what their thinking was to solve the problem.

To plan a re-engagement lesson, the team examines the student work from the CFA and chooses two or three solutions that represent different ways to solve the problem—not all have to be accurate solutions. They plan the questions that will guide the lesson ahead of time. Students are given the multiple solutions (without student names) or the solutions are provided on large chart paper in the room. The teacher asks students the series of questions about the various responses and allows them to talk to a partner before answering to the whole class. The purpose of this is to reach a deeper level of conceptual understanding for all students. If the answer is inaccurate, the questions help students to see the underlying misunderstanding in the solution. In order to design a successful re-engagement lesson, the original tasks the students did as the assessment must have multiple ways of solving it and the mathematical concepts must be attached to the current lesson.

Going Beyond Tier 1

Teams in a professional learning community understand that some students need more time and support more often than others. They also believe that teachers must provide this time and support as the foundation of good teaching and, of course, student learning. However, when your Tier 1 response still isn't enough for certain students, your team will want to consider how you will find additional time for the students who continue to need it. This is the underlying thinking behind the response to intervention (RTI) model. We believe that this model is the best hope we have for ensuring that all students will learn and know many teams who are able to create success for students on these more rigorous standards as a result.

We're sure that your team feels it's equally important to respond to those students who have already reached proficiency by providing them some additional challenge. Chapter 11 describes this response in more detail.

Tips for Teams New to the PLC Process

Many of the teachers we work with who are new to the PLC process find planning and responding to the results of their CFAs a little overwhelming because they don't see how this is different from the work they try to do every day individually in their classrooms. Understanding the differences will help you and your team feel more confident that you can do this well. The first difference is that the collaborative team has a greater capacity to plan *and* carry out responses that are more effective than any one individual teacher can do in isolation. The second difference happens as a result of planning an effective assessment—one designed to assess a small number of learning targets. These quality assessments provide the specific information your team needs to plan most effectively. If teachers follow the steps we've laid out—identify essential or power standards, unwrap the standards into learning targets, and write short formative assessments around a small number of learning targets—they will find that they get back the information that makes this step much easier.

Often teams will get started by planning the response together but keeping all of their own students together for the actual response. This is a great first step. You will see that all of your students get a response—some corrective instruction and some enrichment. Once you feel more confident that you are getting the right data and creating quality responses, however, you can lead your team to try sharing students among teachers if the master schedule permits. You will then recognize how much more intensive you can make your response. This also builds a sense of all of the students belonging to all of the team members. Be aware that being willing to work this way means that teachers have to trust each other to be able to respond as effectively as they believe they can. Trust may take time to build, but planning together will be an important first step in establishing trust.

Additionally, it is important to provide time in the pacing guide after each common formative assessment to respond to the results of that assessment. This means carefully choosing the power or essential standards as the focus of your assessment system. We must be upfront—no team can effectively teach, assess, and respond to every standard teachers teach. Teams must collaboratively agree on their focus and their guaranteed curriculum.

If you are beginning to develop a systematic response in your school or district, *Simplifying Response to Intervention* (Buffum et al., 2012) provides a thoughtful explanation of how to use the culture you've built with your PLC practices to structure a strong response program.

Tips for Principals and Leaders

At the foundation of all good teaching practices is the importance of being able to respond in a way that gives each student what he or she needs. In education, we frequently talk about differentiation as the answer to this issue; however, many teachers see differentiation as an overwhelming goal. If teams consider the response we described in this chapter, they will be differentiating in a manageable way. They agree collaboratively on what is most important and plan differentiated responses on those specific learning targets.

Because the CCSS are likely more rigorous than your current state standards, it's really important for teams to see how understanding learning progressions and scaffolding learning strategies will benefit their response. This may be a new idea even for teams who have operated in professional learning communities for a long period of time. You may want to emphasize the commitment to continuous improvement to help them see that this is an extension of their previous work.

The best way to get good at this process with these new standards is to practice this process. That means that teams should start on this work at whatever part of the curriculum they are currently teaching. Try it out with a unit. Don't expect perfection, but be willing to learn together. As the leader, help teams to see that this can't be accomplished all in one year. Put a few common formative assessments in place this year and add to them each year.

In the past, many teachers have expected that students who need more help are either pulled from their classroom or have a support teacher "push in" to the classroom to provide that support. We believe that the teacher teams who are the experts on their own curriculum best provide Tier 1 support. Having the support from specialists to create smaller groups and to plan more effectively is certainly a bonus. However, the reality is that teams can do this work effectively without any additional personnel. As the leader, you must continue to communicate the value of the team response and help teachers see that their expertise is needed to make this work effectively.

Be aware that high-performing teams will have much greater success in helping students. Consider what skills your team leaders must have and provide them the training and support they need to manage and lead this work on their team.

11

Responding When Students Are Proficient

- Meeting the needs of students who are already proficient is more effective when collaborative teams work together to examine student data and plan instruction.

- Effective instruction that meets the needs of diverse learners begins with collaborative teams who have clear answers to the first two questions that guide their work in a professional learning community.

- Collaborative teams must have clear, focused, data-driven agendas and plans to ensure that all students reach their highest potential.

In what way does the thoughtful, strategic planning that teams engage in related to the first question, "What do we want our students to learn?" and the second question, "How will we know if our students are learning?" help collaborative teams to meet the needs of all students? We believe the true power of clear learning targets becomes evident when teams learn how to use the data from target-aligned assessments to make instructional decisions for students. We also believe it is even more powerful when students begin to understand themselves better as learners by using their own assessment data to determine learning targets of strength and those they might need to continue working on. In this chapter, we'll explore what happens when we encounter students who demonstrate that they *already* know the learning we identify as essential, or they demonstrate mastery early in the instructional cycle. How do we meet their needs? What do teams need to think about related to using the information from learning target-aligned assessments to extend and enrich learning for these students? This chapter is not about specific instructional strategies for differentiation, as there are many wonderful resources available for that. Instead, we focus on how collaborative teams successfully use assessment information about their students to determine that there is a need for differentiated instruction, focusing on what the students already know, and how that learning can be extended and enriched.

The Power of Preassessment

Gayle Gregory and Carolyn Chapman (2007) say it best in their book *Differentiated Instructional Strategies: One Size Doesn't Fit All*: "Yet for years we have planned 'The Lesson' and taught it to all, knowing that we were boring some and losing others because they were not ready for that learning" (p. 2). This problem occurs not because teachers are unaware of the differences in their students, but rather because they lack the specific information they need to tell them which students already know which learning targets. The reality is we don't always know who is bored and who is lost until they already are bored and lost.

One way to avoid this dilemma is to use a preassessment before instruction begins or shortly after a brief introduction to the lesson to find out what students already know. A common question is, "What happens if my team discovers that many students already know what we are about to teach? What do we do then?" Our answer is always, "Celebrate!" You have bought time for more in-depth learning regarding the concepts and skills students are not as proficient in. If we think of assessment as a part of the instructional process, it is only natural that we would want to know what students know prior to beginning instruction, throughout instruction, and when instruction is complete. Preassessment data provide formative information that teams can use immediately to guide instructional planning. Its purpose is to help the team make decisions about appropriate pacing and choosing the most effective instructional strategies for the students they are currently working with. As Diane Heacox (2009) states, "Without preassessment, you do not know the preparedness of your students for new learning, the specific learning differences amongst your students, or where to begin devising new curriculum goals" (p. 27).

We've seen teams successfully approach preassessment in three ways: (1) preassessment before starting a unit of instruction, (2) preassessment as daily end-of-period activity, and (3) preassessment after a brief period of initial instruction.

Preassessment Before Starting a Unit of Instruction

A more formal approach is to develop a preassessment for each unit of instruction and give that assessment at least one or two weeks prior to the beginning of instruction. Ideally, your team will want to have a team meeting after you gather the data to discuss how the results will impact your planning; therefore, having a week or two lead time is crucial.

The assessment itself can be created in a variety of ways. Some teams we have worked with use more summative, end-of-unit assessments as their preassessment without changing the assessment at all. In other words, teachers give the exact same assessment in the pre- and postassessment. Other teams select and use representative questions from the final summative assessment to preassess. This results in having a shorter, more focused assessment. Finally, some teams write questions that are similar to, but not exactly the same, as their final summative assessment. Keep in mind that the purpose of preassessment is to provide direction about what specific students already know about what is to be taught as well as about patterns of learning for this particular group of students.

Let's look at an example of a team that uses this more formal approach. Two weeks before the team is to begin instruction for a mathematics unit on decimals, students are given the end-of-unit summative assessment as a preassessment. Each teacher grades his or her own students' preassessments and enters the data into a shared spreadsheet in preparation for a team meeting focused on review of the preassessment data. (Many teams we work with are finding great success using Google Docs for shared data.) At the team meeting, the teachers review the data with a focus on not only the students within their own class that are already proficient on the learning targets but also on patterns that emerge from the entire grade level. These patterns help the teachers determine several strategies that could be used in individual classrooms to meet the differences in student learning and ways in which they could flexibly group the entire grade level in order to meet the needs the preassessment data identified. Discussions focus on enrichment activities that could deepen and extend learning for students who already know the skills and concepts that will be addressed in the upcoming unit of instruction. It is important to the team that these students be engaged in meaningful learning opportunities, not just more problems, harder problems, or activities to simply keep them busy. The teachers discuss ways to provide enrichment activities that provide students opportunities to pursue their interests, extend their understanding, and broaden their learning experiences (Guskey, 2010).

The team also plans more formative, informal checks for student understanding throughout the unit, so they can make adjustments to the plan along the way. They also arrange to give the same summative assessment at the end of the unit. One interesting question this team grapples with is whether to give the postassessment to the students who already demonstrate proficiency on the preassessment. Initially, as they are unsure about the implications of assessing some students differently, the teachers decide to give all students the postassessment. Later, after going through this cycle with several units, they begin to differentiate the assessments based on data from the preassessments as well as the data they gathered throughout the unit. Each student receives a postassessment that includes only questions aligned to the learning targets on which the teacher still needs additional information for each student. Being this sophisticated in differentiating their assessments is a result of experience as well as developing trust in their own assessment abilities.

Preassessment as Daily End-of-Period Activity

The second successful approach to preassessment we've used is a more informal approach. By using less formal assessments, the team can still gather data about both student knowledge and patterns, but the assessment itself is less obtrusive to the students.

Let's look at how the mathematics team in the previous example might use a more informal approach. A week or so before the team is to begin instruction for a mathematics unit on decimals, teachers present students with a daily end-of-period mathematics problem involving decimals to solve as their ticket out the door. One teacher explains to her students that they should do the best they can on the decimal problems, but that she does not expect them to know the information just yet. She explains that she wants to find out how much they already know before beginning the decimal unit. The teacher stands at the door collecting each ticket as the students exit the classroom. The teacher reviews the tickets each day, making three stacks of tickets by levels of mastery—the students who demonstrated complete mastery in one stack, partial mastery in another, and no mastery in the final stack. At the team meeting, the teachers review their stacks, focusing on how to meet the needs of students at all three levels of mastery, but particularly those who already know the information they were about to teach. Just as in the more formal example, the team discusses several strategies that teachers could use in individual classrooms and ways in which they could flexibly group the entire grade level in order to meet all three levels of mastery the informal preassessment identified. The team also plans more formative, informal checks for student understanding throughout the unit, so it can make adjustments to the plan along the way. The informal preassessment measure in this example is simply one way to approach preassessment informally. There are many options including ongoing student journals, focused observations, homework as preassessment, and so on.

Preassessment After a Brief Period of Initial Instruction

The third way we've seen teams successfully use preassessment is to give the preassessment after a very brief period (one class period or less) of initial instruction or review of the concepts. Some teams we worked with have found this method preferable, reporting that there is a difference in the depth of instruction that students need in order to demonstrate mastery. Certain students only need a brief review of the skills and concepts to demonstrate mastery, while others need more in-depth, thorough instruction.

This is an example of how as the teachers became more comfortable and skilled with the preassessment cycle, they began to adapt it based on what they knew about their students and the student data.

You might be asking, "What if my team is not ready for formal or informal preassessments yet, but we still want to use student data to adjust instruction and meet the needs of the different levels of learners in our classrooms after initial instruction?" It's certainly possible to provide challenge and enrichment for students without the benefit of preassessment data. In fact, some teams wait until later in their own learning about assessment to tackle the preassessment decision. When they do, however, it means that teams must use common formative assessments throughout their instructional unit and stop periodically to plan together for students who are demonstrating learning at mastery levels and beyond.

Let's look at the same team in the previous examples, but this time acting without the use of a formal or informal preassessment. The team is about to begin instruction for a mathematics unit on decimals, and teachers begin by reviewing the learning targets that will be addressed in the unit. Instruction related to one or two of the learning targets for the unit begins. After a team-designated period of instruction related to these targets, teachers give students a CFA. Each teacher brings information from this formative check to the team meeting. At the meeting, the same conversation from the previous examples ensues. The teachers review the data, discussing ways they can enrich and extend for students who are already proficient and provide more focused instruction for those that are not yet proficient. They discuss several strategies that could be used in individual classrooms and ways in which they could flexibly group the entire grade level in order to meet the needs identified from this formative data. The team also plans how teachers will address the next cycle of instruction within the unit, keeping in mind the information they now have related to student proficiency. This process requires that teams plan time in their schedule to meet the needs the student data identified. This could require an entire class period or more depending on the variance and depth of need they discovered in the student data.

All of these examples provide opportunities for teams to use assessment data to make instructional decisions for all learners, so that the students who are already mastering benefit as much as the students who may need more intensive instruction. It is imperative that teams learn strategies that will give students meaningful learning experiences when data show that they already know the skills or concepts. Clearly, the collaborative process is essential to the success of meeting all students' needs. Collaborative teams must have clear, focused, data-driven agendas and plans to ensure that all students reach their highest potential.

Scaled Learning Targets Enhance Differentiation

In chapter 5, we discussed the benefits of scaling learning targets to determine what each learning target would look like per level of proficiency. How can teams use scaled learning targets to provide even more focused enrichment and extension for students who already know the content and those who are not quite at expected proficiency? By using questions written for each level of the scale, the team is more accurately able to know exactly what the student has learned for each of the learning targets being assessed, and the planned instruction is likely to be better matched to the needs of the students.

"At its most basic level, differentiation consists of the efforts of teachers to respond to variance among learners in the classroom. Whenever a teacher reaches out to an individual or small group to vary his or her teaching in order to create the best learning experience possible, that teacher is differentiating instruction" (Tomlinson, 2000, p. 1).

Let's look at an example of how this will look in practice. A second-grade team begins a unit of instruction with a scaled preassessment. Prior to planning the unit, the team members scale the following Language standard: "Demonstrate understanding of word relationships and nuances in word meanings" (L.2.5; NGA & CCSSO, 2010a, p. 27). Table 11.1 shows this scaled learning target.

Table 11.1: Scaled Learning Target for Second-Grade Language Standard L.2.5

Level of the Scale	Powered Learning Target
Proficiency Level 4.0	Evaluate a piece of writing illustrating how carefully choosing words and looking at word nuances would enhance the piece.
Proficiency Level 3.0	Demonstrate understanding of word relationships and nuances in word meanings.
Proficiency Level 2.0	Identify the definitions of word relationships and nuances in word meanings.
Proficiency Level 1.0	With help, partial success at score 2.0 content and 3.0 content
Proficiency Level 0.0	Even with help, no success

The preassessment the team develops includes questions that assess student knowledge about targets at proficiency levels 4.0, 3.0, and 2.0. As second-grade teacher Amanda Smith examines her results from her class preassessment, she discovers that nine students in her class (35 percent) are already mastering the questions aligned to the proficiency level 2.0 and 3.0 learning targets, and four students (15 percent) demonstrate mastery on the questions aligned to the proficiency level 2.0, 3.0, and 4.0 learning targets. This indicates that 50 percent of her students are already mastering the expected learning target she will address in class over the next week. That is, they could go beyond the expectations she has set before instruction has even started.

Additionally, she learns that eleven students (42 percent) are mastering the proficiency level 2.0 learning target, but not the proficiency level 3.0 learning target, while two students (8 percent) are not mastering the proficiency level 2.0 or 3.0 learning targets. Figure 11.1 (page 174) lays out Mrs. Smith's data. This figure is available as a reproducible "Preassessment Data and Instructional Planning Chart" in the appendix (page 204).

Overall, Mrs. Smith establishes that her students are in very different places before instruction even begins. She knows that 50 percent of her class would not benefit from a basic lesson on figurative language and word choice, while others need exactly that. She begins to plan how she might approach each group using the assessment data and instructional planning document her team developed for this purpose. (See the "Instructional Plan" column in figure 11.2, page 175.)

She is particularly concerned about how to address the needs of students who already know the concepts and skills as she was unsure how to meet their needs. She needs the support of her teammates. She wonders what her teammates have found in their preassessment data, and she could not wait until the next team meeting to compare results, discuss strategies, and determine ways the team could meet the needs of each group of students. Figure 11.2 (page 175) shows the data for the second-grade teachers on the collaborative team. The team uses the same reproducible template "Preassessment Data and Instructional Planning Chart" (pages 204–205).

Figure 11.3 (page 176) shows the data for the second-grade team's instructional plan.

Teacher name: Mrs. Smith

Instruction start date: Monday, November 19

Learning target: Common Core Language standard (L.2.5)—"Demonstrate understanding of word relationships and nuances in word meanings."

Level of Scale	Preassessment Proficiency	Instructional Plan
Mastering levels 2.0, 3.0, and 4.0 learning targets "Evaluate a piece of writing, illustrating how carefully choosing the words and looking at word nuances would enhance the piece."	Lisa, Kevin, Lucas, and Staci (Four students: 15 percent)	**Individual Classroom (Classroom Teacher or Support Staff)** • Use more advanced vocabulary. • For students level 4.0 proficient, create peer-tutoring opportunities for other students who need support with these concepts. **Flexible Grade-Level Groups (Grade-Level Teacher or Support Staff)** • Put together a minimagazine or collection of writing.
Mastering levels 2.0 and 3.0 learning targets "Demonstrate understanding of word relationships and nuances in word meanings."	Kathy, Laurie, Nick, Brandon, Jon, Michelle, Connor, Shaun, and Liz, Lisa, Kevin, Lucas, and Staci (Thirteen students: 50 percent)	**Individual Classroom (Classroom Teacher or Support Staff)** • To move students to 4.0, present a minilesson on evaluating a piece of writing for inclusion of figurative language and specific word choice, identifying the effect on the overall quality of the piece. **Flexible Grade-Level Groups (Grade-Level Teacher or Support Staff)** • Evaluate writing for figurative language and word choice.
Not mastering level 3.0 learning target Mastering level 2.0 learning target "Identify definitions of word relationships and nuances in word meanings."	Lauren, Quin, Julie, Paul, Kim, Mike, Randy, Beth, Melissa, Becky, and Scott (Eleven students: 42 percent)	**Individual Classroom (Classroom Teacher or Support Staff)** • Present new lesson on understanding how to use specific word choice. • Create more opportunities for students to practice skills. • Work with peer tutor (level 4.0 students). **Flexible Grade-Level Groups (Grade-Level Teacher or Support Staff)** • Create opportunities for continued learning and practice.
Not mastering levels 2.0 or 3.0 learning targets	Samuel and Heather (Two students: 8 percent)	**Individual Classroom (Classroom Teacher or Support Staff)** • More intensive, focused instruction and practice with understanding the concepts of word meaning and choice **Flexible Grade-Level Groups (Grade-Level Teacher or Support Staff)** • Create opportunities for continued learning and practice.
Pattern Variations Mastering level 4.0, but not level 3.0 learning target Mastering level 3.0, but not level 2.0 learning target	None	If students fall into either of these patterns, first: • Check the assessment question. • Review the scale. • Check student answer again. • Have discussion with student to gather more information.

Figure 11.1: Sample second-grade teacher's preassessment data and instructional planning chart.

Team: Second-Grade ELA (Mrs. Smith, Mr. May, Mrs. Nielsen, and Mr. Ryan)

Instruction start date: Monday, November 19

Learning target: Common Core Language standard (L.2.5)—"Demonstrate understanding of word relationships and nuances in word meanings."

Level of Scale	Preassessment Proficiency	Instructional Plan
Mastering levels 2.0, 3.0, and 4.0 learning targets "Evaluate a piece of writing, illustrating how carefully choosing the words and looking at word nuances would enhance the piece."	Lisa, Kevin, Lucas, and Staci (Mrs. Smith) Hector, Leila, and Sammy (Mr. May) Liza and Joey M. (Mrs. Nielsen) None (Mr. Ryan) (Nine students: 9 percent)	**Individual Classroom (Classroom Teacher or Support Staff)** Differentiate in classroom Monday, Wednesday, and Thursday. **Flexible Grade-Level Groups (Grade-Level Teacher or Support Staff)** Work with Extended Learning Specialist on Tuesday and Friday.
Mastering levels 2.0 and 3.0 learning targets "Demonstrate understanding of word relationships and nuances in word meanings."	Kathy, Laurie, Nick, Brandon, Jon, Michelle, Connor, Shaun, Liz, Lisa, Kevin, Lucas, and Staci (Mrs. Smith) Robert, Cindy, Juan, Sophia, Isabella, Jacob, Mason, Emily, Molly, Madison, Ethan, Alex, Hector, Leila, and Sammy (Mr. May) Daniel, Anthony, Alissa, Anna, Sarah, Timmy, Olivia, Ilza, and Joey M. (Mrs. Nielsen) Colleen, Noah, Leah, Maya, Maria, and Zac (Mr. Ryan) (Forty-three students: 33 percent)	**Individual Classroom (Classroom Teacher or Support Staff)** Differentiate in classroom Monday, Wednesday, and Thursday. **Flexible Grade-Level Groups (Grade-Level Teacher or Support Staff)** Split group between Mrs. May and support staff or specialist on Tuesday and Friday. (Assess 4.0 again on Friday.)
Not mastering level 3.0 learning target Mastering level 2.0 learning target "Identify definitions of word relationships and nuances in word meanings."	Lauren, Quin, Julie, Paul, Kim, Mike, Randy, Beth, Melissa, Becky, and Scott (Mrs. Smith) Sydney, Riley, Jimmy, Kyle, Claire, Taylor, Audrey, and Toby (Mr. May) Ben, Logan, Lucy, Jocelyn, David, Morgan, Gavin, Julia, Luke, Evan, and Khloe (Mrs. Nielsen) Colton, Chrissy, Brody, Nate, Diane, Brooke, Anna, Luis, Cameron, Katie, Eli, Lynn, and Mia (Mr. Ryan) (Forty-three students: 42 percent)	**Individual Classroom (Classroom Teacher or Support Staff)** Differentiate in classroom Monday, Wednesday, and Thursday. Flexible Grade-Level Groups (Grade-Level Teacher or Support Staff) Split group between Mrs. Smith and Mr. Ryan on Tuesday and Friday. (Assess level 3.0 again on Friday.)

Figure 11.2: Sample second-grade team's preassessment data and instructional planning chart.

Team: Second-Grade ELA (Mrs. Smith, Mr. May, Mrs. Nielsen, and Mr. Ryan)

Instruction start date: Monday, November 19

Learning target: Common Core Language standard (L.2.5)—"Demonstrate understanding of word relationships and nuances in word meanings."

Level of Scale	Preassessment Proficiency	Instructional Plan
Not mastering levels 2.0 or 3.0 learning targets	Samuel and Heather (Mrs. Smith) Leona, Nicole, and Freddy (Mr. May) Adam, Oliver, Carson, and Brianna (Mrs. Nielsen) Aly, Jose, and Liam (Mr. Ryan) (Twelve students: 12 percent)	Individual Classroom (Classroom Teacher or Support Staff) Differentiate in classroom Monday, Wednesday, and Thursday. Flexible Grade-Level Groups (Grade-Level Teacher or Support Staff) Work with Mrs. Nielsen on Tuesday and Friday. (Assess levels 2.0 and 3.0 again on Friday.)
Pattern Variations Mastering level 4.0, but not level 3.0 learning target Mastering level 3.0, but not level 2.0 learning target	None (Mrs. Smith) Nicholas: 4.0, but not 3.0 (Mr. May) Anna: 4.0, but not 3.0 Blake: 3.0, but not 2.0 (Mrs. Nielsen) Thomas: 4.0, but not 3.0 Nolan: 4.0, but not 3.0 (Mr. Ryan) (Five students: 5 percent)	If students fall into either of these patterns, first: • Check the assessment question. • Review the scale. • Check student answer again. • Have discussion with student to gather more information. *After review with students, place them into one of the four groups.

Figure 11.3: Sample second-grade team's planning chart.

Just as Mrs. Smith uses the planning sheet, prior to the team meeting, the other team members enter their student results into a shared team document. The four teachers on the team previously decided it was more efficient to enter the data prior to the meeting so the team time could be focused on instructional planning instead of data entry.

The team data indicate that of the 103 students on their second-grade team, forty-three students (33 percent) are already mastering the questions aligned to the 2.0 and 3.0 learning targets, and nine students (9 percent) demonstrate advanced understanding of the concept by mastering questions aligned to both the 3.0 and 4.0 learning targets. This shows that nearly half (42 percent) of the students are already able to demonstrate mastery of the expected learning target prior to instruction.

These data are quite surprising to the team, as the teachers did not expect that so many students would already know the concepts and skills prior to instruction. Initially, this type of finding was stressful for the team because the data clearly indicate that these students need something different, and the teachers were not sure they knew what to provide. However, this finding compelled them to learn how to provide meaningful extension and enrichment.

They acquire strategies for differentiation in many different ways, many of them through job-embedded learning. Because they had studied the principles of professional learning communities, they knew that building shared knowledge would help them with their own learning. They investigate various resources, learning together the best way to meet the needs of their students. One of the teachers had been reading some literature on differentiation, and she created a summary of the ideas she found most interesting. They also worked with their building instructional coaches who supported their learning by providing resources, building their knowledge through minilessons, and modeling extension and enrichment lessons. One of the team members was able to participate in a workshop related to meeting the needs of diverse learners. The teachers realized that understanding how to meet the needs of their diverse learners was much more than creating some new activities for this unit of instruction. They needed to consider how to use time, student groups, and varied instructional strategies throughout their lesson designs.

The team also discovers that forty-three students (42 percent) are able to master the 2.0 learning target, but not the 3.0 learning target, while twelve students (12 percent) are not mastering the 2.0 or 3.0 learning targets. These students represent the typical group of students the teachers had planned for in the past—students who needed instruction on the learning targets in the unit.

Five students demonstrated an unusual pattern of mastery. Four students mastered the 4.0 learning target questions but did not master the 3.0 learning target questions, while one student mastered the 3.0 learning target questions but not the 2.0 learning target expectations. These unusual patterns do not happen often, but when they do, the first step is to investigate why this may have occurred. In our work with teams using scaled assessments, we have found that when there are just a few students with these unusual patterns, it means that there was some student misunderstanding related to the question or the student did not read the directions carefully. Usually, a brief conversation with the student to check for understanding solves the problem. On the other hand, if there are many students with these unusual patterns, it often suggests a problem with either the assessment question or the learning target. Once the issue is thoroughly investigated, the students with these patterns should be identified as either beyond mastery, mastering, partially mastering, or not mastering the learning target.

Thinking Differently About Time

Once the team identifies the patterns in the student data, the teachers discuss the best way to approach instruction for each group. First, they explore how they could best use their time and how they could group students to maximize their different current levels of knowledge. The team has access to additional support staff and a specialist at certain times during the week and wants to use those extra adults in their planning, so teachers decide to differentiate instruction within their own classrooms on Monday, Wednesday, and Thursday and to mix up their student groups for flexible grouping on Tuesday and Friday.

Teachers share ideas for differentiating instruction within the classroom at the team meeting, with each teacher sharing his or her ideas from their individual classroom planning sheet. Each teacher would be responsible for planning lessons for Monday, Wednesday, and Thursday, and the team would plan together the lessons for the flexible groups on Tuesday and Friday.

Thinking Differently About Student Groups

The team divides the students in the largest subgroup, made up of forty-three students who mastered the proficiency level 2.0 learning target questions but not the proficiency level 3.0 learning target questions, into two smaller groups. Each smaller group works with one classroom teacher during flexible grouping, receiving instruction focused on building knowledge and skills related to the proficiency level 3.0 learning target. These are the students who met the traditional expectations of having some prior knowledge about the learning target but needed the regular instruction for the learning target itself. These students are able to show that they know the simpler concepts and could do the simpler skills outlined in the level 2.0 learning target, which provides the teacher with valuable information about what the student can do, providing a good starting point for instruction. In this school, students also now know what they can do, where they currently are, and where they need to go in order to master the proficiency level 3.0 learning target expectation.

The twelve students who did not master the proficiency level 2.0 learning target questions or the proficiency level 3.0 learning target questions need the most direct, intensive instruction as even the simpler concepts and skills are difficult for them. A different classroom teacher works with these students during flexible grouping, scaffolding learning to enable the students to move from mastery of the level 2.0 learning target to eventual mastery of the level 3.0 learning target.

The forty-three students who are already proficient on the levels 2.0 and 3.0 learning target questions and the nine who are already mastering the levels 3.0 and 4.0 learning target questions participate in instruction focused on deepening and extending their learning related to this target. The forty-three students who are already mastering the proficiency levels 2.0 and 3.0 learning target questions but not the level 4.0 learning target questions work with one classroom teacher and a support staff on mastery of the proficiency level 4.0 learning target expectation.

This team has access to a specialist who works to support students at any time they demonstrate advanced understanding of learning targets and need extension and enrichment. This specialist works with the nine students who are already mastering the levels 3.0 and 4.0 learning target questions during the flexible grouping on Tuesday and Friday with instruction focused on even more advanced extension of the learning target. She also supports teachers in learning how to meet the needs of these students in the classroom. All students, with the exception of the nine students who demonstrated advanced understanding of the learning target, will be assessed again on Friday to check for understanding after instruction has occurred. The team will discuss this data to determine any remaining student needs and devise a plan to meet these needs.

We know that many of you must be thinking that this team has a lot of resources and support, and that is what makes this work. While we agree that access to resources, including support staff and time, makes it easier to provide this type of focused, differentiated reinforcement for students, we also know that teachers can do it with limited or nonexistent resources and support. All it takes is a dedicated, motivated team of teachers willing to get a little creative in planning and instruction.

Thinking Differently About Instructional Strategies

Many teachers worry that they don't know enough about how to plan instruction for the students who need more challenging activities. You may have noticed that this team was able to work with a specialist; however, it isn't necessary to have a specialist for this type of extension to happen. We have worked with teams who did not have any support staff available to them but still found ways to adjust instruction to meet the needs of all learners in their classrooms. One team focuses on making sure that every teacher on the team is skilled in differentiation, particularly for students who needed extension and enrichment within their own classrooms. Team meetings are focused on strategies teachers tried, discussing what was working, what was not working, and how they were adjusting to make instruction as effective as possible. Instead of assuming that the answer would come from somewhere else, the teachers realize that they already have lots of knowledge and ideas about how to challenge students. When they look at their scaled targets, it becomes much more apparent how they would teach students to "Evaluate a piece of writing" differently than it would be to teach "Demonstrate understanding of word relationships." By having worked through the scaling process, they tap into their own knowledge about matching instructional strategies to student needs. They also realize that by focusing their differentiated instruction on specific learning targets and identifying exactly what students could benefit from, they are much more confident that they can respond appropriately.

Many other teams have found creative ways to flexibly group students, using only the classroom teachers and within the constraints of their schedules. Most importantly, effective teams, regardless of resources, feel compelled to act when they focus on student data and use them to make instructional decisions.

Clearly, not every preassessment will provide these types of varied results. There will be times when it will not be necessary to differentiate on such a large scale before instruction begins, as it is likely that the majority of students will not be able to demonstrate proficiency on the preassessment. However, we have seen it happen many times in our work, and when teams are prepared, it is exciting to watch students thrive as a result of carefully planned instruction designed specifically to meet individual student needs.

What about preassessment? This example shows the team's response to preassessment data, but could this be done without preassessment? Absolutely. The scaled common formative assessment could be given after instruction, using the same planning chart in figure 11.3 (page 176). The same team conversations could occur as outlined in the preassessment example, only this time the conversations will focus on postinstruction data. In this case, the data tell you where each of your students is after instruction has occurred. Are the students clear on the simpler concepts and skills but not quite proficient on the expected concepts and skills, or are they proficient on the expected concepts and skills and the more difficult or extended concepts and skills? Once you know where the students are in their learning, you and your team can work together to determine how to respond.

It will still be essential that your team build in instructional time to respond to the student needs identified from the assessment. One teacher we worked with describes her experience this way, "It is obvious that in all classrooms, the needs of students are very different. The scaled assessment results provide a starting point for differentiation as well as a way to help teams of teachers discuss differentiated instruction, especially for the students who already knew everything I was about to teach! Student data from scaled assessments help drive initial instruction as well as intervention and assessments."

Secondary Classrooms

As we discussed in chapter 10 (page 158), the master schedules for secondary schools often limit the way that teams can flexibly group their students for differentiation. If the school's master schedule is designed so that there are always two sections of a class meeting during a particular period, the teachers could regroup their students for instruction at two or more levels. However, if this isn't the case, the team would still benefit from planning their response together. By having the right data to know exactly where students are in their learning, the team would plan for different levels of instruction.

The collaborative team structures outlined in this chapter can be useful in helping teams discover how to meet the needs of diverse learners. Each can be adapted to work within the context of your school, district, or team. They also deepen the capacity of collaborative teams to function as an effective community of learners focused on meeting the needs of all students. These structures rely on teams to keep the focus on learning as their main outcome, to collectively learn how to meet student needs based on student data, to take action based on what they learn from the data, and to commit to continuous team improvement as well as student improvement.

Tips for Teams New to the PLC Process

A good place for your team to start is by having discussions regarding how you are currently meeting the needs of students who already know the standards in an upcoming unit. This discussion can center on the strategies each individual has tried or strategies the team may have used in the past. You may find that some of the strategies that you are using are working well, while others need to be tweaked. Think about how you currently identify students as needing enrichment or extension and whether or not the strategies you are currently using provide true extension opportunities for these students. You can also begin to explore how preassessment can help you determine the students who already know the concepts and skills that will be taught. If you are not ready for the preassessment discussion, then decide how you will use common formative assessments or informal checks for understanding to know where students are in the learning process, so that you can respond appropriately.

Tips for Principals and Leaders

How to effectively meet the needs of students who are already proficient is one of the most challenging questions for teams to consider. Teachers may not know how to differentiate instruction effectively for these students or even what data to use to determine who needs extension. You will need to be clear about what constitutes appropriate extension strategies and what does not, as well as your expectations for using assessment data to determine students who need extension. For example, it would not be appropriate to give students extension worksheet packets and leave them on their own to complete them. It is possible that worksheets can provide appropriate extension, but the teacher will need to closely monitor student progress. Similarly, teachers should be able to tell you exactly how they know who needs extension, how they are providing extension, and how they know if students are meeting their extension expectations.

As we have stated in this section in other chapters, you will need to be in touch with teams often regarding how they are approaching extension and providing a balance of pressure and support as they determine together the best ways to address this issue.

Final Thoughts

Consider this school. The fifth-grade team is exiting its monthly staff meeting bearing grim faces. Pausing together in the hallway of their school, the teachers look at each other, alternating glances between the shocked faces of their colleagues and the three-ring binders containing their Common Core documents. Almost in unison they cry, "Where do we get started?"

This scene is one we didn't want you to experience. We know the power of working together. We know that the guiding questions used within a PLC will light the way to clarity. Rather than letting the thought of transitioning to a new set of standards overwhelm you, standards that represent a more rigorous and integrated view of what students need to know and do, we want you to feel empowered with the comfort that you're part of a team that puts student learning in the forefront as its beacon and purpose. As a team focused on student learning, we wanted to make sure you have the tools—a set of processes that you can walk through to get common clarity and make appropriate adjustments to your curriculum design, instructional practice, assessments, and differentiated support for students. This was our purpose for writing the book.

As we close this book, we want to encourage you on this journey. While we don't promise it will be easy, we do promise that approaching it as a team will bring about a sense of accomplishment, satisfaction, and efficacy—knowing that your hard work pays off. Knowing that this is about continuous improvement, we'll end our book using the words from the beginning: Happy learning!

Appendix

Reproducibles

Loose Versus Tight Decisions

For each of the following decisions, the leadership team should decide whether it is a *loose* decision (left up to the team) or a *tight* decision (left up to leaders).

Activity, Process, or Task	Loose	Tight
Question One: What Do We Want Our Students to Learn?		
Who will determine the power or priority standards—each school or a team of representatives for the entire district?		
Which subject or grade-level standards will be done first, next, and so on?		
Who will decide the completion date for power or essential standards?		
Who will determine when and how the vertical alignment process for power or essential standards will occur?		
Who will decide the pacing for the power or essential standards?		
Who will make specific curricular decisions (textbooks, instructional strategies, and so on)?		
Question Two: How Will We Know If Our Students Are Learning?		
How frequently will teams use common formative assessments?		
Who will write the common formative assessments?		
Will we use technology to score common formative assessments?		
Will we use technology to warehouse data from common formative assessments?		
What, if any, interim or benchmark assessments are used?		
Question Three: How Will We Respond When Some Students Don't Learn?		
How will we provide time for each tier of response?		
Who will provide each tier of response?		
What universal screener and progress-monitoring tools will be used to identify students?		
How will students be moved between tiers?		
What data will be kept on students for providing RTI?		
Question Four: How Will We Extend and Enrich the Learning for Students Who Are Already Proficient?		
Who will provide response for these students?		
How will the results be reported?		
How will students be identified for each tier?		

Protocol for Powering the Common Core

To answer the first question a collaborative team asks (What do we want our students to learn?), the team identifies power/essential standards. This protocol provides a step-by step process to do this work.

Preparation

1. Make sure the team is familiar with the three appendices for the ELA standards and appendix A for the mathematics standards and have copies on hand.

2. Each team member will need a copy of the grade-level or course standards the team is powering, and a copy of the standards for the grade level before and the grade level after or the course before and the course after.

3. Teams will use chart paper to write the initial draft list of the standards.

4. Provide copies of sample items (or whole test blueprint, if available) from PARCC or SBAC for each team.

5. The team should review what the criteria (endurance, leverage, and readiness) mean.

6. The team should review all of the grade-level standards to see how they are organized.

Process

Step One: Identify Potential Power Standards Using the Filtering Criteria. Each teacher privately reads the standards and identifies which standards he or she believes should be a power standard.

Step Two: Develop a First Draft Based on Team Members' Recommendations. The team works to build consensus on which standards should be powered for specific grade levels or courses.

Step Three: Determine Alignment Between Draft Power Standards and Other Related Documentation. The team considers PARCC and SBAC documents and reviews any data or test blueprints that provide information about which standards should be given more priority.

Step Four: Review for Vertical Alignment. All of the teachers review all of the standards on the draft list vertically, to see if there are gaps or redundancies. A final list of power standards for the school or district is compiled.

Basic Unwrapping Template

Standard to Address:

Context or Criteria:

| Learning Targets: | **Knowledge or Concepts Students Need to Know:** |
| | **Skills Students Will Do:** |

Academic Language and Vocabulary:

Unwrapping Template With Formative and Summative Measures

In this template, teams will list the concepts and vocabulary they must establish in support of the standard. Then, they can decide the formative measures to monitor student progress on those factors and the summative measures to determine overall achievement.

Standard to Address:		
Learning Targets	**Aligned Assessments**	
Knowledge or Concepts Students Need to Know	**Formative Measures**	**Summative Measures**
Vocabulary		
Skills Students Will Do	**Formative Measures**	**Summative Measures**

Leveled Unwrapping Template

This template can be used by teams to unwrap standards, and organize the learning targets into categories of "simple" and "complex." It also provides space for members to note any assessment ideas.

Guiding Questions

- What standards will we prioritize in our teaching during this instructional unit?
- What specific concepts or information do we want students to know? Are they simple or complex?
- What skills do we want them to be able to do? Are they simple or complex?
- What assessment will we use to ensure students successfully learned the concepts and skills?

Standard to Address:			
	Learning Targets	**Depth of Knowledge (DOK) Level**	**Assessment Ideas**
Context or Criteria:			
Knowledge or Concepts Students Need to Know	Simple		
	Complex		
Skills Students Will Do	Simple		
	Complex		
Academic Language and Vocabulary			

Protocol for Team Review of Unwrapped Standards

Purpose: This team protocol is to collectively examine standards that have already been unwrapped. The goal of this examination is to build common clarity of the skills and concepts teams identified for teaching and assessment in the unwrapped version, and provide an opportunity for modification or adjustments of those learning targets based on the professional experiences of the group.

Materials: Copies of unwrapped standards for a unit of study (one copy per participant)

Time: Approximately twenty minutes

Roles: Facilitator, notetaker, and timekeeper

Process

Step One

(Two to five minutes) Please note that there are optional structures provided within this step which may be selected depending on the desire of your team or structure of your meeting.

> Option one: Each member of the team reads the standards to examine and quickly circles the verbs, underlines the nouns, and places brackets around any information related to how well or in what context students will be expected to demonstrate their knowledge and skills.

> Option two: Teams work in small groups using a document camera or chart paper. Participants will engage in identifying key words while one member circles, underlines, and brackets the standard.

Step Two

(Five minutes)

1. Members examine the unwrapped standards, what they've written for the knowledge or concepts students need to know, and the underlined nouns. They pose the following questions. "Are all of the critical pieces of knowledge or concepts that we need to develop in this standard addressed in the unwrapped version? Do we see any that are missing? Any we might add? Are we all clear on the terminology the standards use?"

2. Members note any additional concepts or pieces of knowledge they would want their students to have and discuss work to clarify any confusing elements.

Step Three

(Five minutes)

1. Members examine the unwrapped standards, what they've written for the skills students will do, and the verbs they have circled. They pose the following questions. "Are all of the critical skills that we need to develop in this standard addressed in the unwrapped version? Do we see any that are missing? Any we might add? Are we all clear on the terminology the standards use?"

2. Members note any additional skills they would want their students to have and discuss work to clarify any confusing elements.

Step Four

(Five minutes)

1. Members discuss the context or criteria the standard implies. If they are unable to extract this information from the language of the standard, they examine the previous grade's standards or those in subsequent grades. Teams can also examine the CCSS appendices and the exemplars they provide to gain further information and build clarity about the intent of the standards. Some unwrapped standards also provide sample guiding questions and big ideas that can be used to frame instruction. If available, teams can examine them during this process to gain information about the context for learning and assessment.

2. What is our picture of success for our students? In what context will they be required to perform this task? With what level of complexity or rigor? Are there exemplars that we might find to inform our team of the picture of success?

Step Five

(Two minutes)

1. Members discuss the academic language or vocabulary that would be critical to emphasize within instruction and assessment.

Collaborating for Success With the Common Core © 2014 Solution Tree Press • solution-tree.com
Visit **go.solution-tree.com/commoncore** to download this page.

Comparison of Taxonomies

Bloom's Revised Taxonomy	Marzano and Kendall's New Taxonomy	Webb's Depth of Knowledge
Level Six: Create Generate Plan Produce **Level Five: Evaluate** Judge Critique	**Level Four: Knowledge Utilization** **Decision making** Decide: What is the best way? **Problem solving** Adapt: Figure out a way to … **Experimenting** Generate and test: What would happen if … **Investigating** Research: Take a position on …	**Level Four: Extended Thinking** Design Connect Synthesize Apply concepts Critique Analyze Create
Level Four: Analyze Differentiate Organize Attribute Compare	**Level Three: Analysis** **Matching** Create an analogy, Distinguish **Classifying** Organize, Sort, Identify **Analyzing errors** Identify errors, Critique, Diagnose **Generalizing** Draw conclusions, Create a rule **Specifying** Predict, Judge, Deduce	**Level Three: Strategic Thinking** Revise Construct Compare Hypothesize Cite evidence Formulate Draw conclusions
Level Three: Apply Execute Implement Carry Out	**Level Two: Comprehension** **Integrating** Describe the relationship between, Paraphrase, Summarize **Symbolizing** Depict, Represent, Illustrate	**Level Three: Skills and Concepts** Infer Predict Interpret Use context clues Estimate Compare Organize Graph
Level Two: Understand Interpret Summarize Classify Explain **Level One: Remember** Recall Identify Recognize	**Level One: Retrieval** (These aspects are hierarchical within this level only.) **Executing** Use, Show, Demonstrate **Recalling** Name, Describe, List **Recognizing** Select or identify from (a list) Determine (if statements are true)	**Level One: Recall** Define Identify List Measure Arrange Calculate Recall

Adapted from Anderson & Krathwohl, 2001; Marzano & Kenall, 2007; Webb, 2005.

Unwrapping Template With Taxonomies

This is a variation of the unwrapping template that can be used by teams to list their learning targets as they are identified. Teams then use this list when they are writing their common formative assessments.

Focus on Key Words:			
Standard to Address:			
Skills Students Will Do	**Knowledge or Concepts Students Need to Know**	**Context or Criteria**	**Level of Thinking**

Bloom's Revised Taxonomy	**Marzano and Kendall's New Taxonomy**	**Webb's Depth of Knowledge**
Remember Understand	Level One: Retrieval	Level One: Recall (DOK1)
Apply	Level Two: Comprehension	Level Two: Skills and Concepts (DOK2)
Analyze	Level Three: Analysis	Level Three: Strategic Thinking (DOK3)
Evaluate Create	Level Four: Knowledge Utilization	Level Four: Extended Thinking (DOK4)

Scaling Form

Level of the Scale	Powered Learning Target	Taxonomy Thinking Level	Suggested Assessment Strategies and Items
Proficiency Level 4.0			
Proficiency Level 3.0			
Proficiency Level 2.0			
Proficiency Level 1.0	With help, partial success at 2.0 content and 3.0 content		
Proficiency Level 0.0	Even with help, no success		

Planning Common Formative Assessments

Learning Target	Bloom: Remember/Understand Marzano: Retrieval DOK: Recall	Bloom: Apply Marzano: Comprehension DOK: Skills and Concepts	Bloom: Analyze Marzano: Analysis DOK: Strategic Thinking	Bloom: Evaluate/Create Marzano: Knowledge Utilization DOK: Extended Thinking	Total Number of Questions

Assessment Plan for Scaled Assessments

	Bloom: Remember/ Understand **Marzano:** Retrieval **DOK: Recall**	Bloom: Apply **Marzano:** Comprehension **DOK: Skills and Concepts**	**Bloom:** Analyze **Marzano:** Analysis **DOK: Strategic Thinking**	**Bloom:** Evaluate/Create **Marzano:** Knowledge Utilization **DOK: Extended Thinking**	**Total Number of Questions**
4.0 Target					
3.0 Target					
2.0 Target					
4.0 Target					
3.0 Target					

Analytic Rubric Template

Learning Target or Criteria to Assess	Beyond Proficient	Proficient	Partially Proficient	Not Proficient

Collaborative Scoring Protocol

In order to ensure that all members of your collaborative team are scoring student work consistently, your team should practice collaborative scoring. This protocol provides a step-by-step process to guide you through that activity.

Materials: Copies of the rubric, sticky notes, one or more pieces of unscored student work from each teacher's classroom

Step	Procedure	Time Allotment
1	Team reviews the student assignment and the rubric and discusses any scoring procedures that apply to the task.	Five minutes
2	Each team member scores one piece of student work without discussion and puts the rubric score he or she believes is appropriate on a sticky note on the back of the work.	Five minutes, depending on the length of the task
3	The team members pass the pieces of student work to a new team member who also scores the work and puts another sticky note on the back. This process continues until everyone on the team has scored all pieces of student work.	Up to twenty minutes
4	The team turns over a piece of student work to reveal the teachers' scores. The team members discuss the differences in the scores and explain why they each scored it the way they did. This continues until the team has discussed all pieces of student work or until the team feels confident teachers are applying the rubric in the same way.	Varies by the amount of discussion
5	The team makes any needed changes to the rubric to reflect new understanding.	Five minutes
6	The team discusses implications for future instruction and how to respond when students need more time and support.	Ten minutes

Variation on Collaborative Scoring Protocol

In order to ensure that all members of your collaborative team are scoring student work consistently, your team should practice collaborative scoring. This protocol provides a step-by-step process to guide you through that activity.

Materials: Document camera, copies of the rubric, three pieces of student work from each team member expected to represent various levels of performance

Step	Procedure	Time Allotment
1	Team reviews the student assignment and the rubric and discusses any scoring procedures that apply to the task.	Five minutes
2	The team displays the first piece of student work on the screen via the document camera. The team discusses each criterion on the rubric and builds consensus on the appropriate rubric score for each criterion.	Varies depending on the amount of discussion needed to build consensus
3	Team members score additional pieces of work one at a time while they build collective agreement about how to apply the rubric to various levels of student performance.	Varies depending on how many pieces of student work the team discusses
4	The team makes any needed changes to the rubric to reflect the members' new understanding.	Five minutes
5	The team discusses implications for future instruction and how to respond when students need more time and support.	Ten minutes

Developing a Response to a Learning Target

This template is provided for teams to use when discussing how to plan their response after a common formative assessment. For each learning target assessed, the team should plan what they will do for students who need more support to meet the proficiency target or extension to go beyond the proficiency target.

Learning Target	Planned Response
Proficiency Target	
Simpler Content for Target	

Developing a Response to Scaled Learning Targets

This template is provided for teams to use when discussing how to plan their response after a common formative assessment. For each level of the learning target assessed, the team plans an appropriate response—either supportive or challenging.

Scale	Learning Target	Planned Response
Level 4.0		
Level 3.0		
Level 2.0		
Level 1.0		

Survey on Team Norms

Team: _____ Date: _____

Use the following ratings to honestly reflect on your experience as a member of a collaborative team:

Strongly Disagree	Disagree	Agree	Strongly Agree
1	2	3	4

1. _____ I know the norms and protocols established by my team.

Comments:

2. _____ Members of my team are living up to the established norms and protocols.

Comments:

3. _____ Our team maintains focus on the established team goals.

Comments:

4. _____ Our team is making progress toward the achievement of our goals.

Comments:

5. _____ The team is having a positive impact on my classroom practice.

Comments:

Preassessment Data and Instructional Planning Chart

Teacher Name:
Instruction Start Date:
Learning Target (LT):

Level of Scale	Preassessment Proficiency (List student names.)	Instructional Plan
Mastery on 2.0, 3.0, & 4.0 LT		**In the Individual Classroom** (Classroom Teacher/Support Staff) **Flexible Grade-Level Groups** (Grade-Level Teacher/Support Staff)
Mastery on 2.0 & 3.0 LT		**In the Individual Classroom** (Classroom Teacher/Support Staff) **Flexible Grade-Level Groups** (Grade-Level Teacher/Support Staff)
Not Mastering 3.0 LT Proficient on 2.0 LT		**In the Individual Classroom** (Classroom Teacher/Support Staff) **Flexible Grade-Level Groups** (Grade-Level Teacher/Support Staff)

page 1 of 2

Collaborating for Success With the Common Core © 2014 Solution Tree Press • solution-tree.com
Visit **go.solution-tree.com/commoncore** to download this page.

Not Mastering on 2.0 or 3.0 LT		In the Individual Classroom (Classroom Teacher/Support Staff) Flexible Grade-Level Groups (Grade-Level Teacher/Support Staff)
Pattern Variations *Proficient on 4.0, but not on 3.0 *Proficient on 3.0, but not on 2.0		If students fall into either of these patterns: **FIRST** • Check the assessment question. • Review the scale. • Check student answer again. • Have discussion with student.

References and Resources

Ainsworth, L. (2003). *Power standards: Identifying the standards that matter the most.* Denver, CO: Advanced Learning Press.

Anderson, L. W., & Krathwohl, D. (Eds.). (2001). *A taxonomy for learning, teaching, and assessing: A revision of Bloom's taxonomy of educational objectives.* New York: Longman.

Arter, J. A., & Chappuis, J. (2006). *Creating & recognizing quality rubrics.* Portland, OR: Educational Testing Service.

Bailey, K., & Jakicic, C. (2012). *Common formative assessment: A toolkit for professional learning communities at work.* Bloomington, IN: Solution Tree Press.

Beck, I. L., McKeown, M. G., & Kucan, L. (2002). *Bringing words to life: Robust vocabulary instruction.* New York: Guilford Press.

Beck, I. L., McKeown, M. G., & Kucan, L. (2008). *Creating robust vocabulary: Frequently asked questions and extended examples.* New York: Guilford Press.

Bellanca, J. (2010). *Enriched learning projects: A practical pathway to 21st century skills.* Bloomington, IN: Solution Tree Press.

Black, P., & Wiliam, D. (1998). Inside the black box: Raising standards through classroom assessment. *Phi Delta Kappan, 80*(2), 139–144, 146–148.

Buck Institute for Education. (n.d.). *What is PBL?* Accessed at www.bie.org/about/what_is_pbl on September 22, 2012.

Buffum, A., Mattos, M., & Weber, C. (2012). *Simplifying response to intervention: Four essential guiding principles.* Bloomington, IN: Solution Tree Press.

Calkins, L. (2013). *Units of study in opinion, information, and narrative writing (K–5).* Portsmouth, NH: Heinemann.

Carnevale, A. P., Smith, N., & Strohl, J. (2010). *Help wanted: Projections of jobs and education requirements through 2018.* Accessed at www9.georgetown.edu/grad/gppi/hpi/cew/pdfs/FullReport.pdf on March 6, 2013.

Chappuis, J. (2009). *Seven strategies of assessment* for *learning.* Portland, OR: Educational Testing Service.

Common Core Standards Writing Team. (2012). *Progressions documents for the Common Core math standards.* Accessed at http://ime.math.arizona.edu/progressions on July 1, 2012.

Conzemius, A., & O'Neill, J. (2002). *The handbook for SMART school teams.* Bloomington, IN: Solution Tree Press.

Council of Chief State School Officers. (2012). *Framework for English Language Proficiency Development Standards corresponding to the Common Core State Standards and the Next Generation Science Standards.* Washington, DC: Author.

Daggett, B. (2012). *Rigor/relevance framework.* Accessed at www.leadered.com/rrr.html on September 1, 2012.

Darling-Hammond, L. (2010). *The flat world and education: How America's commitment to equity will determine our future*. New York: Teachers College Press.

David, J. L. (2008). Pacing guides. *Educational Leadership, 66*(2), 87–88.

Davis, L. (2012). *5 things every teacher should be doing to meet the Common Core State Standards*. Accessed at www.eyeoneducation.com/bookstore/client/client_pages/pdfs/5ThingsCCSS_Davis.pdf on July 1, 2012.

DuFour, R., DuFour, R., & Eaker, R. (2008). *Revisiting professional learning communities at work: New insights for improving schools*. Bloomington, IN: Solution Tree Press.

DuFour, R., DuFour, R., Eaker, R., & Many, T. (2010). *Learning by doing: A handbook for professional learning communities at work* (2nd ed.). Bloomington, IN: Solution Tree Press.

DuFour, R., & Marzano, R. J. (2011). *Leaders of learning: How district, school, and classroom leaders improve student achievement*. Bloomington, IN: Solution Tree Press.

EngageNY. (2012). *Instructional shifts for the Common Core* [PowerPoint slides]. Accessed at http://engageny.org/resource/common-core-shifts on July 1, 2012.

Ermeling, B. A. (2013, January 18). PLCs and the Common Core: Are we leaving instruction behind? *Teachers College Record*. Accessed at www.tcrecord.org/Content.asp?ContentId=17001 on January 20, 2013.

Ferriter, W. M., & Garry, A. (2010). *Teaching the iGeneration: 5 easy ways to introduce essential skills with web 2.0 tools*. Bloomington, IN: Solution Tree Press.

Fisher, D., & Frey, N. (2008). *Better learning through structured teaching: A framework for the gradual release of responsibility*. Alexandria, VA: Association for Supervision and Curriculum Development.

Fisher, D., & Frey, N. (2012). The perils of preteaching. *Principal Leadership, 12*(9), 84–86.

Fisher, D., & Frey, N. (2013a). *Common Core English language arts in a PLC at work, grades K–2*. Bloomington, IN: Solution Tree Press.

Fisher, D., & Frey, N. (2013b). *Common Core English language arts in a PLC at work, grades 3–5*. Bloomington, IN: Solution Tree Press.

Fisher, D., & Frey, N. (2013c). *Common Core English language arts in a PLC at work, grades 6–8*. Bloomington, IN: Solution Tree Press.

Fisher, D., & Frey, N. (2013d). *Common Core English language arts in a PLC at work, grades 9–12*. Bloomington, IN: Solution Tree Press.

Fisher, D., Frey, N., & Lapp, D. (2012). *Teaching students to read like detectives: Comprehending, analyzing, and discussing text*. Bloomington, IN: Solution Tree Press.

Fisher, D., Frey, N., & Uline, C. L. (2013). *Common Core English language arts in a PLC at work, leader's guide*. Bloomington, IN: Solution Tree Press.

Foster, D., & Poppers, A. P. (2009, November). *Using formative assessment to drive learning* (The Silicon Valley Mathematics Initiative). Accessed at www.svmimac.org/images/Using_Formative_Assessment_to_Drive_Learning_Reduced.pdf on July 5, 2013.

Frey, N., Fisher, D., & Everlove, S. (2009). *Productive group work: How to engage students, build teamwork, and promote understanding*. Alexandria, VA: Association for Supervision and Curriculum Development.

Gareis, C. R., & Grant, L. W. (2008). *Teacher-made assessments: How to connect curriculum, instruction, and student learning*. Larchmont, NY: Eye on Education.

Graham, P., & Ferriter, W. (2010). *Building a professional learning community at work: A guide to the first year*. Bloomington, IN: Solution Tree Press.

Grazer, B. (Producer), & Howard, R. (Director). (1995). *Apollo 13* [Motion picture]. United States: Imagine Entertainment.

Gregory, G. H., & Chapman, C. (2007). *Differentiated instructional strategies: One size doesn't fit all* (2nd ed.). Thousand Oaks, CA: Corwin Press.

Greiner, A., & Simmons, C. (2012). *The write tools for Common Core State Standards: Narrative—Real or imagined*. New York: Raindance Press.

Guskey, T. R. (2010). Lessons of mastery learning. *Educational Leadership, 68*(2), 52–57.

Hall, G. E., & Hord, S. M. (2006). *Implementing change: Patterns, principles, and potholes* (2nd ed.). Boston: Pearson.

Hattie, J. A. C. (2009). *Visible learning: A synthesis of over 800 meta-analyses relating to achievement*. New York: Routledge.

Hattie, J., & Timperley, H. (2007). The power of feedback. *Review of Educational Research, 77*(1), 81–112.

Heacox, D. (2009). *Making differentiation a habit: How to ensure success in academically diverse classrooms*. Minneapolis, MN: Free Spirit.

Heritage, M. (2008). *Learning progressions: Supporting instruction and formative assessment*. Washington, DC: Council of Chief State School Officers.

Hess, K. (2009). *Hess' cognitive rigor matrix*. Accessed at www.nciea.org/publications/CRM_ELA_KH11.pdf on April 30, 2013.

Kanold, T. D. (2011). *The five disciplines of PLC leaders*. Bloomington, IN: Solution Tree Press.

Kanold, T. D. (Ed.). (2012a). *Common Core mathematics in a PLC at work, grades K–2*. Bloomington, IN: Solution Tree Press.

Kanold, T. D. (Ed.). (2012b). *Common Core mathematics in a PLC at work, grades 3–5*. Bloomington, IN: Solution Tree Press.

Kanold, T. D. (Ed.). (2012c). *Common Core mathematics in a PLC at work, high school*. Bloomington, IN: Solution Tree Press.

Kanold, T. D. (Ed.). (2013a). *Common Core mathematics in a PLC at work, grades 6–8*. Bloomington, IN: Solution Tree Press.

Kanold, T. D. (Ed.). (2013b). *Common Core mathematics in a PLC at work, leader's guide*. Bloomington, IN: Solution Tree Press.

Kay, K. (2010, October 11). *21st century readiness for every student*. Keynote speech presented at the 21st Century Learning Summit, Rosemont, IL.

Killion, J. (2011, September 1). *Theory of change and Common Core standards* [Web log post]. Accessed at http://blogs.edweek.org/edweek/learning_forwards_pd_watch/2011/09 on January 2, 2013.

Kotter, J. P. (1996). *Leading change*. Boston: Harvard Business School Press.

Kotter, J. P. (2008). *A sense of urgency*. Boston: Harvard Business Press.

Marzano, R. J. (2003). *What works in schools: Translating research into action*. Alexandria, VA: Association for Supervision and Curriculum Development.

Marzano, R. J. (2004). *Building background knowledge for academic achievement: Research on what works in schools*. Alexandria, VA: Association for Supervision and Curriculum Development.

Marzano, R. J. (2006). *Classroom assessment & grading that work.* Alexandria, VA: Association for Supervision and Curriculum Development.

Marzano, R. J. (2007). *The art and science of teaching: A comprehensive framework for effective instruction.* Alexandria, VA: Association for Supervision and Curriculum Development.

Marzano, R. J. (2009). *Designing & teaching learning goals and objectives.* Bloomington, IN: Marzano Research Laboratory.

Marzano, R. J. (2010). *Formative assessment & standards-based grading.* Bloomington, IN: Marzano Research Laboratory.

Marzano, R. J., & Kendall, J. S. (2007). *The new taxonomy of educational objectives* (2nd ed.). Thousand Oaks, CA: Corwin Press.

Marzano, R. J., & Kendall, J. S. (2008). *Designing & assessing educational objectives: Applying the new taxonomy.* Thousand Oaks, CA: Corwin Press.

Marzano, R. J., Pickering, D. J., & Pollock, J. E. (2001). *Classroom instruction that works: Research-based strategies for improving student achievement.* Alexandria, VA: Association for Supervision and Curriculum Development.

Marzano, R. J., Waters, T., & McNulty, B. A. (2003). *School leadership that works: From research to results.* Alexandria, VA: Association for Supervision and Curriculum Development.

MindTools. (n.d.). *Kotter's 8-step change model.* Accessed at www.mindtools.com/pages/article/newPPM_82.htm on March 7, 2013.

National Governors Association Center for Best Practices & Council of Chief State School Officers. (2010a). *Common Core State Standards for English language arts & literacy in history/social studies, science, and technical subjects.* Washington, DC: Authors. Accessed at www.corestandards.org/assets/CCSSI_ELA%20 Standards.pdf on January 4, 2013.

National Governors Association Center for Best Practices & Council of Chief State School Officers. (2010b). *Common Core State Standards for English language arts & literacy in history/social studies, science, and technical subjects: Appendix A—Research supporting key elements of the standards and glossary of key terms.* Washington, DC: Authors. Accessed at www.corestandards.org/assets/Appendix_A.pdf on January 4, 2013.

National Governors Association Center for Best Practices & Council of Chief State School Officers. (2010c). *Common Core State Standards for English language arts & literacy in history/social studies, science, and technical subjects: Appendix B—Text exemplars and sample performance tasks.* Washington, DC: Authors. Accessed at www.corestandards.org/assets/Appendix_B.pdf on January 4, 2013.

National Governors Association Center for Best Practices & Council of Chief State School Officers. (2010d). *Common Core State Standards for English language arts & literacy in history/social studies, science, and technical subjects: Appendix C—Samples of student writing.* Washington, DC: Authors. Accessed at www .corestandards.org/assets/Appendix_C.pdf on January 4, 2013.

National Governors Association Center for Best Practices & Council of Chief State School Officers. (2010e). *Common Core State Standards for mathematics.* Washington, DC: Authors. Accessed at www.corestandards .org/assets/CCSSI_Math%20Standards.pdf on January 4, 2013.

National Governors Association Center for Best Practices & Council of Chief State School Officers. (2010f). *Common Core State Standards for mathematics: Appendix A—Designing high school mathematics courses based on the Common Core State Standards.* Washington, DC: Authors. Accessed at www.corestandards.org /assets/CCSSI_Mathematics_Appendix_A.pdf on January 4, 2013.

National Governors Association Center for Best Practices & Council of Chief State School Officers. (2010g). *The standards*. Washington, DC: Authors. Accessed at www.corestandards.org/the-standards on August 31, 2012.

National Governors Association Center for Best Practices & Council of Chief State School Officers. (2012). *Common Core State Standards official identifiers and XML representation*. Washington, DC: Authors. Accessed at www.corestandards.org/common-core-state-standards-official-identifiers-and-xml -representation on January 4, 2013.

National Governors Association Center for Best Practices & Council of Chief State School Officers. (n.d.a). *Application of Common Core State Standards for English language learners*. Washington, DC: Authors. Accessed at www.corestandards.org/assets/application-for-english-learners.pdf on January 4, 2013.

National Governors Association Center for Best Practices & Council of Chief State School Officers. (n.d.b). *Application to students with disabilities*. Washington, DC: Authors. Accessed at www.corestandards.org /assets/application-to-students-with-disabilities.pdf on January 4, 2013.

Partnership for Assessment of Readiness for College and Careers. (2012a). *Advances in the PARCC ELA/literacy assessment* [PowerPoint slides]. Accessed at www.parcconline.org/sites/parcc/files/PARCC_Shifts%20 and%20Sample%20Items%20Overview_ELA%20Literacy%2008182012_0.ppt on August 27, 2012.

Partnership for Assessment of Readiness for College and Careers. (2012b). *Item and task prototypes*. Accessed at www.parcconline.org/samples/item-task-prototypes on September 1, 2012.

Partnership for Assessment of Readiness for College and Careers. (2012c). *PARCC model content frameworks*. Accessed at www.parcconline.org/parcc-model-content-frameworks on August 31, 2012.

Partnership for Assessment of Readiness for College and Careers. (2012d). *PARCC model content frameworks: English language arts/literacy—Grades 3–11*. Accessed at www.parcconline.org/sites/parcc/files /PARCCMCFELALiteracyAugust2012_FINAL.pdf on March 11, 2013.

Partnership for Assessment of Readiness for College and Careers. (2012e). *PARCC model content frameworks: Mathematics—Grades 3–11*. Accessed at www.parcconline.org/sites/parcc/files /PARCCMCFMathematicsNovember2012V3_FINAL.pdf on March 11, 2013.

Partnership for 21st Century Skills. (n.d.a). *Professional development for the 21st century*. Accessed at www.p21 .org/storage/documents/ProfDev.pdf on January 2, 2013.

Partnership for 21st Century Skills. (n.d.b). *P21 Common Core toolkit.* Accessed at www.p21.org/tools-and -resources/publications/p21-common-core-toolkit on April 28, 2013.

Pearson, P. D., & Gallagher, M. C. (1983). The instruction of reading comprehension. *Contemporary Educational Psychology, 8*(3), 317–344.

Popham, W. J. (2003). *Test better, teach better: The instructional role of assessment*. Alexandria, VA: Association for Supervision and Curriculum Development.

Public Schools of North Carolina (2012). *English language arts and math unpacking standards.* Accessed at www.ncpublicschools.org/acre/standards/common-core-tools/#unpacking on April 30, 2013.

Reeves, D. B. (2002). *The leader's guide to standards: A blueprint for educational equity and excellence*. San Francisco: Jossey-Bass.

Reeves, D. (2007). Challenges and choices: The role of educational leaders in effective assessment. In D. Reeves (Ed.), *Ahead of the curve: The power of assessment to transform teaching and learning* (pp. 227–251). Bloomington, IN: Solution Tree Press.

Richardson-Koehler, V. (Ed.). (1987). *Educators' handbook: A research perspective*. New York: Longman.

Robinson, K. (2006, February). *Ken Robinson says schools kill creativity* [Video file]. Accessed at www.ted.com/talks/ken_robinson_says_schools_kill_creativity.html on September 23, 2012.

Sadler, D. R. (1998). Formative assessment: Revisiting the territory. *Assessment in Education: Principles, Policy and Practice, 5*(1), 77–84.

Schmoker, M., & Marzano, R. J. (1999). Realizing the promise of standards-based education. *Educational Leadership, 56*(6), 17–21.

Sinek, S. (2009). *Start with why: How great leaders inspire everyone to take action.* New York: Portfolio.

Smarter Balanced Assessment Consortium. (2012a). *Content specifications for the summative assessment of the Common Core State Standards for English language arts and literacy in history/social studies, science, and technical subjects.* Accessed at www.smarterbalanced.org/wordpress/wp-content/uploads/2011/12/ELA -Literacy-Content-Specifications.pdf on January 2, 2013.

Smarter Balanced Assessment Consortium. (2012b). *Content specifications for the summative assessment of the Common Core State Standards for mathematics.* Accessed at www.smarterbalanced.org/wordpress /wp-content/uploads/2011/12/Math-Content-Specifications.pdf on January 2, 2013.

Smarter Balanced Assessment Consortium. (2012c). *Smarter balanced assessments.* Accessed at www .smarterbalanced.org/smarter-balanced-assessments on July 6, 2012.

Smarter Balanced Assessment Consortium. (2012d). *Smarter Balanced Assessment Consortium: Technology-enhanced item guidelines.* Accessed at www.smarterbalanced.org/wordpress/wp-content/uploads/2012/05 /TaskItemSpecifications/TechnologyEnhancedItems/TechnologyEnhancedItemGuidelines.pdf on September 2, 2012.

Stiggins, R., Arter, J. A., Chappuis, J., & Chappuis, S. (2004). *Classroom assessment* for *student learning: Doing it right, using it well.* Portland, OR: Assessment Training Institute.

Tomlinson, C. A. (2000, August). Differentiation of instruction in the elementary grades. *ERIC Digest.* Champaign, IL: ERIC Clearinghouse on Elementary and Early Childhood Education. (ERIC Document Reproduction Service No. ED443572) Accessed at www.eric.ed.gov/PDFS/ED443572.pdf on May 1, 2013.

Trilling, B., & Fadel, C. (2009). *21st century skills: Learning for life in our times.* San Francisco: Jossey-Bass.

Van Driel, J. H., & Berry, A. (2012). Teacher professional development focusing on pedagogical content knowledge. *Educational Researcher, 41*(1), 26–28.

Washor, E., & Mojkowski, C. (2007). What do you mean by rigor? *Educational Leadership, 64*(4), 84–87.

Webb, N. L. (2002) *Depth-of-knowledge for four content areas.* Accessed at http://facstaff.wcer.wisc.edu/normw /state%20alignment%20page%20one.htm on April 26, 2013.

Webb, N. L. (2005). *Web alignment tool.* Accessed at http://wat.wceruw.org on September 16, 2012.

Wiggins, G., & McTighe, J. (2005). *Understanding by design.* Alexandria, VA: Association for Supervision and Curriculum Development.

Index

Common Formative Assessment
Kim Bailey and Chris Jakicic
The catalyst for real student improvement begins with a decision to implement common formative assessments. In this conversational guide, the authors offer tools, templates, and protocols to incorporate common formative assessments into the practices of a PLC to monitor and enhance student learning.
BKF538

Making Teamwork Meaningful
William M. Ferriter, Parry Graham, and Matt Wight
Focus on developing people—not just improving test scores. The authors examine how staffing decisions can strengthen professional learning communities and explore actions that can help school leaders safeguard their schools against complacency.
BKF548

Common Core Mathematics in a PLC at Work™ series
Edited by Timothy D. Kanold
These teacher guides illustrate how to sustain successful implementation of the Common Core State Standards for mathematics. Discover what students should learn and how they should learn it. Tools and strategies will help you develop and assess student demonstrations of deep conceptual understanding and procedural fluency.
Joint Publications With the National Council of Teachers of Mathematics
BKF566, BKF568, BKF574, BKF561, BKF559

Common Core English Language Arts in a PLC at Work™ series
Douglas Fisher and Nancy Frey
These teacher guides illustrate how to sustain successful implementation of the Common Core State Standards for English language arts in K–12 instruction, curriculum, assessment, and intervention practices within the powerful Professional Learning Communities at Work™ process.
Joint Publications With the International Reading Association
BKF578, BKF580, BKF582, BKF584, BKF586

Wait! Your professional development journey doesn't have to end with the last pages of this book.

We realize improving student learning doesn't happen overnight. And your school or district shouldn't be left to puzzle out all the details of this process alone.

No matter where you are on the journey, we're committed to helping you get to the next stage.

Take advantage of everything from **custom workshops** to **keynote presentations** and **interactive web and video conferencing**. We can even help you develop an action plan tailored to fit your specific needs.

Let's get the conversation started.

Call 888.763.9045 today.

 solution-tree.com